majak

After eight years as a television news journalist, in 2008 Heath O'Loughlin became the General Manager of Media, Communications and Marketing at North Melbourne Football Club. At Arden Street, O'Loughlin formed a close bond with the players, particularly Majak Daw. He also helped Brent Harvey with his autobiography, and wrote the book *Sons of God*, about Victoria Police's Special Operations Group. In 2021, O'Loughlin joined the National Basketball League as its General Manager of Media, PR and Communications.

majak
MAJAK DAW

with HEATH O'LOUGHLIN

VIKING
an imprint of
PENGUIN BOOKS

VIKING

UK | USA | Canada | Ireland | Australia
India | New Zealand | South Africa | China

Viking is part of the Penguin Random House group of companies,
whose addresses can be found at global.penguinrandomhouse.com.

Penguin
Random House
Australia

First published by Viking, 2021

Cover design by Alex Ross © Penguin Random House Australia Pty Ltd
Cover photograph by Julian Kingma
Typeset in Sabon by Midland Typesetters, Australia
Printed and bound in Australia by Griffin Press, part of Ovato, an accredited
ISO AS/NZS 14001 Environmental Management Systems printer

 A catalogue record for this
book is available from the
NATIONAL LIBRARY OF AUSTRALIA
National Library of Australia

ISBN 978 1 76089 965 3

penguin.com.au

MIX
Paper from
responsible sources
FSC® C009448

This book contains references to suicide and suicidal ideation. If you or a loved one need support, you can call Lifeline on 13 11 14 or chat online at lifeline.org.au.

Contents

1 **Tök**   1

2 **Rou**   6

3 **Diäk**   14

REFLECTIONS: Augustino Daw   24

4 **Ŋuan**   26

REFLECTIONS: Augustino, William and Elizabeth Daw   31

5 **Dhiëc**   37

REFLECTIONS: Augustino Daw   44

6 **Detem**   46

REFLECTIONS: Augustino, William and Elizabeth Daw, Joey Halloran   63

7 **Dhorou**   70

REFLECTIONS: Shane Sexton, Joey Halloran, Matthew Lloyd, Shane Casley, Augustino Daw   90

8 **Bët**   103

REFLECTIONS: Shane Casley, John Lamont, Brad Scott   111

9 **Dhoŋuan**   125

10 **Thiäär** 146

REFLECTIONS: Brad Scott, Shane Casley 153

11 **Thiär ku tök** 159

REFLECTIONS: Scott Thompson 179

12 **Thiär ku rou** 182

13 **Thiär ku ďïäk** 195

REFLECTIONS: Joey Halloran, Augustino Daw, Shane Casley 216

14 **Thiär ku ŋuan** 223

REFLECTIONS: Joey Halloran, Augustino and William Daw, Luke McDonald, Andrew Oppy 233

15 **Thiäku ku dhiëc** 255

REFLECTIONS: Andrew Oppy, Alex Moore 264

16 **Thiär ku detem** 274

17 **Thiär ku dhorou** 280

REFLECTIONS: Shaun Atley 304

18 **Thiär ku bët** 306

19 **Thiär ku dhoŋuan** 320

20 **Thiërrou** 331

REFLECTIONS: Brad Scott, Shane Casley, Sonja Hood 341

A letter to Majak 351

Acknowledgements 353

1

Tök

I was on the verge of securing the biggest deal of my career. As the end of my breakout 2018 football season approached, my value as a player had significantly increased. Although I was already under contract with the North Melbourne Football Club for 2019, my manager convinced the club to consider negotiating a new deal, for more than $400000 a year, which would have set me up financially and put me back on my feet after a tough period.

Twelve months earlier, and eight seasons into my AFL career, I was treading water and couldn't cement a spot in the senior side as a ruck/forward player. I was 27 years old and had just 32 games to my name. Everything pointed to my AFL career being over in a matter of months, and my ambitions remaining largely unfulfilled. But just when I had almost lost all hope of being a first-picked player at the Kangaroos, my then coach, Brad Scott, spoke to me about a change of role. With Ben Brown and Jarrad Waite holding down key spots in our attack, and both able to pinch-hit in the ruck when Todd Goldstein needed a rest, and Braydon Preuss next in line for a ruck role, Brad told me my only chance to break into the side was as a key defender alongside veterans Scott Thompson and Robbie Tarrant. I wasn't in a position to pick or choose where I wanted to play at the time, so I agreed to start training immediately in the backline group under then assistant coach Josh Drummond. Brad wanted to give me some clear direction and told me that if I trained hard, he'd try me out in defence in the upcoming pre-season practice matches.

I had a lot to learn, having never played as a defender before, and went to Robbie Tarrant and Scott Thompson, who were the best in the business, for help. Playing back is very different to playing forward, but the good thing is that it's probably easier to play back on someone than have someone play on you. As a forward, you have to be proactive and initiate the running and leading to the ball, but when you're a defender, most of the time you're reacting to the forwards' movements. With my power and speed, I was able to give my man a few metres' head start on a lead to the ball, but close the gap on him quickly enough to get into a position to spoil his mark, or mark it myself. If the ball was kicked in high and on top of our heads, I had the strength to out-muscle and push my opponent off the ball. While it wasn't that simple, I did feel comfortable in the position pretty quickly and felt that the change of roles was a good move for me and my career.

Full of confidence and ready to test my abilities against genuine opposition, Brad and the North coaches threw me in the deep end for a practice series, the AFLX, where I played okay against Carlton. But it was a match against Melbourne down at Kingston Twin Ovals in Hobart, Tasmania, as part of the full-length practice games, where I found out just how hard the role of a defender could be. Just when I was starting to feel good about my football transformation, I was given an absolute bath by Jesse Hogan and Christian Petracca. They outmanoeuvred me, out-muscled me, outplayed me and, to be honest, embarrassed me. I conceded several goals and looked completely out of place. It prompted talk in the media about whether my role change was a silly experiment. Brad reassured me that I was worth persisting with, but, later that week, I was dropped for the second game of the pre-season and sent back to play a scratch match in the VFL with Werribee against Williamstown.

I wasn't brought back in to play our final practice match against reigning premiers Richmond, in Carlton, where we got smacked by a whopping 70 points. I started the season proper on the outer too, and missed games against Gold Coast and St Kilda. In Round 3 against Melbourne at the MCG, I got my chance for redemption. After initially being named as an emergency, I was brought in to play alongside Scott Thompson when Robbie Tarrant pulled out with hamstring soreness. Within seconds of the game starting, the Demons booted the ball long and high into their forward line, looking for Bayley Fritsch or Christian Petracca to mark it. I had left my direct opponent, having identified where the ball was going, and leapt from the back of a pack to take a soaring mark right in front of their goal. It was a real confidence booster for me and set the tone for the rest of the afternoon. I was also able to line up Jordan Lewis with a nice hip and shoulder, as I was trying desperately to prove to Brad and the coaches that I had the aggression and determination to play as a defender regularly. While we ultimately lost the match, I ended up with five contested marks, seven tackles and a contender for mark of the year after sitting on Fritsch's head late in the first term – it was a productive day for a defender and I felt like I had passed an important test.

My effort against Melbourne was good enough to see me hold my spot the following week against Carlton, despite the fact that Robbie Tarrant was declared fit to return. I was getting games and building my form slowly, when disaster struck. A Hawthorn player accidentally landed on my foot and caused a small crack in my navicular, which is a small bone that sits in the middle of the foot between the ankle and the toes. Breaks in this area are troublesome and can take a long time to heal, because the navicular is a bone that bears weight. Navicular injuries are notorious for ending football players' careers prematurely because they're so delicate and hard to repair. After an assessment by the club's doctor during the week and a subsequent visit to a specialist, we decided to continue the season without surgical intervention, which was a risk. The thought process was that if the fracture broke all the way through the bone, we would get it fixed, but until then it would be more of a pain-management issue for me.

So, before each game that year, I had an injection in my foot to numb the pain. At the three-quarter-time break each week, the pain-killing medication would wear off and severe pain would kick in. Some of my teammates, who knew I was battling with the injury at the late stages of games, would get behind me and implore me to grind the games out until the final siren, which I always did. The club's medical team members were astounded that the bone never cracked all the way through despite the fact that I played 15 games on it. I managed to play 18 games that season, by far eclipsing my previous best tally of nine games in 2016. At the end of the 2018 season, I had surgery to repair the fracture, but I was in a good place football-wise and was about to put pen to paper on my new deal. Off the field, however, things were starting to unravel like never before. I was in a bad place mentally, but even I had no idea just how bad things were about to become.

2

Rou

I knew our pet lion was hungry because he hadn't eaten for several days. Sometimes my family didn't have anything to give him after feeding ourselves. On this particular day, the lion had a very distinct look about him that signalled 'approach with extreme caution!' and when he was in that sort of mood, it was a bad idea to go anywhere near his cage. Despite all the warning signs, I found a small piece of leftover meat for him and approached his small enclosure. It wasn't much, but I knew it would get him through the next few days until we could spare him some more.

A naïve seven-year-old, I slowly moved towards the steel bars. 'Here you go,' I uttered nervously and watched as he got up off the ground and came towards me with his ears folded back slightly. He seemed to become relatively docile and didn't growl or gnash his teeth – his usual signs of aggression. He was panting, though, and looked very tired. He turned his head towards me and our eyes locked. I sensed he knew I was there to help him. I reached out with the lump of meat in my hand and he started sniffing the air. The scent of sun-baked, rotting animal flesh suddenly brought him to life. We were less than a half a metre away from each other, my hand edging ever closer to his mouth. I pushed the meat through the bars, his eyes stayed fixed on mine and his mouth began to open. What happened next is a blur. I remember him lunging forward and I instinctively let go of the meat and fell backwards to the ground.

There was blood everywhere. It was on my clothes and smeared across the bars of the cage. I looked down at my left hand – the one that had the meat in it – and it too was covered in blood, but at first I felt nothing. Then the pain kicked in. My hand started throbbing and I saw that the top of my left ring finger was missing. I screamed out for my mum and then I must have passed out.

That was almost 20 years ago, so you will have to forgive me; my memory is very clouded. In fact, it's so clouded that our pet was actually a tiger, not a lion. Yes, that's right – our pet tiger bit my finger off! No, no, no – he wasn't a pet. He was a wild beast that roamed around the outskirts of our village in Sudan and attacked me without warning one day when I was walking home from school and took a chunk of my finger. Or was the missing part of my finger self-inflicted? So hungry as a child in a developing country, perhaps I had to eat my own finger just to survive.

What *is* true is that I am missing a quarter of my finger on my left hand and I've been lying to people for years about how it happened. Only now have I figured out why I have been so guarded and protective of that story. When I arrived in Australia in 2003, I was asked about my missing finger a lot. I have pretty big hands, so the short, stumpy, deformed-looking ring finger on my left hand does stand out to people when they first meet me. It has no nail and was severed at the first (distal) knuckle. The stories I told you before, about the lion, the tiger and me biting it off for food, were all various versions of long-winded tales I made up to avoid telling anyone the actual truth, and in my mind, to avoid them judging me for coming from a poor African country. I thought if I injected some stereotypes, like wild or pet lions, tigers, starvation and a bit of humour, it would distract people from finding out the real story – and funnily enough, it always seemed to work.

Many people were understandably curious about my early life in Khartoum, Sudan, and later in Egypt, but there were some things I never felt comfortable sharing with them, and my missing finger was one of them.

Since joining the AFL, I've had many opportunities to tell my life story, with many people asking me to write a book, film a documentary, do a podcast or sit down for various radio interviews. While writing a book was always most appealing to me, I never felt it was the right time – but things changed after I became a father. With all that's happened to me and with the environment we're all living in, I decided now was the right time to share my journey and hopefully help others overcome the types of challenges and obstacles I have faced and worked through.

So, while I was kidding around with the story of how I lost my finger before, I make a promise to you as a reader of my story that from this moment on I will tell you nothing but the truth. And to prove it, here is the real story about why I had the top of my finger amputated at around the age of eight, and why I've been so sensitive about revealing the real story behind it.

After my early life during the civil war in Sudan, my parents decided to leave in search of a better future for their then eight children – I will elaborate on this later, but for context it's important to touch on it now. While awaiting a visa to gain entry to a country like Australia, Canada or the United States, we spent three years in Egypt, initially without my dad, William, who stayed back in Sudan to work and send money across to us. We were lucky enough to have some extended family in Cairo – a second cousin on my dad's side who we called an uncle. He and his wife had six children and lived in a tiny three-bedroom house. Despite already being overcrowded in their family home, they allowed us to stay. You can do the maths – that's 15 people under the one roof. It goes without saying it was cramped and extremely awkward, but we had nowhere else to go and were very lucky our uncle agreed to take us in.

After a period of time, it became very clear to me and my two older brothers, Peter and Augustino, that our mum, Elizabeth, was struggling financially to pay the rent and couldn't afford food for us all. None of us were attending school at the time because of our finances – Mum couldn't afford to send us and it just wasn't a priority, and our days basically involved sleeping in and playing with the other neighbourhood kids. Mum couldn't work because she had to look after my younger siblings, Teresa, Anthony, Sarah, Angelina, and Mary. Being the eldest, Peter decided to find work and had some success at a mechanic's garage. Augustino followed his lead and worked in a factory of some sort.

Although I was only nine years old, I too ventured out to assist my family in any way I could. When I look back now, the thought of walking the dangerous city streets at such a young age and searching for full-time work is hard to comprehend, but back then, I didn't have any perspective to even question it. After various attempts and knock-backs from several business owners who had no need for a child who wasn't their own, I eventually had some luck at a furniture maker's factory and started work immediately. My days involved helping the carpenters with the joinery, clamping and general cleaning of the workshop floors and benches. I was also responsible for making cups of tea and coffee for them and all the other workers. I can't recall exactly how much I got paid – it would have been very little – but the look of gratitude on my mum's face when I gave her my earnings each evening made it well worth the effort and made it easier for me to go back every day.

Although things started off okay for me at the factory, it didn't stay that way for long. After about a year, one of the carpenters started mistreating me – mainly for being young, vulnerable and Sudanese. Many local Egyptians hated the Africans who moved to Cairo for two main reasons: racism or religion. This particular man would occasionally hit me or abuse me when I had to work with him. I put up with it for a long time, and never told my mum or brothers about what he did, but eventually I made the decision to leave and find other work, as his treatment of me was getting worse and I feared for my safety.

It wasn't until I stumbled across a small family-owned sewing shop that I had any luck with getting other work. With their own children also employed to help with tailoring and curtain making, I don't actually think the owners had any work for me, but out of the goodness of their hearts they took me in. I felt very safe and welcome there. They were all so kind, even feeding me lunch and making me feel part of their family. I have really good memories of being with them and will be forever grateful to them for their generosity.

My role was to take the curtains after they'd been sewn and hemmed, cut holes in the fabric with large, sharp scissors and then clamp big metal eyelets onto them so they could be hung on a rail in people's homes. That's right, an eight-or-so-year-old using scissors and a metal clamp – you'd be forgiven for thinking they had something to do with the severing of my finger, but no, it was actually my own stupidity rather than an accident of that nature.

After several months, when the monotony of the work I was doing got to me, I'd often go over to the station where the eldest sister of the family worked and have a chat. She operated an old sewing machine with a rubber band looped over a metal wheel that spun around. While talking, I was running my fingers around the outside of the metal balance wheel, just playing, and my finger got caught between it and the rubber belt. The mechanism crunched down on my finger and caused the sewing machine to come to a grinding halt. I wrenched my finger out with force and blood spilt everywhere. All the bones in my finger had been crushed. I don't recall being in much pain, probably due to the shock. The family rushed me to the nearest hospital and called my mum. The damage was so significant, they couldn't save all of my finger and had to amputate part of it at the first knuckle. I was lucky it wasn't further down on my hand.

I know while reading this, you're probably thinking, *That's exactly what a child would or could easily do in that situation*, and *There's no shame in what happened*, but for me, the story holds so many different uncomfortable feelings and connotations.

In Egypt and other developing countries, a child having to forgo school and an education in order to work to help his family pay the bills is commonplace, but in Australia it's a storyline you'd only see or read about in a movie or an article in a *National Geographic* magazine. I've told a lot of my friends about where I grew up and various stories about my family, but I've never really discussed with them the levels of hardship we endured. I suppose I was always worried about what they might think of me, and deep down I feared they'd view me and my family as poor and inadequate.

As I've grown older, it's one part of my life that I've had to learn to become more comfortable with. With one finger three-quarters its original length, I have a very real reminder of what we suffered through as a family, and it's something I'll have to carry with me forever.

There's no point hiding my past anymore, and you're about to learn all about it.

3
Diäk

Had we stayed in Sudan, I don't think there would have been any way to keep our family together. I've heard so many stories over the years about other families who elected to stay back in Sudan, and they're really struggling. We often send money back to those in need so they can afford food and other items. Several of my cousins, uncles, aunties and others I know have passed away before reaching their thirties or forties. My parents had decided to leave our native home in search of a better life. The civil war made for a terrifying backdrop and the risk that it could flare up at any time and harm or kill someone close to us was all too real.

Whether you have a lot or very little in life depends on your perspective, in my experience and opinion. When I look back on my early childhood in Khartoum, Sudan, my siblings and I wanted for nothing. We weren't a wealthy family by any means, but we weren't considered poor, either. As the saying goes, 'You don't know what you don't know.' As a toddler, I didn't know anything about the material items, appliances and gadgets that people and kids in other parts of the world had. Most things Australian kids would have had growing up and perhaps took for granted – like toys, PlayStations and Xboxes, Nike clothing and Air Jordan shoes – I wasn't aware even existed.

We lived in a village that forms part of Omdurman, which lies on the western banks of the Nile River, and has the biggest population of any city in Sudan. Omdurman is about five minutes away from the capital Khartoum. We lived there until 1996, and then moved to an area called Jabarona. In Omdurman, we lived in a gated community along with my grandparents, some aunties and other extended family. The entire complex was surrounded by these big stone walls and it had a large gate at the front that I don't remember ever being closed. The roads inside the village were barely wide enough for a car, so donkeys and horses were used to transport goods and materials to people.

Our house was very basic. It was made from mudbrick and had a densely thatched roof made from straw and other materials. Inside the home was small and pretty bare as we didn't have much furniture. There was one big bedroom that we all slept in, as well as a living area and small kitchen area. We didn't have a TV and we ate family meals in the bedroom area. Our beds were rectangle-shaped mudbrick slabs, cemented to the walls like shelves, with very thin mattresses on top. They weren't that comfortable, but it was a real luxury to have a proper bed. There were several beds in the room, and anyone who couldn't squeeze onto one slept on a mattress on the floor. The floor was made of a mud and clay that had been rendered. It was smooth and would get terribly dusty, so sweeping was a common chore for us all.

We all had responsibilities as kids. Some of us had to feed the chickens and pigeons, while others were tasked with fetching buckets of water from the main water pump in the village. We'd use the water for drinking, cooking and bathing. There was no shower, so we'd have to stand in a large bucket and hope that someone could tip a smaller bucket of water over us. If no one was able to help you'd have to bathe yourself, which I hated. I would always argue with my parents to try to get out of it because it was so tedious and messy. In the language we spoke, Dinka, the word for wash is *wak*.

We didn't have an electric iron. Instead, Mum had to pack the inside of an old iron box with hot coals. We used oil lamps and torches to light the way at night and much of what we did day-to-day involved a lot of manual labour and a lot of effort. It was never as easy as just flicking a switch, like I'm accustomed to now. Clothes washing was all done by hand and the toilets were communal; I think you would call them a 'drop toilet' – basically just a hole you'd squat over to do your business. There was no toilet paper either, just a water jug to clean yourself up with, so you'd always hope for a clean drop and pray the jug had water in it.

Mum did all of the cooking for our family. The food we ate was like Indian food: lots of stews, gravies and curries. It usually involved cooked meat and vegetables, some rice and a sour bread called *kisra*. There was a food market not far from the village and my parents would often do the food shopping after church. If we bought any meat or fish, usually once a week, it would have to be eaten that day, because there was no way of preserving or refrigerating it. It would usually be dried before it was cooked. One of Mum's specialties was traditional Dinkan balls made of wheat and vegetables.

Family was everything to me growing up, and I was always around a lot of people, with my cousins staying over or other relatives visiting our place. My mum's family lived in the city areas, but my dad's family lived in the country areas. It's common to take things or gifts from people's houses whenever you visit, so when family visited us, they'd always leave with a random item like a chicken, a chair or a cushion. Our culture has lots of traditions, but one of the strangest ones happened on my dad's side. Stay with me here, because this gets confusing – even to me.

My dad's mum's first husband was named Majak, but he passed away before my dad was born. In Dinka culture, if a deceased man has a brother, the brother has to assume the role of father in that family and must continue raising and creating a family with his sister-in-law, even if he has his own family. So, Majak's brother took over as father and husband, and had a baby with Majak's widow. That baby was my dad. So, the man who should have been my dad's uncle ended up being my dad's biological dad, and the man who was supposed to be my great-uncle became my grandfather or 'pop'.

My parents were, and still are, extremely proud people, and seeing the way they went about everyday life in Sudan to ensure their kids never went without is inspirational to me. In a rich country like Australia, you can always go and get new clothes, food, furniture or an appliance to make your life easier, but back in Sudan, we didn't have those options. In fact, we didn't know certain things had even been invented or were on the market and available to normal people. We weren't exposed to any of it, so we never felt like we were missing out on anything – it was, in a strange way, blissful ignorance.

While some wealthier families in our village wore nicer clothes and had nicer things, there were also many people and children who couldn't even afford shoes. When the sun was really hot in the middle of the day, walking outside without shoes on was painful, but some kids didn't have a choice. Some had holes in their shoes, or no shoes at all, and their feet would bleed from the heat and from all the nasty blisters they'd get.

Our family was middle-class as far as life in Sudan went, but my parents would never show that we were better off than some others. We never lived beyond our means. One year, Dad became the principal of a local school and then he was promoted to become the head of the school district, and his bosses offered him a car and driver, but he refused to accept the perk. He felt having someone pick him up every morning and drop him off every evening was unnecessary and a misuse of resources. He was too humble and never the type to show off. Having a car and a driver would have made him very uncomfortable. He much preferred to ride his bike to and from work.

The people who lived in northern Sudan were considered better off and wealthy, but there was a lot of poverty around us in the south. People relied on each other a lot. There were times when families didn't have anything to eat and had to depend on the generosity of their neighbours to help get them through. There were always people begging on the streets and a lot of people struggling to get by.

Police brutality was common. With alcohol consumption illegal, because it was an Islamic country, people would make home-brew beer and vodka from dates, and a lot of drunks would be regularly beaten by the police. The way petty criminals were treated was terrible. I saw many men and women beaten severely with batons, with no mercy shown at all. One time after school, I saw a drunk and disorderly man in the streets, which prompted the police to be summoned. A military-type lorry truck arrived and several officers piled out, like it was some sort of ambush. They attacked the man and split his head wide open, causing his wife to leap to his aid. But in doing so, she too was bashed and loaded into the truck and taken away. I was always fearful of the police and never had any trust in them to protect me or my family. They were very corrupt and would often abuse their power.

When someone died in our area, an ambulance would park at the front gates of our community and the deceased would be carried through the village in a canvas sheet. It was tradition for all the adult males to shave their heads out of respect. Other families would bury the bodies of their loved ones on their property. I remember several funerals taking place when I was younger. Lots of people would visit the deceased's family home. The body would be placed inside the house for viewing until the burial. Death was very common and, looking back, people would die for the simplest of reasons – things you wouldn't need to worry about in a country like Australia. Because we didn't have great access to medicine or health professionals, the ill would often be left to fend for themselves. I remember lots of people dying from malaria and severe diarrhea because they couldn't get to hospital in time. If a person got sick and couldn't convince someone with a car to take them to a hospital, the lack of transport or an ambulance meant they'd have to try to get themselves to the local market and then find a taxi, bus or a lorry truck to take them to a hospital. Small things would become fatal very fast without the necessary treatment and care. There was a doctor in the village, but there was only so much he could do as he was vastly outnumbered.

This also meant that childbirth was carried out at home. I can remember many of my siblings being born inside our house. My dad, older brother, Peter, and cousins would help unfurl a big blue tarp that was left over from building some part of the house, and would spread it out in a bed-room for Mum to lay on during labour. There was always a lot of chaos during this time, with a lot of family and friends coming around to offer help and best wishes. Our neighbour was a village midwife, and she was always on hand to help Mum. On the day following the birth of a child, the placenta would be buried in the backyard. We'd always have to spend the next few days stopping our dog, Kolagnyak, from digging it up.

School started at 7 a.m. and finished at 12 p.m. Those odd but short hours were set so we could avoid the heat of the day. It was always scorching hot outside after midday, and we'd stay indoors until it cooled down and then play soccer until dusk. It used to get so hot and dry, the ground would crack. In the wet season the rain would pour non-stop. The cars and lorry trucks couldn't even get around because the rain was so intense and the mud it created was so thick. A large pool of water would always form at the front of our house, which would be full of birds and frogs. Some houses would get washed away and others would be badly flooded. The blue tarp that we'd used for building and childbirth always came in handy at this time. In terms of air temperature, I don't remember it ever being very cold.

A short walk away was a desert and another village that we would sometimes visit. We played outside all the time and crafted toys out of clay. We'd dry out all sorts of animals and trinkets in the sun and keep them. We tied old balls of socks to a stick and hit them with our hands – like totem tennis. We played marbles and soccer and flew kites. There was lots of wrestling and walking on our hands – I can still do that now! I was so good at it I could walk more than ten metres on my hands without toppling over.

Life was simple, but despite the fact we were relatively settled and comfortable in Sudan, my parents knew that life could be much better for us all. In 2000, they decided that Mum would take all of us kids and move to Egypt.

Our departure was very hush-hush. It was the middle of the night when I was woken by one of my brothers. Tired and grumpy, I reluctantly got out of bed and gathered my belongings. It was time to say farewell to my birthplace and start a new life. We had to get to the train station quite early, about 3 a.m. Being so young, I was really dragging the chain for the rest of the family – I remember Augustino holding my hand to make sure I didn't fall behind.

Out the front of our house there was an old ute called a 'boxy', waiting to take us to the station. These types of vehicles were everywhere in Sudan. I'm sure you can picture them: the cabin up the front could seat about three people, and then the tray on the back was just a wooden box tacked on, which you could cram upwards of 15 people into. Twenty if you really wanted to push it and got creative.

Being so young, I had no idea why Dad wasn't coming with us. Everything was happening quickly, and no doubt it was hard for my parents to explain. I knew we were going to Egypt, but it was all so confusing. I didn't know what was going to unfold or if we were ever going to see Dad again. I just put all my trust in my Mum and had to believe she'd look after us all.

We embarked on a three-day train ride to Aswan, Egypt's southern gateway. It was a really old train – like one you'd see in an old western movie. There was first class, second class, and then our class, which was very cheap and nasty, with disgusting drop-toilets in the carriages.

Looking out the window, there was nothing to see along the way, just sand and desert. The train would stop intermittently in the middle of nowhere to allow people to get off and stretch their legs, and to let the Muslim passengers pray. If you didn't get back on in time, the train left without you; I spent a lot of time amusing myself by watching people trying desperately to catch up and get back on board the train as it picked up speed. Some didn't make it and would have to wait for another train to come by – whenever that would be.

When we arrived in Aswan, we had to stay in a hotel for a night, which was terrible. It was so cold, and there was no mattress on the bed. It was a bad night's sleep for us all.

The next day we got our passports stamped and boarded a ferry that travelled along the Nile river towards Cairo. Before we reached the capital of Egypt, we had to get another train, which was only a two-hour journey.

My first impression of Cairo was that the amount of buildings, cars, pollution and noise was overwhelming. It was a lot to take in. It was probably the first time in my life that I'd seen that much traffic and chaos.

REFLECTIONS

Augustino Daw

My second-oldest brother, Augustino, remembers me as a bit of a handful growing up. He and my oldest brother, Peter, were always very busy keeping me out of mischief.

Maj was a – what-do-you-call-it? – we don't call him a naughty man, but he was a kid who was very hyperactive and would always get himself into trouble. Peter and I were constantly getting him out of trouble and sorting everything out for him. He was very cheeky. If you told him, 'Don't touch that!' he would touch it as soon as you turned your back on him. If you said, 'Hey! Don't do that!' he would break the rules and do it. He was the kind of kid who wouldn't do something if you asked him to. He loved to get out of his comfort zone, and he was a very adventurous young fellow.

Maj used to wake up at around five-thirty or six in the morning. He was an early riser, and he used to eat a traditional dish called *ful*. When he got up, he'd go to a restaurant and would be the first customer to be served. I mean, he was around four or five years old and the restaurant owner got to know him. One morning an incident happened. Maj had gone to the restaurant at around 5.15 a.m. and the food wasn't ready yet. He decided to pop his head inside to see what was happening and he ended up burning his face on the steam. He'd lifted the lid on a pot and, little did he know, it was actually piping hot. If you look at him closely as an adult today, he's got three dots under his nose – scars from the accident.

When we left Omdurman, we moved to an area called Jabarona. We had a massive boulder at home and Maj decided to go and push the boulder and cut open his hand. The third incident I can remember was we were playing around the house, and he decided to run and struck his head on a doorknob. You can see today there's a massive gash on his head. Another time he climbed on top of a fence and then decided to jump. He fell awkwardly on his shoulder and dislocated it. And then there was the story about him cutting off his finger.

He couldn't fight his own battles. He would get into trouble with a group of older boys and would go and tell them, 'Look, if you touch me, I'll go and call my older brother, and my older brother will come and teach you a lesson.' When Maj came running home, I'm like, 'What trouble have you got us into now?' Maj would say, 'That boy tried to beat me up.' I had to stand up for him knowing that he might have been in the wrong, but I'd be like, 'Hey, that's my younger brother. You ever touch him, you're dealing with me from now on.' That's the upper hand he had. He had two older brothers, so no one could really touch him – and he used that.

4
Njuan

I sat bolt upright in bed and took a few seconds to gather my thoughts and senses, as I had been startled by an incredible amount of shouting and yelling that was coming from outside. The sounds were full of angst and lots of aggression. It was late at night in Cairo, and I got out of bed and ran to my mum's room to make sure she was up. She was already awake when I got there, and she was climbing out of bed to see what all the fuss was about. Together, we walked cautiously to the front door, opened it slowly and peered outside.

Down the street, a mob of people had surrounded a young man who was trying to walk by. He had his head down and was clearly trying not to make any eye contact or provoke them, but he was being attacked, harassed and taunted.

I could see they were angry at him and were holding sticks and flick knives or pocket knives, waving them in his face, threatening to slash and stab him. Others slapped him across the head, grabbed at his clothes and kicked him from behind as he continued to make his way down the road. As he and the angry mob neared us, I could make out some dimly lit faces. Some of them were children, others were young adults, and some were even friends of our family – people we'd come to know from the neighbourhood. I wondered what had made them so angry and why they were acting in that way towards this particular man.

My mum stepped outside to get a better look at what was going on, as had many other people in the street, and that's when she cried out, 'Peter!' She was suddenly running towards the group, yelling, 'Get away from him! Peter!' It was at that moment I realised the young man under attack was my eldest brother, Peter, who was only about 12 or 13 at the time. Now that Mum had yelled his name, I could see it was him from the way he looked and walked. He was in real trouble and zigged and zagged around the men who moved to block his path home from work. He was unable to run because so many people were in his way; it was a real pack mentality and they were swarming him.

My mum was closing in, waving her arms and yelling at the men to stop hitting Peter and threatening him. She had no concern for her own safety, only that of her first-born son. She eventually broke through the ring that had encircled Peter and took him in her arms, shielding him from the torment and angry cries of 'monkey!' and other derogatory names.

Her presence and intervention had an immediate impact, as those fearing she'd recognise them ran back to their homes like cowards. For now, Peter was safe, and Mum ushered him inside and slammed the door behind them. It was one of the most terrifying experiences I can remember in all my time in Egypt. I honestly thought they were going to kill Peter, such was their level of hate.

When we first arrived in Egypt, life seemed pretty straightforward, but as we began to explore our surroundings and venture further into the city of Cairo, we discovered there was danger lurking around every corner for people like us; that is, people with our skin colour and religious beliefs. There were a lot of South Sudanese people in Egypt, all from different tribes, although not that many from ours: Dinka – the largest ethnic group in the country. The common language in Egypt was Arabic and that took some getting used to. As we began to integrate with the locals, we learnt a lot about them and, disappointingly, there was a lot of conflict, prejudice and hate stemming mainly from differing religious beliefs. The majority of people in Egypt are Sunni Muslim, and the second most popular following is Coptic Christian. Growing tensions between the two groups often led to violence, and it was extremely dangerous to be alone, especially as a young Sudanese Christian.

It was common to hear people yell out 'monkey!' and mimic ape-like behaviours when I walked by. I had nappies full of shit thrown at me from balconies and out of windows. If it wasn't a nappy, then it might be someone's spit. Regardless of the treatment we received, one thing we were told was to never retaliate or provoke anyone regardless of what they did to us. Locals would always receive preferential treatment from the authorities, and the word of a foreigner, especially a Sudanese kid, didn't carry any weight whatsoever. There were numerous stories about kids, as young as nine-year-old me, being hit by cars and left by the road for days or weeks with no calls to the police or action taken.

The black market was in full swing with human organ trafficking, too. I heard a kidney could fetch up to US$100 000. Some migrants would voluntarily give up an organ for money, so they could afford to pay for a visa or passage through to their next destination. But the human organ traffickers didn't always have to pay. If they stumbled across a defenceless foreign kid, they would just kidnap them, take what they wanted and leave them to die, knowing there'd be little or no consequences or enquiries made by the local police. Even with something as minor as a fight or scuffle, if you lashed out at an Egyptian in retaliation, you would likely be arrested with no questions asked.

To be safe, it came down to being street-smart. You had to be aware of your surroundings and avoid travelling alone if possible. If I was alone and someone asked me what my religion was, I'd always tell them I was Muslim to avoid being ostracised, targeted or assaulted. If someone wanted to fight me for whatever reason, I just had to keep my mouth shut and take a beating. One day, on my way back from my cousin's house, we were surrounded by a small group of teenagers. They demanded to know where we were going and spoke to us in a threatening manner. They wanted to know who we were and what our religion was. We immediately lied to them, saying we were Muslims and that our names were Mohammed and Ahmad. They weren't overly convinced, but thankfully they let us go without incident. We knew if we hadn't thought on our feet and lied, we would have copped a fierce beating or possibly worse.

Having to pretend to be someone else and deny my identity never sat well with me, but as a nine-year-old, I didn't have much choice. Everyday life, in fact, was full of compromises and there were a lot of grey areas. You always had to have your wits about you. There was an ill-feeling about the place, and I can say, as a family, we never felt like we belonged in Cairo. That's a terrible way to live, but after leaving our home in Sudan, it was unfortunately something we just had to get used to.

I don't want to paint Egypt as an evil place or make out that everyone there was nasty and racist, because a lot of amazing people there went out of their way to make us feel welcome and help us out. One family, in particular, went to great lengths to assist by giving us US$1000 a month, just because they wanted to help us and ensure that we were able to live comfortably. When my dad eventually joined us in Cairo, he met a French priest who, after returning home, arranged a big fundraiser at his local church to help pay our visa fees, which exceeded US$20 000. It was incredibly generous, and I don't know how we would have afforded it had he not stepped in to help. For us, it meant being able to start our new life much sooner than we otherwise could have.

REFLECTIONS

Augustino, William and Elizabeth Daw

The racism and violence we witnessed in Egypt remains vivid in all our memories. Augustino recalls similar experiences.

In Egypt, we would get called every single derogatory name in the book. There were even incidents where if you'd walk underneath a building, someone could chuck rubbish on top of you. If you walked down the street, they would try to beat you up or try to harass you. Some people would come up to you and spit on your face. Some would come and grab your hand and be like, 'Ah! Chocolate man! Let me come and eat a bit of chocolate!' and they would lick you. And you just look at them and be like, 'Wait, are you for fucking real? You are licking me . . . you're licking my body.' They would say, 'Yeah, I'm just eating a bit of chocolate out of you.' Eventually, you just had to learn to swallow your pride.

Those things were very common in Egypt. We had to live very cautiously. Most people in Egypt, they would just go out and say, 'Look, if you do come back by the end of the day, perfect. You made it to another day.' You learn how to mature very quickly. At the age of seven, Maj was coming of age and we had to let him know what was happening and what was going on. When Mum took up work as a cleaner, the responsibility was on us. She'd say, 'Guard your younger brothers and make sure you nurture them.' So, we'd go to school, come back from school and then go to work after that.

Things became very difficult in Sudan for my father, William. Although it must have felt impossible, in the end he knew leaving the country was the right thing for his family.

Majak was a very active child, always wanting to try things and test them by himself. He was a very thoughtful and considerate boy. Where we lived in Sudan, there were people from all different backgrounds, with different skin colours, nationalities and religions. We had never told him about the general differences between people, but when he was only two or three, he chose to greet Arabic people in the Arabic language and South Sudanese people in Dinka. I asked him, 'How do you know all of this?' I was expecting him to just greet people in one language, but he was learning to talk to these people in their own languages, by his own choice.

Leaving Sudan was one of the toughest decisions I've had to make in my life. I never thought I'd leave, but it happened that people like us were having problems with the Sudanese government. I was so close to my church, and this was a big problem, because Sudan is an Islamic country. Other things concerned me too. There was fighting, with the war going on between the north and the south of the country. There was political fighting, and ethnicity issues, too. If you weren't lining up with the government and what it was doing, then you were an enemy of the government. If you were not a Muslim, you were their enemy.

At one point I was detained by national security forces for being at a church gathering. We were at a house, having a meeting, and the guards came over the compound's walls, broke into the house and took me away. My family didn't know where I was until I was returned home, at which point I was put under house arrest. On a few occasions, I was beaten unconscious. I lost a day from my memory because I was beaten so badly.

We lived in fear because we knew that, legally, they could stop me in the street and detain me, or pull my car over in the middle of the street without a reason. I used to carry my toothbrush and some toothpaste around because I never knew if they were going to grab me and take me away. Some of my colleagues were taken and never returned – they died. I was prepared to continue living this way, but my mother and Elizabeth's mother said, 'Look, this situation – you may lose your life. Your children will be vulnerable, and we do not want to see that. Please, can you leave the country?' It took me a long time to accept their position.

When I made the decision to leave Sudan with my family, one of my lawyer friends told me to separate the passports, and to issue Elizabeth with her own passport. This was because if my name was listed on the passport, our request to leave would be rejected. Splitting the passports was the only chance we'd have of getting out. I had to stay back in Sudan and try to find a legal way for me to get an exit visa too, which took me almost six months.

I struggled while I was away from my family. My mother kept asking me, 'Why have you lost weight? Why are you losing so much weight?' I told her, 'I'm worried about my family, my children. I don't know what's happening. I have dreams that there's a car accident and one of my kids is killed.' That was a constant nightmare for me. Living without my children was the first time I had to make such a sacrifice, leaving them on their own. I didn't even know anything about Egypt.

Even when I finally got my visa, I wasn't sure if I'd be allowed in. I was unsure right up to the point when I reached the border of Sudan and Egypt, travelling on a steamboat on the Nile. Thankfully the Sudanese guards handed my passport over to the Egyptian authorities, which meant that not only was I allowed to leave, I would also be allowed back into Sudan at a later date.

When I got to Egypt, I got a job straight away. I said to my kids, 'Thank you, you have done your role by working for the family. I am here now and you don't have to work anymore. Go back to your schools, your time to work will come.'

As difficult as it was for my father, it was even harder for my mum, Elizabeth, looking after all of us kids by herself, in a country that was completely alien.

In Sudan, Majak was always on the move, a very busy little boy. I always had to keep an eye on him as he was always opening the windows and the cupboards in the kitchen. One day he decided to try and fix the old coal iron we had, and I said, 'No! How do you even know how to fix it?' But he just took it and tried to fix it anyway. He was a very good boy, and friends with lots of other children. When he decided he wanted to do something, there was really no way of telling him no – he was very certain.

It was very hard for me in Egypt with the kids. It was a tough life. One of the houses we moved into had only one bedroom, but five families lived there. Some of the places we stayed in had a bed but no mattress, no pillow, no bedding – it was terrible. The desert, the cold weather. I didn't know any of the language, so I couldn't shop; it was lucky I had carried so much food with me on the way over.

When we went to Cairo, we went to a place that people go when they come from Sudan. William's friend took us in, but it was a one-bedroom house with about five families and twenty people. All the children in one room with only blankets. We were kicked out of three houses in total. Many houses we weren't allowed into because we weren't Muslim. Others wanted $2000 a month, which I couldn't afford. I cried a lot. It was very hard for me.

One day, after work, I got back to the house we were staying in and my children were gone. A lady who lived nearby told me the owner had kicked the kids out of the house while I was away. I didn't know where they were. I searched for them for twelve hours, until 4 o'clock in the morning. I went to the church and the priests came, and, thank God, helped me find my kids. We found another place to stay, but that was another one-bedroom house. It was so dirty and full of rubbish. I spent hours cleaning it – no one slept that night.

5

Dhiëc

We'd been knocked back so many times for a migrant visa, from so many different countries around the world, that it got to the point where I thought we'd be in Egypt forever. We had been in Cairo for three years and had been forced to watch other extended family members come and go before us to places like America, Canada, the Netherlands, Australia and New Zealand, despite the fact that we had been waiting much longer than them. There were no rules with the process as far as we knew, no guarantees that we'd ever get out of the country, and definitely no orderly queue to stand in. All we could do was wait and hope for our turn to come.

One thing we did learn, however, was that our family's large size was a major stumbling block in our application being accepted and processed. We eventually had to apply for a humanitarian visa, because we didn't fit the criteria as refugees. One main difference is that you have to foot the bill and pay your own way on a humanitarian visa, which is in the tens of thousands of US dollars. When Dad joined us in the country, there was Mum and Dad, then Peter, Augustino, me, Teresa, Anthony, Sarah, Angelina and Mary – Ajak hadn't been born yet. So, in total, we were a family of ten looking to relocate. It would obviously have been much easier for a family of just three or four to get accepted.

Despite the painstaking delays and lack of transparency from various countries' immigration departments, as far as the visa application process goes, my parents never wavered in their determination to secure us kids a better way of life and a new home. The feeling that we were being constantly overlooked and somewhat forgotten was significant, but they never gave up hope and constantly reassured us that 'everything would work out fine' and that we'd be 'on our way soon'. It was a tough time for us all, but especially for them. The stress of being stuck in Egypt, treading water and not being able to provide the life they so desperately wanted for their kids was very hard.

Eventually their faith and our patience paid off when we received word that the Australian government had granted us a migrant visa. The feeling was surreal. We immediately called our relatives all around the world to share our news and told them everything we knew about what was to be our new home 'down under'. We received lots of information in return from them about Australia. Our uncles told us the streets in all the cities there were made of glass and that you could get cow's milk out of the taps in all the houses, schools and other buildings. We heard about kangaroos, platypuses, koalas and all the other amazing animals that roamed freely. The kangaroos raising little joeys in their pouches fascinated me the most. Without any access to a computer or any information from the internet, we had to rely on what we were told about Australia, which led to our imaginations running wild. Let me tell you, I thought Australia sounded pretty hi-tech and futuristic, with streets of glass and milk coming out of the taps. C'mon, that's pretty amazing!

With our migrant visa administrative and approval fees paid, we had to wait for about three more months before any official documents came through and we could be on our way. My dad had to do a lot of paperwork to prove to the Australian government that when we arrived, we'd have somewhere to stay and would be able to afford to live and look after ourselves.

At the airport, I remember my aunty crouching down and resting on her knee, lowering herself to my eyeline. She had tears streaming down her face and threw her arms wide open, inviting me in for one last hug. Like a magnet, I threw myself into her chest and held on tightly. I couldn't stop crying, and nor could my brothers, sisters and mum. My aunty kept telling me to 'be happy' but I couldn't let go that easily. We'd all grown up together and the gravity of the situation really hit me hard. I kept thinking that it would be the last time I'd ever see her, and also many of my uncles and cousins, because I'd been in their exact position so many times before – farewelling family members who had secured a better life in some far corner of the world. We'd had extended family move to the United States, Canada, the Netherlands, Australia – all over the world, really. I'd lost count of how many times we said goodbye to relatives on both my mum's and dad's sides of the family – and after farewelling them, I never saw them again. This time, it was me and my family who would be disappearing beyond the glass walls at the departure gates.

None of us had been on a plane before. We'd seen them in American movies on TV, so we knew what a plane looked like, but to be on the verge of boarding one and experiencing flying for ourselves was hard to comprehend. So, mixed in with the emotions of being separated from our extended family forever, we also had this sense of excitement and wonder because we were about to take to the skies and start our new life – something our parents had long dreamed of and worked extremely hard for.

We flew out of Cairo and had a brief stopover in Dubai, and then another in Singapore – but that turned out to be a much longer delay than we'd expected. Because our family was so big, there weren't enough seats on the plane for the Singapore-to-Melbourne leg on this particular day. While that would be an inconvenience for most people, for us it ended up being a blessing in disguise and a most memorable occasion. We were told that we'd have to stay overnight in a hotel before getting another connecting flight to Tullamarine Airport.

Mum and Dad's initial panic about not being able to afford a hotel room or dinner for us all was quickly alleviated by an airline staff member, who told us that the bill for everything would be taken care of. The woman told my dad through an interpreter that the room and all our meals were to be 'free of charge' – a term none of us had ever heard before.

Knowing what I know now, it wasn't a super-fancy hotel by any stretch of the imagination, but back then it was the most luxurious and opulent place I'd stayed in, or even seen, for that matter – and by a long way. It was the coolest thing ever! The wow-factor was overwhelming, and we all felt like royalty. Located inside the airport precinct, the hotel's lobby was adorned with large water fountains and even had a shopping centre. We all couldn't believe how advanced and extravagant everything was. Our hotel room was amazing, too. The airline had arranged some two-bedroom apartments for us, and I shared a room with Augustino. That night we went to a restaurant, and because we barely spoke a word of English, we struggled to order food from the menu. Dad could speak some broken English, so they found a translator to help take down our order. We ate like kings and queens and took full advantage of what was on offer.

When we returned to our rooms after dinner, we couldn't comprehend the number of channels we could choose from on the TV. Flicking through them over and over was entertainment in itself. Augustino and I settled on some cartoons, and as a result, we had very little sleep that night because there was just too much to take in and experience. We knew if we went to sleep, we would have been missing out on so much fun.

We touched down in Melbourne on Australia Day – Sunday, 26 January 2003. For some reason we had thought it was going to be really cold; clearly we had no idea it would be summer when we arrived. Before we left Egypt, my parents took us all shopping for new clothes, and we all got some jeans, pants, t-shirts and shoes. Mum and Dad wanted to make sure we would be warm enough and bought us all these ridiculously big puffer jackets. So here we were in Melbourne on a hot summer's day, looking like we were headed to the snow. I think it was about 25 degrees that day and we were all sweating!

Friends of Dad's arrived at the airport in a mini-van they'd borrowed from their local church to collect us, and they took us back to their house in Maidstone. Again, we were taken in by people who really had no room for us. They were a family of six, and we were ten – so 16 people were under the one roof in a three-bedroom house. When we arrived, dozens of people were waiting to welcome us to Australia. It was all a bit overwhelming, and I remember going to bed very early that afternoon as I was completely exhausted from all the travel, emotional turmoil and excitement from the previous few days.

When I woke up the next morning, people were sleeping all around the house. It was super-crowded and wherever there was enough space for a human, someone was lying in it. I was lucky enough to get a queen-sized bed, which I shared with Augustino and Anthony, but my other siblings had to settle for a couch or a mattress on the floor in the living room. As kids, all we wanted to do was play and explore, but with so many people in the house, we were constantly getting into trouble for bumping into things and breaking stuff. I remember kicking the soccer ball over the fence and getting into so much trouble from my mum and dad.

After a few weeks of staying there, my parents were able to get a house of their own not that far away in Footscray, and we also registered as new citizens. The school year was about to begin, and we had to decide how I'd start my education, keeping in mind I didn't speak a word of English. My parents were weighing up the option of putting me in Grade 6 with students much younger than me, or sending me straight to Year 7 to begin high school. They thought I may have needed an extra year in primary school to get on top of the language and settle in properly. I was keen to go straight into Year 7 and eventually got my way, but it meant going to an English-language centre first to fast-track things. In fact, Mum and Dad decided to send most of us there, and it was full of other newly arrived migrants.

If I had my time again, I would have stayed back a year and gone to primary school to really help with my development and English speaking and writing. I just felt like I didn't have enough time to understand what was going on, and a lot of that first year in high school went over my head. Although maths is the same in every language, there were some little things I just couldn't grasp. My writing skills weren't up to scratch and I felt a little bit embarrassed by that too. While I might've been a year older than some of the kids in Grade 6, it still would have been much better for my education starting at that level.

REFLECTIONS

Augustino Daw

I leant on Augustino a lot when we first arrived in Australia. He was my protector, guide and best friend. Australia was a strange place for us, as he, too, recalls.

We had to do an induction before coming to Australia. We had to know the major cities and what the culture was like. That was done in English. It could have been done in a language that we understood. We were one of the fortunate families because Dad was an English speaker, so he was able to translate a lot of things for us.

At the English-language school, most of the other students were also refugees and our school was very diverse; we had Vietnamese, Kenyans and Zimbabweans. The one thing we all had in common, obviously, was not knowing how to speak English. We couldn't communicate with the Zimbabweans or the Vietnamese, so we kept to ourselves until we picked up the ABCs and could put a sentence together. Even then, we would only try speaking English to ourselves and would always be asking each other,

'Hey, this is how you say that in English, right?' When Maj and I got to high school, we found that no one wanted to be our friends for the first two to three months. Sport became a great language for us to use when our English failed us.

6

Detem

After arriving in Australia, I quickly became aware of this strange game everyone called 'Aussie Rules'. Although I never had the courage or opportunity to give it a go at school, it fascinated me. For me, Year 7 at the Catholic Regional College in Keilor and later years 8 to 12 at MacKillop College in Werribee were supposed to be about my education and, most importantly, mastering the English language, rather than playing games with other kids in the school yard.

Even if I'd wanted to give Aussie Rules a go in Year 7, I didn't really have anyone to play it with. Recesses and lunchtimes involved me and Augustino sitting together in a quiet corner of the school yard eating our lunch. It wasn't that we didn't want to make friends or play, but it became obvious that no one knew how to approach us, because we were very different to all the other kids at school. So Augustino and I would arrive at school together in the morning, spend time together in the recesses and breaks between classes, and then rendezvous at the end of the day and walk home together. When we got home, we ate together, watched TV together and even shared a room. Although we had each other for company at school, it was still a very lonely experience for us not knowing any of the other children. At the time there weren't many kids with our skin colour – a far cry from the demographics of that region, Wyndham, today. Looking back, I can completely understand why the local kids would have been apprehensive about approaching us. It was a pretty isolating experience, though, and we definitely felt we were on the outer and not very welcome there. Again, that terribly familiar feeling of not belonging was ever-present in my life.

After a few months at MacKillop College, the barriers that divided us from the rest of the kids finally started to come down. Other students began to warm to me and my brother, but it wasn't until we showed them what we were capable of athletically that they really started to like us and include us more. In Sudan and Egypt, soccer was the main sport we'd played and watched religiously, so naturally I started playing it in Australia. Augustino was much more skilled than me at it and really dominated games in the school yard. Oftentimes, I would switch between soccer and basketball, but I always had an eye on the Aussie Rules game that a group of kids would be playing on the big oval.

Of course, I knew a little bit about the sport, because in Melbourne and Victoria it's like a religion and you really can't escape it. As a family, we'd see it on TV on Friday nights and on the weekends, but my parents could never understand it and always turned it off. They really didn't like the sport because they perceived the tackling, bumping, wrestling and hitting as unnecessary acts of violence between the players. The occasional all-in brawl that occurred during some games didn't help sway them either.

Back in 2003, the game was a lot rougher and tougher than what it is today, and I always remember Collingwood being on the main stage on Friday nights. The Magpies became my team of choice, and I slowly grew to like the Australian version of football more than world football, or soccer. More and more, I felt an urge to play it.

In the summer, the kids at school would play soccer, basketball and cricket, but come the winter months, it was as if someone flicked a giant switch causing everyone to dump their soccer balls, basketballs and cricket balls in favour of this bizarre oval-shaped red leather ball called a 'footy'. Groups of kids, about ten or more, would stand about 30 to 40 metres apart and play a game called 'Mark's Up', which basically involved one person kicking the ball high into the air to the opposite group of players, who would all jump at the ball in a giant pack to try to catch it – a skill known as a 'mark'. The player who came down with the ball would then have the honour of advancing to the front of the pack to kick it back to the other group, so its players could try to mark it. No score was kept, but bragging rights were always up for grabs. It was fun to watch because oftentimes no one would mark the ball and bodies would fly everywhere and come crashing to the ground. It was definitely a game I could see myself getting into.

After biding my time on the sidelines, restricted to watching only, one of the students finally invited me to play with them. To say I was excited would be an understatement, but I was also extremely nervous. Scared of hurting myself, or someone else for that matter, it would be fair to say I attacked the first few high balls hesitantly and was just enjoying being included by the other students. I mean, I was jumping along with everyone else, but I wasn't trying too hard, because I didn't want to do something wrong and get kicked out of the game. A few of the boys who I had played some basketball with previously, and who knew I could jump high enough to dunk, started to encourage me, yelling, 'C'mon, Maj! Show 'em what you've got!' It was all the encouragement I needed, and the next ball that came spinning through the air had my name all over it. I took a little run-up and launched at the ball with my arms stretched out. I could feel the other kids' bodies crash against mine while we were all in the air, but I kept my balance and never took my eyes off the fast-approaching leather projectile. To my delight, it stuck in my hands and I was able to pull down my first mark.

My joy was short-lived, though, when I realised I had to kick the ball back to the other pack. As those who can remember their first kick of a Sherrin football will know, executing the perfect kick, or 'drop-punt' as it's called, is near impossible the first time around – or the second time, third time, fourth time . . . you get the picture.

The drop-punt is one of the hardest skills to learn, especially when you haven't grown up with a footy to kick around and play with as a kid. I took the ball, walked to the front of the group and tried to remember what the others had done when they'd kicked the ball.

The pressure was immense, and I felt like every kid in the school yard had stopped what they were doing to watch me. I felt like the principal may as well have jumped on the PA and announced, 'Excuse me, students and teachers, please turn your attention to the football oval where young Majak Daw is about to attempt his very first drop-punt!' In reality, I don't think anyone was actually expecting me to be able to kick it properly, but I was so hell-bent on impressing everyone that I felt the weight of the world on my shoulders. With my hands shaking from adrenaline and nerves, I took a giant step with my left leg and swung my right leg backwards. I dropped the ball at about waist-height out in front of me, and then brought my right leg forward in a reverse-catapult action. When the ball was just centimetres from the ground, I kicked at it with my foot and sent it sailing . . . sideways. To my utter embarrassment, the ball connected with the outside of my shoe and shot off to the right, at a very sharp angle. Making matters worse, it barely went 15 metres, let alone the 40 metres it was supposed to go. I threw my face into my hands and shook my head as I turned to walk back to the group. I could hear chuckling and laughter, but it died down quickly as the ball was returned to our end, and another marking contest began.

While I figured the kicking part of the game wasn't for me just yet, marking was right up my alley. I soon discovered that if I had a decent run and jump at it, the ball was mine to be marked almost every time. No one could match my leaping ability and reach, though the smart players figured out that if they blocked my run-up or bumped me off my line before I jumped, it was a more even affair. Aussie Rules became a daily ritual at school, and after some time refining my skills, I started to pick it up quickly. Doors were really starting to open for me, especially socially, and my network of friends expanded substantially off the back of playing footy. It gave me something in common with the other kids, who had no idea about my background and life in Sudan or growing up in Egypt. For me to integrate fully with them, I had to learn more about their way of life and embrace the Australian culture and their pastimes. Football was the ultimate icebreaker, and it gave me a way in and a chance to get to know people and become friends with them.

My improvement led to an invitation to try out with a local football club, Taylors Lakes. One of my new friend's dads was involved in an official capacity at the club and thought I could be a handy player for them. I asked my hesitant parents to let me attend a training session after school one afternoon and, to my surprise, they said yes. I was taller than most of the other kids there, so my height, leaping ability and skin colour made me stand out. I did my best to impress the coaches but felt completely overwhelmed by the occasion and didn't think I was any chance of being selected. However, I was unexpectedly invited back.

While the other boys from my school were selected for the Under 14A side, I was squeezed into the Under 14B side to play in the Essendon District Football League (EDFL). Being allowed to train was one thing, but now that I had been picked, I had to convince my parents to actually let me play.

My first attempt at swaying my dad can only be described as a short and unsuccessful one. 'No!' was his initial response and it was delivered midway through my request. Once he had figured out what I was after, he slammed the door shut on the conversation and wouldn't let me reopen it. Mum was just as adamant as Dad that I shouldn't play, but she was perhaps even more cautious because she saw how physical the game was and feared for my safety. Both of them were concerned about my education and how playing footy might impact my ability to learn English and continue to adapt to the Australian way of life and culture. I was so frustrated by my parents' stubbornness and, for a while, never thought I'd turn them around and convince them to let me play. Looking back now, I think their concerns were quite reasonable, but as a kid, I just thought they were being selfish and difficult.

Another stumbling block was the cost of playing. I recall the registration fee for junior footy being upwards of $250 per season, which was a massive ask for any low-income earning family, let alone one now made up of 11 people. Being young and naïve, I really had no comprehension about how hard it would have been for my parents to somehow find that amount of money for just one child in their already tight household budget. After Ajak was born in 2006 they had nine little mouths to feed, plus bills, school fees, medical bills, a mortgage and other things they were no doubt saving for.

I never gave up on my ambition to play footy and kept badgering Mum and Dad whenever I sensed there was an opportunity to do so. I had to convince them that the game wasn't violent and full of people only trying to hurt one another. It took ages and ages to even get them to listen to my many arguments. Dad just kept saying, 'Why don't you just play soccer with Augustino?' To that I always answered, 'Because I want to try something new. I want to try this footy thing that everyone plays!' Eventually, I wore them down and they agreed to let me play. But unbeknown to me at the time, I would have to jump several more hurdles before I could make my junior footy debut.

What was supposed to be a regular trip to the shops in Footscray to do the groceries one Saturday afternoon turned out to be anything but for my parents. On returning to the carpark, they couldn't find their car – it had been stolen. It was later found burnt out on a highway in Melton. Obviously, this was a huge inconvenience for my whole family, but for me the ramifications were particularly significant. The following day, a Sunday, I was supposed to be playing my first game for the Taylors Lakes Football Club. I was so excited that I had packed my bag the day before and barely got any sleep that night. After losing the car, my parents had to arrange to borrow a friend's car to take me to the game.

I leapt out of the car when we pulled up and made my way over to the change rooms, but when my coach saw me, he said, 'Maj! What are you doing here?' At first, I thought I had the wrong time or place, but then I saw some of my new teammates standing around in uniform, so I knew something else was the problem. I looked at the coach, confused, urging him for more information. 'You're not registered to play yet!' he declared.

It was at that moment I felt my heart sink around my ankles. *The registration form!* I racked my brain trying to remember where I'd left it. Of all the things to forget, besides the money in my pocket for the registration, the form was the most important piece of paper. I knew deep down I didn't have it with me, and I ran back to Mum and Dad to see if they'd brought it with them by chance. To my utter disappointment, neither of them had it or knew where it was. I broke out in a cold sweat and felt completely humiliated and guilty, because I'd dragged my family all this way for nothing. I felt stupid being all kitted-out in my new uniform with my new footy boots on, which some family friends had bought for me, but with no chance of playing.

Where is the registration form? I kept asking myself the same question, hoping the answer would magically pop into my head. And then it dawned on me. I had last seen the form in the boot of our family car. Just as I started to run back to Mum and Dad to get the keys and retrieve it, I realised it wasn't the same car. The car I needed was the one that had been stolen the day before and was sitting on the side of the road, charred and unrecognisable.

After some back-and-forth with the junior footy league officials, and an explanation from us about what had happened to the form and our car, we were still told that without a registration form, I wasn't able to play. Instead, I had to watch the game from the sidelines, miserable and almost bawling my eyes out. Seeing my level of despair, the coach came over and tried to lift my spirits by offering me an all-important role. 'You can be our water boy, if you like?' he said. Not wanting to disappoint anyone else, I took him up on the offer and used the experience to get as close to the action as possible, trying to pick up some things for when I'd eventually be allowed to play.

My failed attempt at playing was soon a distant memory, because after I got myself sorted with the right paperwork and paid my money, there was no holding me back. While my enthusiasm didn't match my skill level, I still loved playing this new and amazing game of Aussie Rules. It was hard to get the hang of it early on, and I remember feeling incredibly frustrated at being unable to get my hands on the ball around the ground. The skill level in the Under 14Bs wasn't the best, and my abilities at the time didn't help, either. Like the school yard game 'Mark's Up', I could take a big grab, but my kicking was still a work in progress. I figured instead of trying to boot the ball to a teammate, handballing it to one of them to do it for me was a much better option. I also battled with the rules and got penalised a lot for holding the ball, running too far without taking a bounce or tackling a player too late after he'd disposed of the ball. Getting the flow of the game and where to run was another big challenge, but with a lot of help and coaching, I started to find my way.

I think my mum was still a bit unsure about me playing, especially after I came home with a dislocated finger one day! She used the incident as an opportunity to try to convince me to throw in the towel, arguing, 'How can you play this game? It is too rough and you are only going to get hurt!'

As the games wore on, I realised I needed to be ultra-careful with my footy boots to ensure they lasted as long as possible. Unlike other kids, who wore about five pairs of boots a season, some maybe more, I needed the single pair my friends had bought me to last a very long time. I knew Mum and Dad wouldn't be in a position to buy me any new ones, having already forked out the money for my registration, so it meant when I got home after every game, I'd go straight to the laundry, clean the mud off my boots and wipe down the leather so it wouldn't get cracked and damaged. That wasn't my only new chore, either. As a result of being afforded the money for my registration, Mum and Dad made sure I did extra jobs around the house to repay them and show my brothers and sisters that I wasn't being favoured in any way.

Playing for Taylors Lake in the EDFL meant a lot of travel to other teams' home grounds in places like Keilor, Strathmore, Pascoe Vale, Greenvale, Jacana, Aberfeldie and Oak Park, just to name a few. The issue for me was that no one in my family knew any of those areas. It meant I had to learn another new skill – reading maps. Dad made a deal with me that if I wanted him to drop me off at games, I had to direct him how to get there. So, every Sunday I was in charge of navigating our way to the game using an old Melbourne map book called a *Melway*, and it was a stressful experience to say the least. I really had no idea how to read a map, and we got lost on so many occasions and were late to more games than I can count. Even getting to and from training was an ordeal as, oftentimes, Dad would forget to pick me up. After training finished, all the boys would gradually start to disappear while I waited for my ride home. I would spend the time kicking for goal with whoever was still around – a lot of the time until the oval lights were switched off. With no mobile phone or ability to call Dad to remind him to come and get me, I'd eventually have to walk home. I used to get so angry at him. It only took about 20 to 30 minutes to walk home and when I got inside, I'd have steam coming out of my ears from the frustration. 'Dad! Where were you?' I'd ask. His response was always the same: 'I'm sorry. I forgot.'

Despite the many hurdles I faced, we had a good year as a team in my first season. We made our way through the finals and into a preliminary final, and I really felt like an important part of the team playing in the ruck and as a forward. It was an overwhelmingly positive experience for me. I also discovered a set of 'second parents', too. Seeing how enthusiastic I was about footy and how good it was for my integration into the Australian way of life, our family friends Hop and Danni went out of their way to help us out by driving me to many training sessions and games.

They even came to the club's Best and Fairest Award night and watched me take home the Coach's Award – given to the player who showed a willingness to learn and improve, and who constantly displayed and lived by all the team's values the most.

Hop was a mad Melbourne Demons supporter in the AFL, and he was always trying to persuade me to drop my team, Collingwood, in favour of them. So, being grateful to him and Danni for their kind investment in me and my football development, I felt the least I could do was switch allegiances. I became a Melbourne supporter and even started watching Melbourne games on TV on the weekends. I followed David Neitz, the captain of Melbourne, very closely. I loved the way he played and tried to model my game on his. I also liked Russell Robertson's high-flying marks and Adem Yze's smooth skills.

My football improvement was rapid, but just when I was getting comfortable at Taylors Lakes, Mum and Dad bought a parcel of land in Werribee. It meant we had to move again and I was devastated. I had just started playing footy and had made all these new friends, only to be uprooted and forced to find my way once more. It was a recurring theme in my early life and this time it really frustrated me.

Thankfully, there was an oval belonging to the Wyndhamvale Football Club right next door to our new house. When the club's pre-season started, Mum and Dad encouraged me to go across and introduce myself. I was extremely nervous but managed to summon up the courage and headed over to see if the coaches would be open to having me play for their club. As I got closer to the training session, I could see there weren't too many Africans out there. To be blunt, it was a pretty white footy club and not very multicultural at all. I found a few friendly faces and told them I was keen to play, but having never seen me in action before, I could tell they were hesitant to let me join. I mean, from their point of view, here's this tall African bloke who no one knows, saying he wants to play Aussie Rules. It was pretty rare back then for someone like me to just rock up to a training and ask to play. Among the many players and coaches who were there that evening, one person really stood out as a super-friendly face. His name was Joey Halloran, and he was quick to see that I was very nervous and uncomfortable, so he came over to introduce himself and make me feel more welcome. It is something I will never forget. He went out of his way to look after me, although he didn't know me from a bar of soap. Joey helped introduce me properly to the club officials, and soon enough, they extended an invitation for me to train with them.

Footy with Wyndhamvale was a very new experience, as things started to get more serious on the field. The jump from school footy to club footy had been big enough, but now I was moving into an age group where the boys were starting to put on some size with respect to height and muscle. Luckily for me, I too had shot up in height, but I was still very skinny. After Under 14s, I moved up to the Under 16s and had two years in that age group. The players in the league were more experienced and skilled as well, and really exposed me for my lack of footy nous and physicality. I have to admit that during the first few months playing with Wyndhamvale, I really wasn't up to it. I started going to the gym regularly with Joey to make sure I didn't fall too far behind, and it paid dividends. Before long, I was dominating in the ruck with future AFL footballer Jack Fitzpatrick, who went on to play for the Melbourne Demons and Hawthorn Hawks.

Joey and Jack got into the development squad for the Western Jets – a club that plays in the premier Victorian Under 18s competition, the NAB League (then called the TAC Cup). To make it with the Jets, you have to be among the best young players in the region. The club has developmental squads in the Under 15s and 16s, but the Under 18s team is the most celebrated side and is closely watched by AFL recruiters. So, if you make it on a Jets list, you can rightfully dream of playing in the AFL.

My continued improvement with Wyndhamvale caught the eye of the Jets regional manager, Shane Sexton, and one day I received a written invitation from him to train with the Under 15s development squad. I was so surprised because there were other players on my team who were far better than me, and they didn't get a look-in with the Jets. Despite the acknowledgement, and the likes of Joey and Jack constantly telling me I was 'on the Jets' radar', I never let being picked in the squad go to my head. I was fully aware that I had a long way to go before I could even think about playing in the VFL, let alone the AFL.

I was 16 when I started training and playing with the Jets and had two years in the system. After graduating from the Under 15s, I made my way up to training with the Under 18s side. The players were so big and intimidating. They were men and I was still a boy. It was so daunting for me as a shy teenager. Jayden Post (Richmond Tigers), Mitch Banner (Port Adelaide Power) and Kyle Hartigan (Adelaide Crows) were also with the Jets during my time. I had a massive learning curve with the Jets and it was my first involvement in a football institution that involved mandatory training, weights programs, fitness regimes, recovery protocols and healthy lifestyle choices – they even prescribed me a diet to help me put on more muscle mass. My strength and conditioning coach there was James Veale and he was a great person to learn from and develop under.

Joey and I started to up the ante with our weights training sessions, going to the local recreation centre three times a week. As we were both from large families – Joey was also one of nine children – we were reluctant to ask our respective parents for more money for a gym membership. Instead, we told the staff member on the front desk at the leisure centre that we only wanted to use the basketball court, and then we would sneak into the gym afterwards to do weights. It was slightly cheeky, and one day we got caught and were warned not to do it anymore or risk being banned for life. We were told we would have to buy a membership if we ever wanted to come back inside. It forced us to plead with our parents for a gym membership, and to our surprise they said yes.

My footy had gone to a new level. While I had struggled to make the school side in Year 9, by Year 11, I had won the School Association's Best and Fairest Award. It was really the beginning of some bigger things to come for me.

REFLECTIONS

Augustino, William and Elizabeth Daw, Joey Halloran

Augustino got caught in the middle of many arguments I had with my parents about playing footy. He knew, more than most, that I would always get my way.

Maj was a great goalkeeper in soccer. Whenever we used to go and play soccer, we would make him be the goalie for the day. He never showed much interest in Aussie Rules until we moved into our second house in Keilor Downs and he went to play for the Taylors Lakes Lions. He didn't know anything about Aussie Rules, but then, by having a go at it, it brought him closer to a lot of people.

None of us really paid much attention to his football because my dad used to think it was a sport where men beat up on each other. He always said, 'We've seen enough violence in our lives and I don't want any of my sons to play a rough sport.' Dad was always going at Majak, saying, 'Look, we've seen enough. I don't think that's a sport. If you want to pick up a sport, go and pick up a basketball or go and play soccer.' But as I said earlier about Majak, he was always going against the grain and was very stubborn. So, the more Dad pushed him against it, the more Majak wanted to play Aussie Rules. He just told Dad, 'I'm just going to play.' Dad was like, 'Well, go ahead and go and break your bones.' I tell you, Maj has always been defiant. Since he learnt how to walk and talk, he would say to any challenge, 'I can do it,' and Dad would always tell him, 'No, you cannot do it.' And he'd be like, 'Okay. You watch me. I'll do it.' When Maj started playing footy, Dad said to me, 'I should have just told him to go ahead and play, and then he wouldn't have done it.'

Eventually, my parents just got used to him playing it and thought that if it kept him on the straight and narrow, then it was a good thing. It also taught him quite a lot about discipline, which was another positive. Footy gave him a bit of a structure and taught him there are things you can do, and there are things you cannot do. There were actions and consequences for him within the football system, and he knew that if he turned up to training and performed well, he would make it into the side that weekend, but if he skipped training or played poorly, he could lose his spot.

Again, none of us actually took much notice of his early footy career until he made it into the Western Jets squads. At that stage Peter and I thought the kid might actually have a chance of playing sport professionally. Little did we realise he was actually being looked at by AFL scouts. He really took his footy very, very seriously and would get home from school at 5.30 p.m. and shoot back out the door to make it to footy training. It was Joey who actually told us, 'Hey, I think your brother might actually get a chance at the AFL.'

When he got picked up, my dad wasn't there as he was overseas, but he wasn't too happy about it. He never wanted Maj to think about footy as a career because he had the mindset that sport is something you play just for the fun of it, but not to play professionally. My dad is a man of books. He has always said, 'Put your heads into the books, but if you need something to keep you straight, you can use sport as an avenue as well.' Little did he actually know that you can actually use sport as a means of being a professional.

When Dad got home from overseas, he grabbed Peter and me and was like, 'Hey, he's my son. He's not your son. You should have told him, "No. Wait for Dad to come back and he will approve it."' I was like, 'Eh. We can't wait for you to come back in order for him to actually make it professionally. If he was picked, then why not? If not, not a problem at all.' I think Dad was kind of grumpy about it for the first two months or so. Eventually he said, 'Look, I don't think there's much I can really do about it, if Maj has already made up his mind.'

Dad always had it in his mind that Maj was going to be a doctor. Maj always said, 'I will be a doctor. I will be a doctor, and all that.' Whatever he puts his mind to, he will work 150 per cent to make sure he achieves it.

Here's how my dad explains it.

When I was a young man, I played soccer. That's the sport that I like. I also used to run. Australian football, I had no idea about. One day, Majak said, 'Dad, I want play Aussie

Rules.' I said, 'No. It's too rough.' In soccer, you don't touch people; you have to be clever and not touch people. So when I saw this other football, it was: 'Wow! It's too rough. Why do they do that to each other? Are they not smart?'

But eventually I said to Majak, 'If you want to do it, you can do it.' We supported him, and he did what he wanted, and that's a good thing.

Mum didn't find it easy either. But in the end, both she and Dad have supported me throughout my footy career, and I couldn't be more grateful for that.

In Sudan people play soccer and some basketball. I remember seeing Australian football on TV and thinking, 'Gosh! This is rough. I don't want my sons playing this game.' It was new to us and it looked dangerous.

I always hoped Majak would be a doctor, from the day he was born. Even to this day, I don't like him playing. I worry. I'm happy for him to continue, but I don't really like it . . . But it's okay, because I'm very proud of what he's achieved. We are proud, as a family, because our name is everywhere and he's doing a good thing. He's done a great job for the family and our community.

Joey remembers how uncomfortable I was when I first arrived on the scene at Wyndhamvale for practice.

The first time I saw Majak was in 2006. I knew he was uncomfortable and in desperate need of a friendly face and some guidance. He stood out on the sidelines at training at Wyndhamvale and was like a fish out of water. I'd gone to school up until that point in West Melbourne so I'd had some exposure to Sudanese people, and even knew some dialect, but a lot of people hadn't had much exposure to Sudanese people back in those days. I was jogging a few warm-up laps and went over to him to say 'hello' – but I didn't say 'hello' in English, I said it in Dinka just to show off a little bit. I think that really resonated with Maj and made him feel comfortable. I invited him to run some laps with me and we basically became friends from that point on. He would have been the only Sudanese player at the club, through all the junior levels, so he was not only the new kid, he was the new kid who was very different to everyone else. For him to come down to the club like that, alone, was very courageous and I immediately had respect for him.

We both got a chance to try out for the TAC Cup squad at the end of 2007, and I saw his competitive desire to improve. Together, we really tried to do everything we could to make a name for ourselves. Every time I doubted whether he'd make it, he'd give me a glimpse of something that would make me go, 'Yeah, maybe he can do it.' He really battled through the Under 18s year of the TAC Cup and came from a long way back to play a full season the following year.

He might not admit it, but I think he's actually a perfectionist. When he wants to improve at something, he actually masters it. His kicking went from being really shaky and unpredictable, to just perfect drop-punts with a sound technique. When he played in the TAC Cup team, in those days they used to release detailed stats, which listed things like effective kicks, ineffective kicks, effective handballs and ineffective handballs. There used to be a running joke, I think for the first six or seven weeks of that season, that Maj hadn't yet registered an effective kick.

It was probably in Round 8 that he actually recorded his first effective kick, so the boys all took party poppers and streamers to school. We waited for him to walk in on Monday morning and he got a little guard of honour on his way in. He found it hilarious and we all had a bit of a laugh. That's a small example, but the same thing can be said for his ruck work; he really worked on his ruck craft and he really worked on his footy nous, his fitness and his strength work in the gym. The way I saw his improvement was that it all came together at the right time, which was towards the end of his draft year in 2009. Even during his draft year, he wasn't really performing that well, but he managed to string together some really strong games late in the season which had everyone's attention. It was just a bit of a culmination of everything he'd been working on and it all just clicked.

Believe it or not, he did actually battle a little bit in the gym early on. He always had the muscle definition and the 'rig', but his strength wasn't always there. That was something that really exploded at one stage. I was a pretty strong kid; I did a lot of weights work early on in my life and developed early, but Maj didn't. There'd be some sessions we'd do where he'd go after me and I'd almost see his eyes pop out of his head; he just couldn't do the same weights. Sadly, for me somewhere along the line that all changed, and he just never stopped growing in strength.

7

Dhorou

Throughout school, it took a long time for me to figure out what I wanted to do for a living. Having had
to learn English from scratch – even though it became one
of my strongest subjects – I wasn't too aware of the options
that were available to me. I felt that I had limited scope, and
I presumed the only work I could probably get and would
be any good at would be some sort of trade. Another option
was to become a teacher like my dad, and that was something I had a bit of a soft spot for. My options, if we'd
stayed in Sudan and Egypt, would have been extremely limited too, because of where I grew up and the money we
had as a family. For example, women who lived where we
did, outside of Khartoum, would either clean other people's
houses, cook for other families or become a midwife to earn
a living – there wasn't much else on offer for them.

Despite living in Australia for five years, a country full
of opportunities, I still felt quite pigeonholed and really
didn't have anyone encouraging me to aim high and show
me what types of jobs were possible for me to do. Moving

from school to school, struggling to fit in and taking time to feel welcome also made things difficult. So, I naturally thought little about my career potential and the possibility I could be anything beyond being some sort of tradesman or teacher.

My eldest brother, Peter, dropped out of high school soon after we arrived in Australia. He started an apprenticeship to be an electrician but didn't finish it, because he decided it wasn't for him. He moved between factory work and being a security guard. Augustino finished Year 12, completed a TAFE course and became a youth worker. As the three oldest siblings, we didn't get the full benefits of our parents' move to Australia – meaning a full education, the ability to learn English from a young age and all the other flow-on effects – that our younger siblings did. They all had a full education in Australian schools, which has afforded them a lot of opportunities and advantages. To be honest, they're really smart compared to me and my older brothers. So far, they have all achieved great ATARs. Teresa is a nurse now and Sarah is going to be one too. Don't get me wrong, I'm not saying that my older brothers and I are in any way ungrateful for what my parents did in moving here, I'm merely trying to explain how difficult it is to come to a country as a teenager who doesn't speak a word of English, and then try to figure out what you want to do career-wise. You need a lot of guidance and good people around you to steer you in the right direction. In my case, I definitely didn't dream too big.

It wasn't until work experience came around in about Year 9 that I started to broaden my horizons and consider shooting for much higher career goals. As most people would know, work experience at secondary school requires students to find a career path they're interested in and arrange a work placement for up to two weeks with a relevant business to gain some insights and determine if it's something they want to pursue. I had no idea what I was going to do for my work placement and didn't have any friends in high places who could help out either.

So, as often was the case, I turned to my best friend, Joey, for advice and guidance. Joey was keen to become a sports journalist and was looking at getting a work placement with a major newspaper or media outlet. After discussing my bleak options with him, I started to like the idea of doing what he was doing. Becoming a reporter or journalist was something I thought I might be able to do and it just so happened that our friends Sam and Danni Hopgood (we called Sam 'Hop') had a connection at the *Herald Sun* newspaper that we could use to get our feet in the door.

Among other titles he held, Chris de Kretser was a veteran journalist and founding editor of the *Sunday Sun*, the first sports editor of the *Herald Sun* and a *Sports Confidential* columnist. He was also Danni's father, and was more than happy to take Joey and me on as 'cadets' for a week, show us the ropes and give us an idea of what being a journalist at a mainstream newspaper was all about. Joey and I would catch the train from Wyndham to Flinders Street each day and make the short walk from the station to the Herald and Weekly Times building in Southbank.

We were lucky enough to tag along with Chris to the AFL's Under 18s competition at Docklands Stadium. The competition is made up of the best young footballers in the country who were all representing their respective states of origin. It's a massive event for the recruiters from all the AFL clubs and a final chance for them to assess the talent on offer for that year's National Draft.

On one particular day, Victoria Metro was playing against Western Australia and this super-talented kid, Nic Naitanui, was coming through the ranks and turning heads all over the country. Along with Vic Metro's Jack Watts and fellow Western Australian Daniel Rich, Naitanui was widely tipped to be the No. 1 pick at the 2008 National Draft. Naitanui's parents, originally from Suvavou, a small village near Suva, the capital of Fiji, had emigrated to Australia and originally settled in New South Wales. After the death of his father, Naitanui's mother moved to Western Australia. He was a young man of colour like me, and I was immediately drawn to him and marvelled at the way he played the game. Standing 201 centimetres tall, he was hard to miss on the field and glided across the ground with so much ease. When the ball was in the air to be marked or punched, he out-jumped everyone, every time. Watching 'Nic-Nat', as he was affectionately known, up close was an experience I never forgot, and somewhere deep inside me, a little fire ignited. It was at that time I realised that I, too, could aim much higher than I currently was with my football and could possibly make a career out of the sport. I knew it would take a lot of hard work and dedication, but as I'd heard a lot of people say since we had arrived in Australia, 'anything is possible' and everyone is entitled to a 'fair go'.

Despite having a desire to play AFL, it was still a far-fetched dream and not something many thought would ever be a possibility for me. It wasn't until the end of Year 12, in 2009, when I was playing top-age TAC Cup footy for the Western Jets, that my chances of getting drafted to an AFL club gained some momentum. A lot of my friends at school and my teammates always talked about themselves getting drafted, but at the time I wasn't as confident about my own prospects. I always thought, *It would be nice to play AFL* and some people suggested along the way that I could make history by being the first Sudanese-born player, and first African player outside of South Africa, to play in the AFL. Previously, Stephen Lawrence was the first African-born person to play professionally, and the first indigenous African-born person to play in the AFL was South African Damian Cupido. Lawrence played 146 games for Hawthorn from 1988 to 1998, and Cupido played a total of 53 games for Brisbane and Essendon between 2000 and 2005.

If I wanted to get drafted, I had to have an amazing year with the Jets as a top-age player and start to show people that I could make it at the highest level. That meant putting a string of solid performances together, not just having a few good highlights within games. Just as I was building some momentum and getting selected regularly, I rolled my ankle pretty badly. It was a few weeks out from a game I had really set my sights on, which was scheduled in Queensland against the Gold Coast Suns in Round 15. The Suns were about to enter the AFL as the competition's newest club and had a year in the TAC Cup to get themselves ready for the big league in 2010. Only a few teams from Victoria were lucky enough to have been scheduled to play them on the Gold Coast, and we were one of them. I had been looking forward to it for so many weeks – I'd been diligent with my ankle rehabilitation and had gone back to playing some local footy with Wyndhamvale – but despite being fit and able to play in time, the coach, Steve Kretiuk, a former AFL player with the Western Bulldogs, didn't pick me in the side. I really thought I had done enough to secure my spot for the plane ride to Queensland, but the coach thought otherwise and sent me back to play local footy to find some form. It was a devastating blow, not only because I was running out of time to impress the AFL recruiters, but it also prevented me from experiencing my first trip out of Victoria since I'd arrived from Egypt all those years ago. I was shattered and angry about being left out, and completely spat the dummy. Only a few games were left in the season and my chances of getting drafted faded with each one I missed. I was so flat about being left out of the interstate trip, I even thought about quitting.

However, there were a couple of silver linings to playing for Wyndhamvale again. In one game, I was named 'best on ground', and when we went back into the rooms to sing the club song after our win, someone handed me an envelope. To my surprise, it was stuffed with cash – my reward for being the best player on the day. In all, it was about

$250 and was the first time I had ever been paid for play-
ing sport. While the unexpected cash was great, the main
benefit for me was playing against a lot of bigger men with
solid bodies, some of them ten or more years older than me,
which made me much tougher. These blokes would crash in
so hard to get the footy and would hit to hurt their opponents. Some guys on the opposing teams targeted me and
came after me physically to test my nerve and resilience.
They didn't have eyes for the ball at all on some occasions
and just wanted to try to roughen me up, hurt me and
intimidate me. I stood my ground, though, refusing to be
bullied on the field and showing that I was no pushover.
TAC Cup footy, on the other hand, was a bit more bruise-
free. So, looking back, what I thought was the worst thing
to happen to me, in being dropped for the game against
the Gold Coast Suns, ended up being one of the best things
that I could have imagined. The physical side of my game
was probably the one thing that had been missing or lack-
ing, as I'd never really looked to impose myself physically
on the game before. Seeing and experiencing how these
blokes at local-level footy did it gave me the idea and courage to be more aggressive in the TAC Cup and make my
presence known on the field when I eventually got back
into the side.

Word quickly filtered back to Steve, my coach at the
Jets, that I was being more physical during my stint on
the outer in local footy, so he finally brought me back into the
side to show what I had learnt. I was so eager to prove
that he was wrong for dropping me, and I tried to use my

experience playing local footy to show that I was worthy of a spot – not only in the Jets but also on an AFL list.

In the final few games of the season for the Jets, I played with a new-found confidence and added aggression. I flew for my marks, hit the packs with real purpose and intent, and was able to boot my fair share of goals along the way too, including five against the Murray Bushrangers. Steve really enjoyed seeing the new attitude and level of aggression that I was bringing, and he could see that I was starting to gather some interest from local media because of my unique background and story. One day he pulled me aside after training to offer some advice. 'Maj, you're going to start getting some more attention in the next few weeks,' he explained to me. 'Make sure you keep yourself grounded and keep doing the hard work at training, and the rest will take care of itself. Don't get distracted by all the outside noise and you'll be fine.' It was great advice and I took it all on board. It was also timely, because not long after our chat I started getting lots of phone calls from AFL player managers, who were interested in representing me ahead of the upcoming National Draft. It just so happened that the volume of phone calls coming in increased substantially after the game I booted five goals in!

Shane Casley was among the first player agents to schedule a meeting with me at our family home in Werribee. I also remember Adam Ramanauskas from TLA talent management coming out to see us. 'Rama' was a former premiership player with the Essendon Football Club and played 134 games from 1999 to 2008. He was part of the famous 'Baby Bombers' side that won the flag in 2000, despite being one of the youngest teams in the competition. He was diagnosed with cancer twice during his career but showed tremendous courage to not only beat it both times, but to make a full recovery and return to professional football. I knew Shane already because I'd played some football with his son, Ben, who was part of the Jets program.

Shane came to my mum and dad's place to make a pitch to us as to why I should sign on to be a part of his player-management stable. We discussed things like my future financial management, what he could do for me and how his connections in the AFL industry and relationships with club recruiters could help get me drafted. Ricky Nixon, Marty Pask and Ricky Olarenshaw also paid me a visit and tried to convince me they were better options. It was a very intimidating experience, made all the harder because my dad was back in Sudan at the time, teaching. It wasn't that any of the agents were pushy or anything – they were all really friendly and accommodating – it was more that the whole scenario was so foreign to me and my mum, and we really had no idea how to do a business deal or what a contract should even look like.

I called on some of the people involved in our footy program at school to come and sit in on various meetings, which was an enormous help. After a lot of meetings with the various agents, I also spoke to a lot of people close to me, even calling Dad back in Sudan for his advice, and eventually decided to sign with Shane Casley. Later, Shane joined forces with Rama. I had watched Rama play a lot of games and had a tremendous amount of respect for him not only as a player, but also for what he'd gone through in fighting multiple bouts of cancer and how he'd showed great determination to defeat the illness and miraculously return to the game. Joey, an Essendon fan, was always ranting and raving about Rama and couldn't believe that he had come to my house and wanted to be my manager. All in all, I think Rama and Shane were just a good fit for me; I felt comfortable with them and knew they had my best interests at heart.

During my last games with the Jets, Shane told me that North Melbourne would be sending recruiters out to get a better idea of my potential and playing capabilities. It was a funny dynamic for me at the time because there was a lot of hype and buzz around at the footy, with all the players hoping to get drafted, but there was no talk of it around my home or with my family, until one of my school teachers, who had a bit to do with my parents, started to make a scrapbook of newspaper articles that featured me or mentioned my name.

Although I was receiving attention from certain circles and people, my expectations of being drafted were still relatively low. I thought, if anything, I might be a chance of getting taken by a club very late on Draft night, somewhere in among the picks that happened late in the Draft order, around the high 60s or in the 70s.

North Melbourne's recruiters came to my house at one point to get to know me a little better. Clubs do a lot of background work on players to make sure they are not only getting talented players, but also bringing good young men with great characters and values into the organisation. On many occasions, super-talented players will get overlooked because they have shady pasts or aren't considered good people. Club recruiters will speak to a prospective recruit's parents, friends, teachers, former coaches, current coaches – really anyone who can give them an insight into the player, the teammate and the person. So, by the time AFL recruiters actually meet with you in person, they already have a fair idea about you and your background. I asked Joey to come along to my first chat with North Melbourne, and he didn't hesitate – he was always there for me. I also met with the Western Bulldogs, Essendon and St Kilda, but I really felt that North Melbourne was the club that was most keen to sign me.

As it turned out, our school graduation night was on the same night as the National Draft, 26 November. I thought I was a chance to get selected and couldn't help but think it could be an amazing night of celebration for me in particular. I mean, how good would it be to get picked by an AFL club right in the middle of my graduation party? I could only imagine the cheers and all the hype that would spread throughout the school if my name was called out. I was really excited to be going to the graduation and kept an eye on all the Draft proceedings on my phone. The party kicked off at around the same time as the Draft started, so I was fairly distracted. I was tempted to find a quiet room somewhere away from all the noise to watch, but I also didn't want to miss out on all the fun.

The Melbourne Football Club was the first cab off the rank and had the first two picks of the 2009 Draft. The Demons selected Tom Scully from the Dandenong Stingrays followed by Jack Trengove from Sturt in South Australia. I put my phone down and focused on the graduation, knowing it could be an hour before the Draft moved into the back end of the order, where I was a more realistic chance of having my name called out.

I checked back in at around pick No. 40 and watched on as North Melbourne was on the clock with selection No. 41. I held my breath and prayed for my name to be called out. To my disappointment, the Kangaroos selected an athletic type in Ayden Kennedy and also passed on me with pick No. 53, instead taking a small forward named Brayden Norris. My hope was fading, fast. The Bulldogs overlooked me at No. 63 and St Kilda did the same at No. 64. The Bulldogs had another pick at No. 76 but I missed out again, and St Kilda baulked me with No. 77. When North Melbourne promoted rookie-listed player Cruize Garlett to its senior list using pick No. 80, I knew it was all over for me. Other clubs started passing on their selections or were also promoting rookie-listed players onto their senior lists. Pick 95 belonged to the Brisbane Lions and after they promoted their rookie Pearce Hanley, the Draft ended and my dreams of becoming an AFL footballer were all but dashed.

It's safe to say the rest of the night was bittersweet and I felt flat as at the graduation. All my friends supported me and told me to keep my chin up, but I couldn't hide my

disappointment. As the night rolled on, other students continued to come up to me and ask if I got drafted, and I had
to tell them I missed out. It was a tough pill to swallow and
I wanted to hide under a rock.

The next day I spoke to my manager, Shane, who told
me St Kilda had been very close to picking me at No. 77.
He consoled me and told me I was still a chance to be
picked up in the Rookie Draft on 15 December. He said he
would continue to speak to recruiters on my behalf and try
to secure a spot on a list as a rookie for me.

After dealing with the major let-down of not getting
drafted, I was invited to a special football camp at the
Australian Institute of Sport (AIS) in Canberra. But it meant
I had another choice to make: either go to the AIS and train
for ten days, or party. All my mates were heading off to
start 'schoolies week' – a time when all the recently grad-
uated Year 12 students head to coastal towns or holiday
locations in Victoria and interstate to celebrate the end of
high school. It's a chance to get a bit loose and party with
your closest friends before the reality of going to university
or working for a living sets in.

Instead of heading off to the beach with them, I decided
to accept the invitation to join the AFL Academy and have
another crack at getting drafted. It was a pretty intense
camp with Under 17s and 18s squads, and it included
younger players such as Luke Parker, who eventually
played at the Sydney Swans; Jarrod Witts, who went to
Collingwood and then the Gold Coast; and Chad Wingard,
who first played at Port Adelaide before joining Hawthorn.

Other players who'd missed out on being drafted were also there, as well as the Queensland Academy and New South Wales Academy players, but it was mainly made up of young draft hopefuls keen on honing their skills ahead of being selected in the coming years.

Former Essendon champion Matthew Lloyd was one of the coaches at the AIS, as was former Brisbane premiership player Luke Power. As a forward, I worked closely with Lloyd, who taught me the importance of having a goal-kicking routine, how to use my body and strength in marking contests, and some leading patterns when charging out from the goal square or roaming inside the forward 50. It was an invaluable experience, and it gave me even more confidence and a greater sense of what it might take to make it on an AFL list. The coaches and staff also put our various attributes to the test, with assessments done on our individual speed, agility, endurance, flexibility, emotional intelligence and mental strength. They measured our reaction time, peripheral awareness, height, weight, arm span, hand span, and then skills such as kicking efficiency, goal-kicking accuracy and decision-making ability, and topped it off with a general medical test. It was extremely thorough, to say the least, and they examined every area to the nth degree.

With the exhausting AIS camp done and dusted, I was invited to attend a Victorian state screening session, where my 70-centimetre standing vertical leap figured in the top 10 per cent of results around the country. I also recorded a 13.6 in the beep test, where the average for tall forwards like me was 12.9. My 20-metre sprint result of 3.03 seconds was also faster than the average for tall forwards at the National Draft camp. Following that, I then got to go down to Arden Street – the home of the North Melbourne Football Club – ahead of the Rookie Draft. Clubs are allowed to seek permission from the AFL to invite non-drafted players down to train with their senior-listed players in order for recruiters and coaches to get a better look at them and decide if they want to draft them. If I thought the AFL Academy experience was daunting, then this was another level. I hadn't even been drafted and wasn't yet an AFL player, and I was being asked to train alongside seasoned and proven footballers, and show the North Melbourne coaching staff and recruiters what I had to offer.

Some of the players there were absolute champions like Brent 'Boomer' Harvey – one of the most skilled players the game has ever seen, and the all-time AFL games record holder, who played an astonishing 432 games; Drew Petrie, an amazing forward and key position player, who played 332 games; Michael Firrito, one of the best defenders in the competition, who played 275 games; and Daniel Wells, a sublime athlete regarded as one of the most damaging midfielders in the game, who reached 258 games. Brad Scott was the coach, and he was new to the role, having only been appointed at the end of 2009. In his playing days, Brad won two premierships with the Brisbane Lions under legendary coach Leigh Matthews, and was known as a fierce defender and competitor who loved to play a physical game and intimidate his opponents. It's safe to say

I was in awe of all these people and taken aback by the pure fact I was suddenly training alongside them.

The other thing that took me by surprise was how involved I was in all the drills and skills training from the get-go. I initially thought I'd be on the sidelines just observing, but they threw me in the deep end from the very beginning. I guess there's no better way to test someone than by throwing them straight in and watching how they respond, adapt and perform under pressure. My first training session was a twilight session, and my head was spinning. I don't know whether I did very well or not; it felt more like I was just trying to keep up with the pace of the drills and the speed of the players' ball movement and running capacity. They were all extremely good athletes and it showed me how far I still had to go in terms of getting my body and conditioning right. I remember being exhausted after the first training session, both mentally and physically, but despite my levels of fatigue, I had to go in and back it up the next day. I couldn't afford to show any weakness or signs that I wasn't coping and just had to put my head down and grind my way through.

After my gruelling two-day stint with the Kangaroos, I was invited to do another two days of tryouts at the Western Bulldogs in Footscray. Rodney Eade was the coach back then, and it was another eye-opening experience. The Dogs were also stacked with amazing players who had a lot of experience, including Brad Johnson, a crafty and durable forward who kicked 558 goals and became the games record holder at the club with 364; the highly intelligent and reliable Robert Murphy, who played 312 games; hard-nut Matthew Boyd, who played 292 games; and the superstar that was Jason Akermanis, who won three premierships and a Brownlow Medal at the Brisbane Lions before joining the Bulldogs at the Kennel. There wasn't much difference between training at North Melbourne and the Bulldogs. The drills and running sessions were incredibly demanding, and despite the fact that I was in way over my head, I think I held my own and impressed.

After a month of solid training with the AFL Academy, North Melbourne and, finally, the Bulldogs, I was completely spent. I felt I had done all that I possibly could to prove I was worth taking a punt on in the Rookie Draft, but I knew my destiny was now completely out of my control.

The day of the Rookie Draft finally arrived, and I was a lot more confident about my chances, having heard some good feedback from my manager, Shane, who had been chatting to various clubs. Then in the hours leading up to the event, which is held online, I received a text message from a number I didn't recognise. I had received a lot of good luck messages and well-wishes throughout the course of the week and day, but this one was particularly special and stood out. It read: *Majak, don't worry, you are going to come to our club, North Melbourne. Regards, Eugene Arocca.* This was significant because Eugene was the boss of the Kangaroos at the time; if he said something was going to happen, then it was going to happen! I think he may have been speaking out of school by messaging me that early in the piece, but I was chuffed that he thought to give me the heads-up and save me a lot of stress and worry.

Not long after I got that text from Eugene, I received a call from the Channel 7 sports journalist, Chris Jones, asking if he and a cameraman could come to my house and film me watching the Rookie Draft unfold, potentially capturing the moment my name was put up on the screen. Having received Euge's SMS and knowing I was all but guaranteed a spot at North, I was happy for it to happen. I was also aware that it could be a historic moment for the sport and serve to inspire a legion of other people with similar backgrounds to me to play the sport and aim big.

I set my laptop up so we could watch the Rookie Draft on our big-screen television in the lounge room, and all my family gathered around to watch the live feed. It wasn't like the National Draft, where the AFL CEO reads out the names of the selected players live on TV, it was merely a blog run by a journalist who worked at the AFL's headquarters at Docklands in Melbourne. He was simply updating the names on a list, from pick No. 1 through to about No. 80, while taking comments from footy fans and answering questions in between selections.

I kept the news of Euge's text message to myself and stayed cool, calm and collected as other loved ones and my manager began to arrive and take up a spot in our lounge room. Some of my uncles, cousins and school friends, including Joey, were there to watch it all unfold with me.

North Melbourne had pick 9 but was involved early when one of their players, Daniel Harris, was selected by the league's newest franchise, the Gold Coast Suns, as a mature-age rookie. In fact, the Suns had the first five selections that year, but I knew I was no chance of going there as I'd had no contact with them at all. Picks 6, 7 and 8 went to Melbourne, Richmond and Fremantle respectively, before North Melbourne's name came up on the screen with its pick 'pending'. My heart started to beat faster and louder as the seconds ticked away while North's recruiters made their decision on who to pick. Despite Euge's text message, I didn't know if they'd take me with their first selection or one of the picks they held further down the order. I also knew if they passed on me first up, I could be headed to the Bulldogs or even to St Kilda. My eyes were locked on the TV screen and then it happened – my name flashed up on the screen next to North Melbourne's: *Pick 9 (North Melbourne) Majak Daw (Western Jets)*. A supporter commented on the blog, *YES. Roos get their man!* I leapt off the couch and screamed, 'YEAHHHHHH! YEAHH!' and fist-pumped the air. Everyone in the room erupted with me and stood up to clap, hug, shake my hand and congratulate me. I hugged my cousin and let out another cry of delight, 'YESSSSSS!' I was ecstatic. My dream had come true.

Within seconds of my name being typed on the screen, there was a knock on the door and in walked Brent 'Boomer' Harvey from North Melbourne. I couldn't believe what was happening. My head was spinning and there was so much to take in. I shook his hand and welcomed him in, and he said, 'Maj, congratulations, mate,' and he threw me my first North Melbourne playing jumper. It was a case of having to constantly pinch myself. I had just been selected to become a professional in a sport that was unknown to me only seven years earlier, a game I'd never tried until four years earlier, and now one of that sport's best players was standing in my living room shaking my hand – it was completely unfathomable. Boomer started handing out North caps and merchandise to all my family and friends, and the vibe in the room was unreal. Being in Werribee and knowing all too well how far away Arden Street was, I was really appreciative of the club and Boomer for going out of the way to come to my house and welcome me into the North family. It's a memory I've always cherished and will never forget. Little did I know at the time, having that connection with Boomer was something that would hold me in good stead for years to come.

REFLECTIONS

Shane Sexton, Joey Halloran, Matthew Lloyd, Shane Casley, Augustino Daw

It's hard to break into the AFL, and you need a lot of things to go your way. If the Western Jets hadn't seen my potential and given me a chance to impress in the TAC Cup, I would never have made it to North Melbourne. For that, I have many people to thank, including Shane Sexton, who worked at the Jets when I was playing junior footy.

I was the talent manager for the Western Jets, so I was pretty much in charge of everything, and I received a bit of a brief from head office about starting a multicultural program. The Jets had had a pretty rough trot in recent times, which all stemmed from the Calder Cannons joining the competition in 1995, which resulted in the Jets being pretty much cut in two. So, we didn't have a lot of success for quite a long while, and had to try some different things – one of those was to start a multicultural program to unearth some hidden talent. I was involved in recruiting and spotting talent, and we kept an eye out for any multicultural kids who could be suited to football. We were one

of the first elite programs to give kids like that an oppor-
tunity or provide a pathway for them to become involved.
The program eventually became known as the 'Majak
Daw Squad'.

Majak came to my attention when he was playing for
Wyndhamvale. He was a big, strong boy and he was playing reasonable footy for his age. He had really good leg
speed and was certainly a player of interest, put it that way.
At TAC Cup level back then, we identified kids when they
were 15 and we ran a program for them called the 'Brad
Johnson Squad'. Majak was good enough to graduate from
the Brad Johnson Squad, which was the Under 16s champion-
ships held in the first term of the school holidays. He played
really well at that stage and was good enough to get an
invitation to join the TAC Cup program with us the next
year as a 2008 bottom-age player.

Majak didn't play his first game with the Jets until 2009,
and even then he wasn't a regular. He was dropped late in
the year. The way the TAC Cup works is you might have
40 kids on the list or in the squad, but only 22 are selected
to play each week. Those who aren't selected go back to
their local footy clubs and play – that's what happened
to Majak. He had to work hard to get a spot in the TAC Cup.
Steve Kretiuk was the coach and we talked about Majak
regularly. I certainly did, because I wanted us to give him
an opportunity. Gradually we got to the stage where he got
a game of footy, and then he sort of kicked on from there,
but it wasn't easy for him – he didn't walk into the team
first-up and play game after game after game. He was still

working on his footy; trying to work it out. We knew he was big, strong and a terrific tackler. He could kick the ball pretty well too.

Towards the end of his draft year, in 2009, he certainly had the attention of all the AFL recruiters. I kept pushing for Majak's selection on a fairly regular basis to give him an opportunity so he could do what he needed to do. He wasn't putting full games together, but at the end of the day, he was showing us enough. I was a believer in Majak, and TAC Cup programs are about getting kids into the AFL; it should never be about winning games at the expense of giving young talent the opportunity to shine.

I was never taken aback by the amount of attention that Majak had follow him throughout his draft year or when he eventually went to North Melbourne. The build that he had was amazing, the leap he had was amazing, the speed that he had to run and tackle was amazing. I mean, you could give a kid ten yards' head start and Majak could chase him down and tackle him, no problems. People saw the things he was able to do and looked forward to seeing him do them on the big stage. These were things not everyone could do; they were unique in a lot of ways, and Majak brought great excitement to an ordinary game of footy.

What Majak did for us at the Jets was terrific. Once Maj got going in the AFL, it helped our multicultural program to no end. At one stage we had 30 to 35 kids coming to training, including kids from Canada, Africa and the Middle East – you name it, they were coming from everywhere. Majak was fantastic and he used to come down as often as he could to see the kids, see how they were going and get to their games. We've had a lot of success and a lot of that is because of the path Majak created for them.

I'm sure it was somewhat of a difficult time for Joey when I got drafted, as he'd always harboured ambitions to play in the AFL, but he never once showed any disappointment or jealousy. He was so supportive of me and even became somewhat of an accidental public relations agent for me.

There was definitely a turning point of sorts in Maj's footy journey, and it came when he was left out of the Jets squad to travel to the Gold Coast. He was absolutely shattered with the decision, and that's the point in time where I thought, *He's not going to get drafted*, because I remember when he found out that he wasn't picked, it really crushed him. Every team and player looked forward to making the trip up there, and it was a big deal that he missed out. I remember he called me and was ready to throw it in.

Thankfully, he stuck with it, and he was brought back in for the final three games of the year and absolutely tore it up. He had three games to go to show what he could produce, and he kicked five goals in one, ran from the half-back flank to half-forward and kicked a goal in another, and took a massive hanger against Geelong at Chirnside Park – those glimpses had everyone sitting up and taking notice, but not without a little help from me. I actually feel a bit guilty now, but I put together a Majak Daw highlight reel and uploaded it to YouTube to try to get some interest in him and raise some awareness, because all the other big names in the Draft had highlights videos. I had only picked the best bits from all his games, and I think I contributed to the hype surrounding him, because people thought that's what they were going to get from him every game. The reality was, however, that he was extremely raw and really couldn't string a four-quarter effort together yet. For 2009 YouTube standards, it went viral as it was the start of that social media period. That might have been why people thought Majak was going to be the full package – the next Buddy Franklin of the AFL. So all the fanfare that suddenly followed him through to the lead-up to the Draft, I feel somewhat guilty about.

I couldn't actually believe the attention he received. It was a big thing when he got drafted, a big high, and then reality kicked in that it was off the back of three really good games, and he still had a lot of development to do. He never asked for the media hype and attention. Getting drafted was a goal he wanted to achieve – it was a personal goal; it wasn't to get rich or famous. The first time he ever mentioned wanting to play in the AFL was at the start of 2009. We'd been to the gym with another friend and he said he wanted to be the first Sudanese-born player in the league. I remember the guy we were with laughed at him, because he was such a long way off at that point. I suppose as the year unfolded, it was looking less and less likely, but he turned things around like he always does, and made his dream come true through nothing but hard work and determination.

At the AIS Academy, I was fortunate enough to spend time with an AFL legend, Matthew Lloyd. While I didn't have too long under his tuition, the time we did have was invaluable to me and gave me great confidence before spending time training with North Melbourne and the Bulldogs.

I remember first meeting Majak in Canberra at the Australian Institute of Sport, where he joined an initial group of players who would all be eligible for the following year's AFL Draft. These players were viewed as the best 30 footballers in their age group in the country. When I was introduced to Maj, his big smile was one thing that stood out to me – it's something I think about every time I hear his name or talk about him. He had this amazing, beaming smile that would light up a room. I also couldn't help but notice his enormous physique and couldn't get over the size of him for his age. The scary thing was, you could see that he hadn't finished developing physically. Some guys come in and you can tell that they're fully developed or won't grow too much more, but with Majak there was still room to improve his incredible body and to put on more muscle and size.

Majak was very confident from the start of the training camp until the very end of it. He wasn't over-confident but was just someone who wanted to learn as much as he possibly could in the short amount of time we had together. He was asking questions of me and all the coaches straight away – about the craft of a forward and also what I didn't like in regards to what defenders would do to play on me. His thirst for knowledge was really encouraging and you could see that he wanted to get better and was desperate to get an opportunity with an AFL club. I find that kids at that age can be really shy and don't look to engage or pick your brain, but Maj was someone who was ready to engage straight away in conversation and someone who had confidence; a nice confidence, not an arrogance.

He had some unique attributes that really stood out, like power and explosiveness, an incredible leap and serious speed off the mark. He was quite raw, though, in terms of his skills and football smarts. He was never going to have someone like Sam Mitchell's smarts, but I felt he could learn enough to make a good career for himself. On the flip side, someone like Sam Mitchell would never have Majak's power and speed.

Majak wasn't a pure footballer and we understood that, given he'd picked up the game so late in life by comparison to the other kids who had grown up with the sport. Kevin Sheehan (AFL national talent manager) and Mick Ablett (AFL academies development manager) had identified Majak because they could see the growth that he would have in his time. From what I saw, he was someone who was good enough to play some good football with what skills he had and could develop, but he didn't probably have the understanding of the game. But in saying that, I was really impressed with him pretty much from day one, from where he was at that point in time. He fitted in really well, to be honest, with the best 30 boys in the country.

I remember speaking about Majak to the young defenders who were on the camp, and because of his size, we used him as a prototype for the types of players these kids would be training with and playing against the following year should they be fortunate enough to get drafted. We spoke about how you'd want to take away Majak's run – you wouldn't want to let him get a clear run and jump at the ball. We identified that Maj was going to be pretty hard to stop, so it was all about body positioning with him. We figured that the best option was to play in front of him and make him try to take a specky over the top. Giving him a metre or a yard advantage was a mistake because of his speed and explosive power. Majak showed some amazing skills on the camp, and you rarely see someone that can take the ball out of the air at such a high point. He was also pretty good at hitting the ball hard and splitting a pack.

My manager, Shane Casley, recalls the hype surrounding me and why he wanted to manage me, even though I was very long odds to get drafted at one point.

My son, Ben, played at the Western Jets as a 16-year-old, so that would've been Maj's first year as a 17-year-old in 2008. I'd go to training most nights and did so for about a three-year period – two of those years were Maj's last two years. I have to be honest, early on, besides his physique and his size, there wasn't much that I saw in Majak that made me think, *He's going to be an AFL player of the future*. He wasn't on anyone's radar. As a manager looking at players, I didn't think of him as a player that AFL club recruiters would be jumping up and down to pick up, or even have a look at. Then in his final year as an 18-year-old, for the first half of that year, he still wasn't really doing anything that made me sit up and take much notice. There were flashes here and there, but he was a long way off.

It probably was around the middle of that season, in about June, that I started to see some real attributes that would potentially make him an AFL player. I started seeing these attributes more and more, but he still wasn't putting full games together. He started to get a little bit of recognition, but only because of a few highlight reels that had been uploaded onto YouTube, rather than great all-round games he was playing. In a night game against the Geelong Falcons in Werribee, he took a great mark and kicked a great goal. If you put that on a highlight reel, it would look fantastic, but if you watched his whole game, you wouldn't be seeing much more than that.

At that same time at the Western Jets, there was a bit of a wave of Sudanese kids coming through the system, and Majak became somewhat of a poster boy. There was a real hope from the Jets program that someone like Maj might develop and make it. But again, as a parent watching all the training sessions and games, Majak certainly didn't stand out on a week-to-week basis, but he did stand out obviously because he was Sudanese, had a great physique, was six foot four and built like Superman. He was always big as a kid.

Very late in his Draft year, 2009, Maj began to emerge as a potential AFL player. I remember one game in particular against the Murray Bushrangers, where he kicked five goals and really dominated. That was the day that I thought, *This kid could actually make it*. He marked everything that day, and what stood out to me was his kicking and his kicking action. He was 50 metres out, and as a kid kicking in the TAC Cup competition, kicking 50 metres is a fairly big kick, but he just did it with ease. He has a beautiful kick. He didn't miss. I thought, *This kid's got something special*. I started to take a lot of notice of him, as not just a dad with a son playing with him, but also as a player agent. I started to get thoughts of maybe getting Majak in my stable of players and managing him as well. He was reasonably close to my son, Ben, so Ben made the introduction and I started talking to Maj about potentially signing him.

As a result of his highlights reel going viral on YouTube, Maj was featured on the TV show Future Stars, which talked up kids from the TAC Cup and discussed their chances of being drafted. There had been a bit of press on him and word got out that Bulldogs and North were potentially keen, as both clubs were very community and multiculturally focused. There was starting to be a little bit of talk about him and that's the point when I got involved. I vividly remember going out to Majak's school and meeting one of the coordinators in charge of their footy program. The school had started to get a lot of enquiries from the media, so we had to work out how we managed that. Majak's dad, William, was away a lot overseas, and his mum, Elizabeth, didn't speak a lot of English, so most of my discussions were really with Maj, and some people he was close to from the Wyndhamvale footy club. He also had some people from the school helping him, and I was dealing with a lot of those people, more than his parents. The school was managing the publicity and media requests, and he really needed a manager or someone who had been through it all before to guide him. There was some familiarity there between us, and he was pretty close to my son, so that made it more comfortable for him, and it opened the door for me to have a chat. The guys at the school were the first ones I had to convince that I was the right person for the job, because Majak's mum and dad didn't know much about footy – it was all very foreign to them.

In managing players for 30-plus years, you might get the odd number-one player or top Draft pick who attracts a lot of attention. Majak was getting that level of attention off the back of three or four games of footy and a bit of a highlight reel. The amount of publicity he got, for somebody who had done so little, really, in his two TAC Cup years, was phenomenal.

When he missed out on the main Draft, we had some dialogue, mainly with North Melbourne. There was some dialogue with the Bulldogs too, but to be honest, North had pretty much made a commitment that they would pick him up in the Rookie Draft. There was still some disappointment that he didn't go earlier, because there had been a little bit of hype. I don't think North and the Bulldogs had a lot of picks in that Draft, and they were the clubs that had shown the most interest. North were clearly the ones we'd been speaking to the most, but we certainly didn't get a commitment that they were taking him in the main Draft.

After I was drafted, my family ensured that I kept my feet on the ground and never got ahead of myself. Augustino was forever reminding me of who I was and where I came from.

As a family, we don't care about possessions, or fame or anything. Maj is my younger brother and whatever so-called status he held was irrelevant to me – it meant nothing. It meant nothing to the whole family, to be honest. As a family, we don't believe in such a thing as someone's stature. You do great in life, but don't accept the lifestyle of having a stature and everything that would have got attached to your name. When we started to realise Majak had this level of fame, popularity and expectation to live up to, we sort of said to him, 'All right, mate. You know what? Enjoy it. Most of us don't like that level of pressure or stature, but if you want it, enjoy it, but do be very careful. Don't let it change who you are, and don't let fame go to your head.' As an older brother, there's always that constant worrying, right? So, we've always worried about him, and the good thing is that we've always kept in touch with him.

One thing we never did is dampen the young fellow's spirit. We let him do what he wanted to do, and we've always watched him from the background. If Maj was going in the wrong direction, we'd pull him back and tell him, 'Remember who you are. Remember where you came from. We think you're getting ahead of yourself. Just sit down and reflect as to where you came from and ground yourself.' Mum would always worry the most, though, especially with any injuries, no matter how small. There was a VFL game where he twisted his ankle and his leg went sideways. She literally broke down. When he got knocked out in his first game in the AFL, she was like, 'I told him not to play this sport.'

8

Bët

As it turned out, getting drafted by an AFL team was the easy part. The reality was, going from being a no-name high-school student to a professional footballer and person with a public profile in a matter of just two months was an incredibly tough adjustment for me to make. From the moment I was picked up by the Kangaroos, my whole world was turned upside down. When all the calls from family and friends congratulating me died down, I had dozens of people from my new club to get back to: the development coaches, the welfare manager, Eugene Arocca, club chairman James Brayshaw, a heap of players and the media managers, and so many others. It was so great to have them all reach out to welcome me to the club and into the North Melbourne family, but it was also very overwhelming.

I had also been contacted by the strength and conditioning staff and had been sent details about training and when to arrive at the club the next day – this is where things got difficult for me. I was 18 years old, my father was overseas, and I didn't have my driver's licence yet – even if I did, I wouldn't have been able to afford a car at the time, nor could my parents have afforded to buy one for me. Suddenly I had to figure out a way to get from my family home in Werribee to the North Melbourne Football Club at Arden Street, which was about 35 kilometres away. And it wasn't like I had to make the trip just once, but most days of the week and on weekends. That journey would normally be about 45 minutes by car, but it could easily blow out to more than an hour in bad traffic – and in Melbourne, there is always bad traffic.

With such a big family and the costs associated with petrol and car maintenance, driving for us was pretty much reserved for essential things like going to do the shopping, medical emergencies or appointments. My mum could drive, but she wasn't very confident and would avoid it if she could. My older siblings, Peter and Augustino, had work of their own to worry about and couldn't afford to prioritise mine. When Peter realised I was completely out of options and in trouble of missing the first day of training, he came to the rescue and figured out a way to juggle his work commitments and get me to and from the city.

It was a huge gesture from him, and the more I reflect on it, the more I realise just how amazing and selfless he was to do that for me. We would get up super-early – at about 5 a.m. – and leave the house by 6 a.m. He would drop me at the club by 7–7.30 a.m. and then head to work back in Werribee. He would then leave his work early in the afternoon and pick me up at about 3 p.m. and drive me home. So, Peter was in the car for at least four hours a day. It was not only the effort it took, but also the cost to him which makes what he did for me all the more generous.

After about two weeks of shuttling from Werribee to North Melbourne and back again, North's welfare manager, Neil Connell, realised my situation with Peter driving me to and from training was untenable. He proposed that I move to a place much closer to the club. Neil, or 'Codge' as he's affectionately known, sat me down and asked if I could cook, knew how to clean properly, do my own washing and shopping, and whether I could fend for myself if I moved out of home and away from my parents. He had a spot in mind for me in a house in Altona with three other players – Ben Speight, Warren Benjamin and Matthew Scott. I told him that I would be fine, that I was more than capable of looking after myself, and I was keen to join the other players in the 'club house' and start standing on my own two feet.

It was at about this time that my first paycheque from the North Melbourne Football Club landed in my bank account. When it came through, I immediately filled up Peter's car with petrol and bought all the groceries for the week for Mum and my family. I paid all the overdue power, water and gas bills, and helped Mum and Dad clear some of their other small debts. I wasn't earning that much, being on a rookie wage, but whatever I had, I was more than happy to share with my family to help everyone out, because they would do the exact same thing for me. Outside of giving Mum a little bit of money when I'd worked in Egypt at the age of nine, it was the first time in a long time that I was able to contribute financially, make a difference and ease the strain on her and my siblings. Mum really appreciated it, and I know it took a huge amount of pressure off her and Dad.

Aside from being a bit closer to the club, moving into the club house in Altona with the other players put me in an environment that was more focused on footy. Back home, all my mates were going out drinking on the weekends and even having a few beers at the local pub on weeknights, which wasn't a lifestyle I could lead if I wanted to make it as a player. So, as much as I loved hanging out with my friends, it was beneficial to remove myself from the temptation of going out with them, and to move in with like-minded people who were on the same training schedule, had the same expectations and ambitions, and who were also trying to make a name for themselves and break into the senior AFL side.

Moving out of the family home was really the best thing for me, and the bonus was it provided me with a regular car ride to the club each day – well, for a period of time, anyway. The boys got sick of taxiing me around everywhere and put a lot of pressure on me to get my licence and buy my own car. I eventually caved and booked in my driving test to get my P plates, but it took me a lot longer than expected. The first test I sat was a computer driving simulation and written test, and I failed dismally. Apparently flunking that test is hard to do, but somehow I managed it. The pass mark was 80 per cent and I fell short by getting two scenarios or answers wrong. It meant that I had to re-book and try again. It was a case of second time lucky, and I passed and progressed to the driving test.

This is where fortune turned in my favour and I first experienced the power of football. It just so happened that the driving examiner I was allocated was a huge North Melbourne fan. When I got in the car, she knew exactly who I was before I even uttered a word or introduced myself. She was very excited to be taking me for my test. At that moment, I felt that I could clip a light pole on my way out of the carpark or drive over a stop sign and still pass (just kidding!). However, she did give me a level of confidence that I wouldn't have had with another assessor. Look, she may have winked at me and said something along the lines of, 'Don't be nervous, Majak. You'll be fine – trust me.' And in my humble opinion I did well during the drive and would have passed regardless of her attitude towards me. I mean, I wouldn't say it was an exceptional display of driving skill, but it was good enough to pass. All in all, I learnt it was definitely a benefit being a football player in Melbourne – a city where the game is treated like somewhat of a religion.

Soon after getting my driver's licence, I bought my own car and no longer had to rely on anyone else to get around. Matt Scott and I were both on the rookie list and had a similar schedule, so we did a lot together and carpooled often. Being rookies, we knew we had a long way to go before we would be in a position to break our way into the club's senior side – we also knew some rookies never even get a crack at the AFL and are delisted after a year or two.

When I started at North, the club's second-tier players had to find form in the VFL and play for either the North Ballarat Roosters or the Werribee Tigers – both teams were North Melbourne's affiliate or 'feeder' clubs.

I was placed with the Werribee squad because it was in my family's home suburb and made the most sense. Instead of playing in the club's first VFL side, however, I had to play in the development side, two rungs down from the AFL level. It was a big hit to my ego – I mean, I had just been drafted as an AFL player and thought I had made the 'big time', only to be told that not only was I not good enough for the AFL yet, I wasn't even good enough for the VFL. It was safe to say I had a hell of a lot of work to do.

Some of my mates from school who didn't follow football closely had no idea what was going on and couldn't understand why I wasn't playing in the AFL and featuring on TV each week. It was hard to explain to them that I was still far from 'making it' as a professional player. The worst part was that the Tigers VFL development side's games started much earlier in the day and acted as a curtain-raiser for the senior VFL side's game. We had to play some games in Ballarat at 11 a.m., which meant we had to leave our Altona house by 7 a.m. to arrive at the ground by 9 a.m. As football is a winter sport, the weather was often freezing at that time of the morning, especially in a place like Ballarat, so it was a painful slog in my early days as an 'AFL footballer'. Those testing times helped me and Matt to develop a very close friendship, as we spent a lot of time in the car together.

Another hit to my ego came one night when we were out at a nightclub in the city. A girl was giving me some interesting looks from across the bar area, and I thought she must have recognised me from all the media I had received after the Rookie Draft. She approached me at the bar and all the boys were getting into me, saying things like, 'Oooh, Maj! She knows who you are!' and 'Look out, Maj! You're famous now!' I was bracing for more flak from them, and things took a turn for the worse when she said, 'Hey, you play for the Werribee Tigers, don't you?' The boys thought it was hilarious. I tried to correct her by saying, 'Nah, I actually play for North Melbourne,' but there was no saving the situation – the boys were already well and truly getting stuck into me, yelling out, 'He plays in the development league – the twos, twos!'

When I first arrived at North Melbourne, I was very shy and didn't speak up too much, but after living in the house with the other boys for a bit, I started to feel way more comfortable than I would've had I stayed at home in Werribee. I was included in everything with the boys and felt a part of everything. I regularly went out with the other young players to bars and clubs and got to meet all their friends too, so it was very rewarding socially. Looking back, it was definitely the right time for me to move out of home, but I never stopped contributing and helping my parents out with whatever they needed. They knew that if they ever needed help financially, I would do my best to provide it. When I'm in a position to help others, my thoughts are to always do it – it comes naturally to me.

Even when it comes to small things, like new footy boots, I've always sent some home for Anthony or Ajak to wear. Sometimes a boot sponsor would send me four pairs at a time, and I'd know I wasn't going to need them all, so I'd pass them down to my brothers or friends.

I never wanted any of my family members to go without, so if I could help them, I would. That's what my parents did for me, and that's how I was raised. If my parents had had a selfish mindset, I wouldn't be here in Australia to take up these amazing opportunities. My parents could have easily stayed in Sudan with their own families and friends close by, but they put me and my brothers and sisters first, making the extremely difficult decision to move to Egypt then to Australia. My offer to help out my family extended to our relatives back in Sudan, too. When someone dies over there or in Egypt, it can be a challenge for the family to pay for the funeral costs. It's not like they have money saved, so sometimes we are called on to help out with those types of things or even to help them pay their rent. To this day, I'll always help those I love whenever I can.

REFLECTIONS

Shane Casley, John Lamont, Brad Scott

I had to rely a lot on the people around me to get me through the early stages after I was drafted. My manager, Shane Casley, was very good for me financially and kept tabs on my spending to make sure I had enough money to get by.

There were some challenges for Maj in those early days. Obviously, coming from such a big family, it was difficult for him to live at home. One of the first things we had to decide was where does he live? Getting him out of home was one of the main things we tried to arrange. We had to buy him a car, pay rent, pay all these other bills, and all on a rookie wage – those first two or three years, he was unable to save any money at all. Everything that was coming in was going straight out. If he did have any extra money, it was going to support the family. When I'd look at Maj's bank account with him, I'd be saying, 'Mate, where's all your money going?' One thing we did do, and have done for a long, long time, is to have a bank account that I had access to, so we could only draw money out together.

We did that to try to create some saving habits, and give me a bit of transparency and control. It also gave him a reason to say to people asking him for money, 'No, I can't help you out because my manager has my money tied up' or something along those lines.

Before I became a North Melbourne player, I met one of the development coaches, John Lamont, who I ended up working extremely closely with as I struggled to grasp the heavy demands and expectations of life as an AFL player. John also became the head coach of the Werribee Football Club later in my career, and I loved playing for him.

My first recollection is that Majak came to the club just before the Rookie Draft for somewhat of a trial with us. As one of North's development coaches at the time, I was asked to assess his kicking technique and skills because our recruiters were a little bit iffy on selecting him, knowing he'd take some time to develop and would require a lot of resources. So, I went off and had a bit of a one-on-one kick with him and put him through various drills and told the recruiters, 'His kicking is quite sound.' He had a good, efficient kick, and definitely left an impression. I can remember having a chat with the recruiters about his kicking, and nothing else. We discussed that if we did decide to rookie him, then we were not going to have to spend a lot of time on his kicking, which was a real bonus, because if a young player comes in with flaws in his kicking technique that result in a compromised kick, it's a lot of work to unravel it and re-teach. Fundamentally, Majak kicked the ball pretty well and most people would agree with that.

The second thing we assessed was his 'know-how': did he know how to play, find the footy, make a lead and see the game properly and all those things that should come naturally to a footballer? The answer to that was 'No'. Maj had a strong-looking body, but when it came to one-on-one marking contests, defenders were able to move him around the place quite easily, because he just hadn't developed any functional strength. So, there was a little bit of work to be done on that. Obviously, he was a late convert to the game, and other kids who have played since they were five or so, and who have got a bit of size to them, have a bit of that 'know-how' and can use their body and throw their weight around. Majak could run and jump at the ball, but if he got underneath it and had to use his body, he struggled with that. He had elite speed and power, but really, really low endurance too. Despite all the areas Majak required improvement in, he was definitely worth taking a punt on, as there was a heap of upside to him as a rookie selection.

When he arrived at Arden Street, it took him a while to get used to the footy environment and the elite lifestyle that players have to live by and adhere to. There's a saying from a famous American National Football League (NFL) coach, Vince Lombardi, that goes, 'If you are five minutes early, you are already ten minutes late.' Majak just had no real concept of that. The schedule would say nine o'clock warm-up, and he'd be walking in at five minutes to nine. It was sort of a boyhood or youthful ignorance, if you like. There was certainly a bit of reprogramming we needed to do with him on that, but he wasn't on his own there. For Majak, it took a few weeks, maybe even a month or two, for him to join the dots. There were several occasions that Majak was late to training or missed a physio appointment, which resulted in the entire squad being punished with a 6 a.m. swim in icy-cold water off St Kilda pier – of course, that doesn't go down well, with the senior players in particular. There was just that learning curve, and it was probably a bit steeper for him because coming into that environment, it's a hell of a shake-up to what you're used to.

I spent a lot of time with Maj in those early years. Not more than I should have as a development coach, but there was a lot of time with him spent on off-field stuff, because he never had any money. He had a lot going on off the field, which meant he couldn't just focus on playing his best footy. There was the family's lack of understanding about what he was trying to achieve and the need for him to help out financially whenever he could. If you haven't got that balanced wheel or your mind is always elsewhere, it's very hard to focus on footy and a career. It took me a while, but he did really share some emotional stuff with me too. There was no way of knowing if his footy was ever going to be any good until such time as he got a handle on his emotions and all that off-field drama. We had some really meaningful conversations over a long period of time about non-footy stuff, to just clear his head, and that gave us a chance, I reckon.

I worked a lot on getting Maj to try to stay in the moment on the ground when he was playing. We were working on things during the week at training, and then we'd get to game day, and he was unable to stay in the moment and execute. He'd go missing at times and struggled to focus for four full quarters, so we saw highlights but not great games. He also struggled to read the ball off the boot. Playing forward, he'd be on a lead and the kick would leave the boot, but he'd be slow to identify where it was going. He'd keep moving and then he would react to where the ball was going, but by that stage, his opponent had picked up the trajectory of the ball and was out-marking him. We worked on retraining his brain to get him to identify the fall of the ball earlier.

When it all clicked for Maj, he was unstoppable, particularly in the VFL. When I was coach of Werribee, he was a real weapon. If he had a clear run and jump at the ball, it was 'good luck' to the opposition. If he didn't mark it, they weren't going to. If he read the ball okay off the boot, he could bring other players into the game and was a very team-orientated player.

I remember a discussion with Brad Scott and the other coaches at North about trying to turn Maj into a midfielder. It was at the same time that Hawthorn coach Alastair Clarkson had used Jarryd Roughead as a midfielder and he was having a good impact as a bigger bodied bloke. Brad thought we could look at a similar role for Majak, but, of course, he didn't have the footy nous of Jarryd Roughead. We wanted him to use his big body to push some blokes out of the way and take up a bit of extra space around the ball, but he just didn't have the capacity to absorb that level of play and it was unfair on him.

Bigger guys always take longer to develop; the male brain reaches maturity at about 25. After years of playing ruck/forward, he had his best year as a defender in 2018. As his fitness grew, he got a bit of a result, but when you look back at his career, the one thing that stands out is that he always suffered injuries at the wrong time. He dislocated his foot one year right in front of me at Werribee, on the wing. That came at a time where – I'll use the analogy of a jet plane taking off: you're going along at speed and something needs to happen for the pilot to take the controls and lift the nose up to take full flight – Maj was just about to take full flight and he did that injury. He missed some big chunks of pre-season on multiple occasions, and if you were going through the North Melbourne playing list, who was the one bloke that couldn't afford to miss three months of training? Majak Daw. I can't say how many times that happened, but I reckon it was at least two or three times that he missed crucial chunks of pre-season training, which he needed. He needed to be doing more than the other blokes, not less, and injury cost him dearly.

Brad Scott always believed in me as a player. He worked hard to help me develop my skills and become a more rounded player at AFL level, but it wasn't easy for him, or me, because I was coming from such a long way back.

We knew we had this guy in Majak, who just had untapped physical ability and natural ability, but when he got to the club, he couldn't do some of the things that should come more naturally to a player who's good enough to be drafted. For example, when he went for his marks, more often than not, the ball would hit his hands and bounce out. I mean, he wouldn't just drop it – the ball would hit his hands and rebound five metres forwards, because he just didn't have any marking technique to speak of. So, we saw his ability to get to the ball, but the first thing that we had to do was work on his ball control and positioning his hands in the right place to actually mark the ball with soft hands, rather than really hard hands. I knew that if we could get that bit right, we could really turn him into something special. He could kick and his kicking technique was really good, and his set-shot goal kicking was really sound. That didn't need a lot of work. It was all about his marking technique, his timing, running and jumping at the ball, so we just did a huge amount of work on that.

When Maj arrived at the club, he certainly looked like the strongest bloke on the list, but on all our measures he was one of the weakest. His functional strength was low, and he had to do a lot of work in the gym to get himself to a point where he could compete with the bigger bodies he was matched up against on the field. There was a time, after a few years in the gym, that I said publicly, 'Maj is now as strong as he looks.' When we were training in 2010/2011 and we put Maj on our All-Australian defender, Scott Thompson, Scotty would easily push him out of the way. Once Maj got functionally strong, and when he got real core strength and balanced up that strength with the power, his absolute power and agility were unbelievable.

After a few years of Maj being on the list and doing the work in the gym, I'll never forget a conversation I had with Scott Thompson one pre-season after we'd matched him up on Maj. We were doing some one-on-one marking work, and while Maj certainly didn't win every contest against Scotty, he didn't lose any, either. I sidled up alongside Scotty at one point and said, 'How do you think Maj went?' and he looked at me and said, 'I can't beat him.' I said, 'What do you mean you can't beat him?' and he said, 'Well, I can't beat him – he's stronger than me. If I try to sit off him, and run and jump, he just jumps over the top of me and marks it. If I take the back position on him, I can't get around him. If I take the front position, he sits on my head. I just can't beat him.'

Maj had gotten to the point where both Scotty Thompson and our other All-Australian-level key defender, Robbie Tarrant, said, 'We can't beat him one-on-one.' That was probably the light-bulb moment for me. When Scotty said that, it was like, *Okay, we can work with this.* But the problem with it was games of football aren't set up like that. In that instance at training, we were just kicking

40-metre-high balls to a stationary one-on-one contest. That just hardly ever happens – or it never happens – in an AFL game. In a game, Maj would be out of position, or he wouldn't be in the right spot. We just couldn't replicate that stationary one-on-one contest in a game, so it was more the game sense – where to be at the right time, timing his jumping and those things – that he had to learn. We initially thought, *Well if he's beating all of our key forwards in training, let's play him as key forward, because it's the obvious place to play him*. We had to simplify the game enormously for him.

What people have got to understand is the hardest things in the game to coach are the things that are ingrained in players from a very young age. Maj was coming to the game very late in his young life, and it's very hard to take a player who hasn't grown up with the game and teach them some of those game-sense principles or how to read the play. Coaching someone how to read the play is easier said than done, because when you get players at AFL level, most of that is a given. You can make some quick changes for some young players, but we had to start at absolute scratch with Majak. I mean, there was one game in the VFL when Maj took the ball out of the middle and streamed forward and booted an amazing goal from a long way out and left everyone in the dust behind him – the problem was, he'd kicked the ball at the opposition's goals and went the wrong way. It was one of the most awesome goals but it obviously didn't count. As a coach, you don't leave the huddle and feel the need to say, 'Hey guys, just remember you're going to the left.' I mean, other players have done that before too, like David Rodan in an actual AFL game, but with Maj it's just a bit of a reminder for everyone of just how raw he was.

My thoughts very quickly went to, *Imagine if we could harness this in the right direction?* I always felt with Maj, in those early years, we were so close. I probably made a mistake in a pre-season interview early on when, as a throw-away line, I said to a reporter, 'Gee, if we can get a few things right, there are certain aspects of Maj's game that are just unstoppable.' So, after I said that – what do you reckon the headline was? I reckon that put a fair bit of pressure on him, and probably got a few scoffs from different people. That was a mistake, in hindsight, but it was probably just reflective of how excited I was about the possibilities.

The other part of Majak that we had to build from the ground up was his resilience and aggression in the contest. When Maj wanted to do something, he could do it as good as anyone. There is some famous footage of me giving Majak an almighty spray down the phone from the coach's box to the interchange bench during one game later in his career. I honestly had to wind myself up at times to yell at a player. I didn't have to get wound up to give a staff member a spray in the coach's box, but the players, I don't know why, I just didn't think yelling at players helped. If they weren't play-ing well, they'd be well aware of it, and my job as a coach was to help them. With Maj, though, he did need a prickle at times, and before I get to the story of me spraying him, there's another story I need to explain, which is the genesis of my thought process around giving him a bake.

When I started at North Melbourne as coach, we took the players to Utah for a high-performance camp. This camp was to build aerobic endurance, which Maj had very little (to none) of. Our overall group had poor running capacity in general, so it was an endurance-based camp, but it was also about building their mental resilience. We were trying to do it in combination: build aerobic endurance and push the players further than they thought they could be pushed, anaerobically. It was all about taking players out of their comfort zone and doing things like eight-hour hikes at 3000 metres above sea level, up steep slopes. It was physically taxing, but Maj was on another level in terms of his aerobic base – he just didn't have any. For anyone who's a power athlete, the idea of an eight-hour hike is a nightmare. I was really conscious that it was going to be harder for him than it was for the other players.

Pretty early on in the hike I could see Maj was struggling, and on every hill, even a slight undulation, he'd fall back behind the pack. We were only walking, and it was like, *Oh my God! He is so far behind aerobically, how is he going to be able to play AFL-level footy?* My biggest challenge was keeping the group together so early into this eight-hour climb. I knew I had to give Maj every bit of help I could, so, up a pretty steep slope, I just went to the back of the line – trying not to let any other players see – and took Majak's pack and carried it for him. I literally put my hand on his back and pushed him up the hill. When we got to the top of the mountain, word had probably got around that I'd been carrying his bag.

He was just jelly-legged, fell to the ground, flat on his back and, because we were so high, 3000 metres above sea level, there was a fair bit of snow on the ground. In parts, it was knee-deep. Levi Greenwood made a snowball and threw it. It whistled past me and hit Maj smack-bang in the side of the head. The players erupted laughing. Maj, who'd just had his bag carried up the mountain and who at one point had looked like death warmed up, bounced up out of the snow, and with his knees up – it almost looked like his knees were up around his chin – he bounded and covered about 40 metres in no time at all, in about two seconds, chasing Levi. Levi just turned and started running the other way. Maj reeled him in and tackled him to the ground within an instant. I was like, *Wow!* This is a guy who looked like he was about to die, then gets hit in the head with a snowball, and this burst of energy comes based on pure adrenaline. It was a sight that I'll never forget. It was unbelievable.

So, with that in mind, we can go back to the game-day story against Essendon, when I sprayed Maj down the phone. Bombers ruckman Tom Bellchambers had pushed Majak out of the way in the ruck contest about four times in a row, and just literally rag-dolled him, took the ball out of the ruck and kicked it forward. We needed Majak in the ruck for us at that stage, and I thought I had to get him off the ground and throw a metaphorical snowball at his head. When he took the phone I said something to him like, 'Fucking harden up, Majak! You don't have to be stronger, you're the strongest bloke on the fucking ground, Maj! If you get pushed out of the way . . . one more time,

I'm coming down there. C'mon, Maj! Show some fuck-ing aggression!' The whole exchange was captured on the broadcast and plenty of people could easily lip-read me, so there was no hiding away from the fact that I'd given him a massive cook, but as the coach who knew Majak better than anyone, that's what I felt he needed at the time.

We had to show Maj, over time, what he was capable of. If you go back and look at his running test results, he was our worst 2-kilometre time-trial runner, for a long time – for years. After we continued to work with his aerobic base, he eventually came out and blitzed the time trial and was running with our midfielders over 2 k's.

There was one other example where we had the boys doing four 200-metre runs, and Majak sat at the back of the first three efforts, looking like his head was going to wobble off. What our conditioning coach, Jona Segal, used to say to the players was, 'We expect your best effort on the last run, or we will keep going.' Maj had clearly been foxing for the first three runs, and on the fourth and final one, he blew everyone out of the water. It was another one of those moments, as a coach, that you stand back and go, *Oh my God, that is unbelievable!* While Maj initially thought he'd done something remarkable, we had to tell him, 'No, mate. You need to push yourself early, and it's going to hurt.'

I remember telling him the story about Sebastian Coe, an idol of mine growing up and an 800-metre world record holder. Sebastian used to say, 'True courage is pushing yourself early in an 800-metre race.' His lesson was, any-one can just cruise through the first 700 metres and sprint the last 100, but real courage is going out hard early, knowing that you're going to be spent. The last 100 metres is going to be a nightmare, because you're trying to hold off. But that's courage, and that's what I was trying to talk to Majak about. Just cruising through and then dominating everyone, that's not helping you and that's not the way AFL-level football is played. Football is about giving your best effort in every contest, knowing that you're going to be exhausted after it. You might have to go again, but that's what we're training. The 200-metre efforts are designed to elicit an anaerobic threshold, and to be able to push yourself through that. The way footy is played, it's a contest – you've got to give your maximum effort in a short period of time. The ball might come straight back, and you might not have time to recover, but you've got to go again. And that's what we were trying to instil in Maj, that he needed to give his best effort first, not last, because by then, the contest is over – you've lost it, it's gone.

The frustrating bit was that we got him to the point where he did build up his aerobic base, and he was running really well, but he'd just get little niggling injuries here and there. I reckon, as much as anything, that was one of the frustrations throughout his career, that he just couldn't take a trick with injuries.

9

Dhoŋuan

I have thousands of photos of my son, Hendrix, on my mobile phone and I cherish them all – except for one. It might seem odd to say that, but there's one photo of him in my photo album that one day I hope to delete, and that day can't come quick enough.

The photo is a beautiful one of him and was taken one morning after we went for a walk along the Maribyrnong River, near where we lived, in 2019. I had 'Hendy' strapped tight to my chest in a baby harness, the sun was out and there was no wind, it was peaceful and quiet – a perfect day in more ways than one. My partner and his mother, Emily, took the photo and sent it to me. Like all proud parents do these days, I posted it on my Instagram account and watched as a flood of great messages and comments came streaming in, like, *He's adorable*; *You two make a great father and son duo*; *Awesome to see you both smiling, Majak!*; *You're an amazing dad, Maj!* They were just some of the things people sent to me, and the general sentiment from my followers was of love, warmth and compassion.

But on social media, the online 'trolls' are always lurking, and there's always one person who has to try to bring hate and negativity into a positive environment and ruin it – and that's exactly what happened.

When I first saw the message, I couldn't believe what I was seeing and reading. And then a second comment by that same user hit me like a savage punch to the gut. This person wrote something so cruel and nasty about Hendrix, it made my blood boil. He also referenced me jumping off a bridge – an incident I will speak about in detail in a later chapter.

I remember the first time I experienced racism in Australia. It wasn't levelled directly at me, like I'd experienced in Egypt. Back in Sudan it was different too, because I had the same skin colour as everyone else; the conflict there was more between the North and South Sudanese because of religious beliefs.

In Melbourne, it was my parents who copped it the worst when we first moved to the Footscray area when I started high school. We didn't have a car when we first arrived, and Mum and Dad would have to walk 2–3 kilometres to the local shopping centre and then push the shopping trolley full of groceries back to our house. Sometimes they caught the bus when the weather was bad – the bus stop was right out the front of our house. One time, some kids on the bus waited for Mum and Dad to get off with all their shopping, and then pelted eggs at them from out the back windows. They called them names and abused them too. I still remember seeing Mum and Dad when they walked through the door, dripping in egg from head to toe. It was a sad and sorry sight, and still to this day, remembering that moment and what they looked like makes my heart ache. They didn't deserve that treatment – no one does.

Despite being humiliated, no doubt angry inside and feeling insignificant, Mum and Dad held it together for us kids on the outside and tried to brush it off, but you could see the look of hurt and embarrassment on their faces and in the way they carried themselves. When we are kids, we all see our parents as our heroes, and we look up to them. So, for me to see mine walk through the front door covered in egg and looking distressed was shattering. At the time, I couldn't grasp the situation or understand why they had been targeted in that way. It was confusing for me to see them set upon and abused.

Not too long after that experience, I too was singled out for being black. To fast-track my language skills, I enrolled in an English-speaking course at the English Language Centre in Footscray. The idea was to be advanced enough to attend high school at Footscray City College and not get left behind. At the beginning of school, I thought I was going to be okay as I wasn't the only black student, nor the only person from a multicultural background; there were also some Vietnamese and Chinese kids in the class. But it didn't seem to matter, as I was quickly made to feel out of place and not welcome.

At Footscray City College, a boy walked up to me one day and called me a 'nigger' right to my face. I felt an intense rage build up inside of me and remembered the moment my parents had walked through the front door covered in egg. I grabbed a pen off a nearby desk and thrust it at this kid's leg. Fortunately, it didn't go in deep or penetrate the fabric of his pants, but it was enough to hurt him, and I know now it could have been a lot worse. A little scuffle followed before a teacher intervened and marched us to the coordinator's office. I couldn't hold back my emotions and started crying, but it didn't stop me from being suspended. The other boy was also suspended.

When I got home that day, I had to hand my parents a letter detailing what had happened and that I was suspended for two weeks. The most frustrating part was that my dad immediately scolded me for my reaction to the name-calling. He was so disappointed that I had been sent home from school and banished for a short period of time. 'Why are you getting suspended from school?' he growled at me. 'Why are you acting on your emotions and getting upset at what these children are saying to you? This is not how we behave!'

I knew I had done the wrong thing in lashing out, but I expected a little more sympathy from him. For my dad, however, two wrongs never make a right. Always, when we were growing up, he'd try to teach us lessons in self-control and knowing what's right from wrong. If two of us kids were fighting in front of the other siblings, the ones who failed to break up the fight would be the ones who got in the most trouble. 'Why didn't you stop your brothers from fighting?' he'd ask the not-so-innocent bystanders. Not wanting to get involved was never an excuse. 'Don't tell me you didn't want to get involved,' he'd say. 'Because you should have gotten involved and you should have looked after your siblings by stopping them from resorting to violence!' My dad had a strong disposition when it came to fairness, equality and kindness. He's always been like that, and I thank him for it because I've grown up with an open mind. I know that in any given situation, you can always react differently; you don't always have to react with your pure emotions. It's a tough lesson, and it's taken me a long time to learn how to control my emotions.

When I returned to school after my suspension, the bullying and racism continued, and so did my tendency to react in the heat of the moment and lash out physically to any form of abuse or intimidation. I didn't know any other way than to stand up for myself, and despite Dad's words of warning and wisdom, I knew these kids would continue to pick on me until I stood my ground and put them back in their place. I even had one of the coordinators on my side, who one day pulled me to the side and said, 'Are you going to let him say that stuff to your face and let him get away with it? Look at you, you are twice as big as he is!' It was the only encouragement I needed, and the next time anyone uttered racist remarks in my direction, I went at them. I didn't physically touch them or anything, but I let them know that if they said anything again, I would make them pay. And it worked. From that moment on, they all backed off and let me be. I put them on the back foot and let them know what they were doing and how they were behaving wasn't acceptable.

Unfortunately, it wasn't the only time I experienced racism. When I moved schools, times were tough, with some kids making remarks here and there, but it was at its worst on the football field. As I got better at the game and was more confident in myself and my abilities, and as my opponents got bigger and more sure of themselves, the stakes were raised in so many ways. In school footy, not only were we playing for bragging rights between us and other schools in the region, but there was the male ego and lots of testosterone flying around, with boys becoming young adults.

Sledging opponents was very common, with guys going back and forth at each other to try to throw them off their game and get under their skin. When I entered the fray, a whole new series of derogatory names got added into the mix. In years 10, 11 and 12, it really ramped up. At MacKillop College, we had a fierce rivalry with Thomas Carr College in Tarneit. One guy from that school went at me all day. It started with some physical stuff: he pushed me, punched me and hit me from behind – all normal things defenders will do to try to unsettle forwards. I had no issues with any of that stuff and could always take care of myself physically. But when he realised it was not having an impact on my game or affecting me in a negative way, he resorted to the lowest of lows.

We got into a little scuffle and started jumper-punching each other – that's when you grab a fistful of someone's jumper, up around their neck area, and punch them in the chin while still holding onto their jumper. For some reason it's not deemed as a straight-out punch if you have some of their jumper in your fists. It's strange, I know, but when you watch the AFL and see the players getting into a fight, only the stupid ones throw punches without some jumper fabric between their fingers.

'You fucken nigger!' he yelled at me. I knew I'd heard it, but I couldn't quite believe I'd heard it. Other players heard it too, and it was like the whole game stopped for a brief moment while we all replayed the words in our minds, let it sink in, and then waited for someone to react to it. I looked at this kid, and I reckon he would have seen actual fire in my eyes. I let go of his jumper and stepped back to create some distance between us and then propelled myself towards him with a clenched fist. I connected with his chin and dropped him. He fell backwards to the ground, and he was out cold.

Both school principals rushed onto the ground with some other staff and players, and I got dragged to the sidelines, while the trainers rushed over to see if he was okay. As I was being led from the ground, I looked over my shoulder and saw that he was slowly getting to his feet, so I knew he wasn't in any serious danger, but it was a stupid thing to have done on my part. Again, I'd let my emotions get the better of me. Yeah, he deserved it for saying what he said to me, but it was weak of me to react in the way that I did, and I knew it was wrong. I could have caused him serious injury, broken his jaw or given him brain damage.

As a footballer, there's an unspoken rule: what happens on the field stays on the field, meaning you don't dob on other players or try to get them in trouble off the field, no matter what they did to you or someone else during the game. My principal ushered me to a place where we could talk in private, behind our team's interchange bench, and he asked me what had happened to cause me to punch this kid. I thought long and hard about whether to tell him the truth, and break the player's trust, and in the end, I felt compelled to call out the racism. Deep down, I knew that I needed to take a strong stance and declare to everyone there that day, as well as other students from both schools who hadn't attended the game but would no doubt be told about it, that it wasn't okay to say such things.

'He called me a "fucking nigger",' I told the principal. I could see the look of horror and disgust on his face as I said the infamous N-word. I feared that another lengthy suspension was on the way or, even worse, that he'd expel me from the school, but to my surprise, he sided with me immediately and gave me the support I needed. He asked me if I was okay and told me that I was within my rights to have reacted the way I did. He said he'd discuss the incident with the principal from Thomas Carr and ensure that nothing more would come of it. Thankfully, he stuck to his word and my dad never found out about it either – but I guess he will now, when he reads this book. Sorry, Dad!

I crossed paths with the guy in question many times after that incident, not only on the football field during school and local footy, but also at various parties and events held in our local area. Without speaking about it, we had come to a mutual agreement that what had happened was in the past and not worth revisiting. For my part,

I held no grudge towards him, and we would say 'Hi' if we ever came in contact with each other.

Many people ask me, 'If the word "nigger" is so offensive to black people, why do they use it too?' I actually never use it and don't agree that it's okay for black people to use it, regardless of the situation or context. I see it as a word that should be banished to the annals of history, forever. If I get offended when a white person calls me a 'nigger', then why should I be okay if a black person says it to me? The argument that black people are trying to reclaim the word and use it for empowerment doesn't make sense to me. We shouldn't tolerate the word in any shape or form. The sooner it is forgotten and stopped from being used, the better.

The word was first used in the 18th century as an adaption of the Spanish word *negro*, which means 'black'. During times of slavery, 'nigger' was the name used to identify all black people. They weren't called by their actual names back then; instead, they were lumped into one big collective 'nigger' category and that's how they were all addressed. It was, and is, derogatory and highly offensive. It strips black people of any individuality and basically says to us, 'You are a commodity, not a person. You are something that should be owned, and you are less of a human than white people are.' In my experience, there's no other word in existence that makes a black person feel more out of place, unwelcome, unwanted, isolated, alone, ashamed, weak, pathetic or small than the word 'nigger'. I hate even writing it here, in this book, but I know I have to address it, as this is my chance to try to educate those who may not have the context or understanding.

Looking back, I think the reason I decked that boy for saying the N-word to me was because when I played football, I felt like I belonged. All my life, I'd been moved around from country to country, and our family had spent more time than most just trying to fit in and find a sense of belonging. I had changed schools many times and had to make friends and then leave them behind, only to start over again. I had to change football clubs too, and fight for acceptance and make my way into various teams. My entire life, up until that point, had been about adapting as best I could, and trying to fit in and seek acceptance, happiness and peace. When I became good at football during school, I finally felt like I had found my niche or calling, and had stumbled on the one thing that would act as a great leveller for me – a young black man from Africa trying to make a new life for himself in Australia.

When I was playing with my teammates, the colour of my skin didn't matter. When I was in space and open, they'd kick or handball the ball to me. When I'd kick a goal, they'd hug me, high-five me and celebrate with me. For perhaps the first time in my life, I was treated exactly the same as everyone else and felt no bias, fear or trepidation towards me. In football, I found my 'bliss point' – a place where I belonged, felt safe and, most importantly, was truly valued and respected. Then that boy from Thomas Carr came along. By calling me the N-word, it felt like he'd stripped me bare in front of everyone and exposed me as a fraud, and revealed to everyone within earshot that I was some 'thing', not someone, and that I didn't deserve to be doing what I was doing. He took away the one thing that I loved doing and made me hate it – for a brief moment. It was a crushing insult that left me feeling so instantly vulnerable and alone, I really had no hope of holding back my fist. Before I'd even realised, I had knocked him out cold – such is the power of that fucking word.

As much as I tried to shield myself from racism and avoid situations where it may occur or I could be vulnerable to it, sometimes its vicious tentacles reached me in places I never expected. In 2011, I was playing in the VFL with the Werribee Tigers at Port Melbourne Football Oval when an elderly white man fired an abusive tirade at me over the fence. 'Go back to where you came from, ya fucken black ape!' I couldn't hold myself back and marched over to the fence, pointing my finger directly at him to single him out. 'What did you fucken say?' I roared back at him. 'What did you say to me? C'mon, say it again! How dare you fucken say that to me!' I was seeing red. I couldn't control myself. 'Fuck you!' I continued. He was an old man, probably in his late sixties or seventies, and the look of fear on his face from my retaliation will stay with me forever. He clearly felt threatened, and I fed off that because I had essentially done to him what he had done to me: made him feel small, unsafe and insignificant. He was suddenly scared, timid and pathetic, and I had taken all his power away from him.

After I gave him a serve, I returned to the field of play and tried to continue with the game, but a wave of emotion had swept over me and I just didn't feel like playing anymore. I didn't want to be out there. The game I loved had become somewhat dirty or tainted for me, and I just wanted to go home and get away. The half-time siren sounded and I retreated to the locker room, where I was met by the then North Melbourne football boss, Donald McDonald. He came over and asked me what had happened, having seen me get upset at the supporter from the opposite side of the ground. When I told Donald what had been said to me, he couldn't have been more supportive and empathetic. He put his arm around me and told me that, unfortunately, there are some people out there who will say nasty things to get players off-guard and rattle them. He assured me the club would find the man in the crowd and have him ejected and would report his actions to the police and to the Port Melbourne Football Club.

Donald knew a lot about racism, as he'd played for North Melbourne back in the 1980s and had a solid track record of sticking up for the club's Aboriginal players, including Jim and Phil Krakouer, who were subjected to frequent abuse and racism. Somewhat of an enforcer for the team and his teammates, Donald was and still is as loyal as anyone, and would never tolerate seeing his friends or loved ones attacked in any way, shape or form. As the head of the football club decades later, the same values and actions applied to him, and he'd always go into bat for his players and staff. With Donald in my corner, I broke down and started bawling my eyes out. Just like my uncontrollable urges to fight and use force when I was racially abused, I was overcome by feelings of sadness and humiliation and couldn't hold back the tears. The feelings of not belonging that formed a common thread through-out my life had returned, and made me feel so alone and vulnerable.

The man, a Port Melbourne supporter, was identified, spoken to and ejected from the ground. Later that week he was told that he'd be banished from the football club for life unless he agreed to a series of conditions, which included sending me a letter of apology and registering for a racial and religious vilification awareness program. The incident made headlines across the country, and with the support of Donald and the wider North Melbourne Football Club, I elected to go public with what had happened, explaining my reaction in an effort to educate others about the hurt and damage that can be inflicted on people from diverse backgrounds through this type of behaviour. The Victorian Premier, Ted Baillieu, spoke out about it too, saying that racist people deserved the 'wrath of the community' and also commenting, 'I despair for moments like that. I think Majak Daw is a hero and there are plenty of other heroes in similar situations.' The CEO of the AFL Players Association (AFLPA), Matt Finnis, said, 'We want to send a strong message that this is our players' workplace and the workplace of other officials and spectators who pay money and who should be able to play the game free of offensive behaviour.'

It was a wonderful feeling to have so much support from people in high places and those who could help make a difference. Other AFL clubs also voiced their disgust at how I had been treated. The Melbourne coach at that time, the late Dean Bailey, called for a harsher response, suggesting people who racially vilified others should be 'named and shamed'. Bailey added, 'I think what happened to young Majak Daw is a disgrace. Here's a young man making his way in life and being a footballer and really representing his people, and to have those slurs on him is just ridiculous.'

Away from the football field, those racist tentacles can reach out and wrap themselves around you on the street too. When I walk into a shop or café, I can feel some people tense up and maybe get a little bit scared of me, becoming more alert or unsure. I can see it in their body language and in their eyes. If I'm getting petrol late at night, the service station attendant will be frightened of me and lock the door, but moments before it was left unlocked when a white person strolled in to pay their bill. People are constantly surprised when they hear me speak. They can't believe how articulate I am. 'Oh, wow! I didn't realise you could speak so well!' people will often say to me. They have a preconceived idea that I should talk in broken English.

On another occasion I had met up with my older brothers, Peter and Augustino, along with my cousin Bol, who I hadn't seen in a long time. We were looking to have a good night out together, so I recommended a cool nightclub that I frequented with some other guys from the football club. I was so familiar with the place that I knew the bouncers and staff by name, and I was always given free drinks and was well looked after. But this time, with my black family members with me, things were much different. We were standing near the bar having a drink, but it felt like everyone in the room was staring at us. We felt unwelcome and out of place, despite minding our own business. Even ordering a drink at the bar was difficult. I could sense the bar staff were deliberately ignoring us and stayed away from our end of the bar to avoid taking our order. Apparently, a girl walked up to one of the security guards, completely unprovoked by us, and told him that she felt threatened by our presence. The guard came over to me and asked me if we'd consider leaving, because we were making people feel uncomfortable.

'But we're not doing anything wrong,' I protested.

'There's some concern that your brothers or cousin might cause some trouble and start a fight,' the guard replied.

I tried to argue he was being unreasonable. 'Mate, what do you mean? These are my brothers and they don't go around causing trouble. We are here for a good time and we don't want to upset anyone.'

'But you see, you are upsetting people, Maj.'

'You know me. I vouch for my friends and family. Just leave us be, and we'll be fine, I promise.'

'Look, maybe you should find somewhere else to have a good time tonight,' he urged.

During my exchange with the security guard, I noticed that some other guards had started to move towards us as reinforcement, and it was creating quite a scene. My brothers were asking me what was going on, and I just kept telling them not to worry. I didn't want them knowing that they were the problem, but eventually I had to explain that we were no longer welcome there. Realising we weren't going to win over the club's management and security guards and be left alone, we decided to leave. I was so disappointed and felt that I had let my brothers and cousin down, because I had recommended this place and thought we'd be okay there. The way the security guards and staff had treated us made it feel like my friends had turned on me. I actually knew the owner of the nightclub very well but stopped myself from ringing him and complaining, because I knew it wouldn't have made a difference or changed any attitudes or behaviours. Even if the owner had intervened and told the security guards to invite us back in, we wouldn't have wanted to go back inside anyway, as the atmosphere and mood would have changed.

In 2014 a Hawthorn supporter at Aurora Stadium in Launceston, Tasmania, apparently yelled to me over the fence, 'Go back to South Africa, you black dog!' I say apparently because I didn't actually hear it; my teammates and opponents did. At the end of the game, the media was asking for a reaction, and although members of our club tried to shield me from the comments, it was impossible for me not to hear what had been said; it was all over social media. The club ensured I didn't have to respond, and instead Brad Scott addressed the comments in his post-match media address saying, 'Unfortunately, there's still idiots out there. If there's any good to come out of it, it was a Hawthorn supporter, but other Hawthorn supporters around him made it known to him it's not on,' Scott said. 'Those Hawks supporters need to be applauded. It's disappointing. Majak has been through a lot in his life, so this is not going to worry him.' My teammate Scott Thompson also came out strongly on my behalf and said, 'It's very disappointing but Majak has a strong character . . . he copes with it really well . . . It was good that supporters stuck up for [Majak] and dobbed that guy in.' Shockingly, the guy that yelled out had a young child aged about five with him when he was thrown out of the ground by security after complaints from nearby fans. A host of players joined Brad's and Scott's condemnation of the remarks, including Hawks superstar Cyril Rioli, who said on social media, 'Very disappointed about what occurred at the footy last night! My support goes out to Majak.'

One of the hardest things for me is that I get stuck in the middle of a lot of racism-related issues, regardless of whether they've affected me or not. While I have been racially vilified and attacked on several occasions, for the most part, I've been very lucky and haven't been exposed to racism anywhere near as much as some of my family members and other people I know. Life has been pretty good for me in Australia in that regard. So, I admit, early on in my AFL career, there were plenty of times when I didn't want to get involved with various issues and causes. I would think, *Why should I always be the one who has to speak up and try to make a difference?* I would get hundreds of requests from organisations and people asking me to speak out on their behalf or endorse a company, mission statement or position, and it's not that I felt uncomfortable doing those things, it's that I saw how my white teammates were allowed to just go about concentrating on their footy, not having to concern themselves with anything else.

It took me a while to realise that I'm in a privileged position and able to be a voice for others, make meaningful change and have an impact. I think about all those other people with public profiles throughout the world who could have buried their heads in the sand and not spoken up for what's right. For me, I decided it's not an option to remain silent and pretend these things don't happen. I have a voice, and I can be a voice for the voiceless. I can use my reputation and various platforms to speak up on their behalf and call out mistreatment or social injustice.

All those who have come before us have paved the way for black people to be in the position we are in – and the position I am in. Even some of my teammates, in the early days, never understood why I kept sticking my neck out for other people or speaking up. 'Why are you always going to these events and putting stuff on social media like that?' they'd ask. Over time, and after getting to know me, my background and my family, they came to realise that I really had no choice but to speak up, and that doing so has become an important part of my life. I'll never take for granted the support my teammates gave me and continue to give me, and I've really grown to appreciate them more, have seen the growth in them and watched as they expanded their levels of understanding. They appreciate how those things affect me, and they realise skin colour actually has no bearing on whether they can help to make change or fix social issues.

So, when I saw what that racist commenter had to say about that photo of Hendrix and me by the river, I felt sad and overwhelmingly disappointed. For him to inject his hate into my life, and into the life of my baby boy, was hurtful and disgusting. I've kept a screen shot of his remarks, because it serves as a reminder that we are nowhere near where we need to be as a society. I have to do more – we all have to do more – to combat racism and stamp it out. It can't be a never-ending battle; there must be a future where it's eradicated. There are times when I think twice about posting something on social media, for fear that someone might say something abhorrent to me, but if I stop posting for that reason, then they've won.

The AFL and the AFLPA have taken a tough stance against online trolls and, as an industry, we've elected to call out those who spread hate and racially vilify others. There's no wrong or right way to go about it, and I don't know if it's working, because many trolls hide behind fake identities on platforms like Twitter, Facebook and Instagram. In my opinion, the best way to combat racism is to keep telling people how it makes us feel and hope the majority of good people out there work with us to extinguish it. We all want to be happy, be loved and enjoy life; it doesn't matter what colour skin you have, we should all have the same opportunities.

People that sections of society don't deem 'normal', like black people, gay people and other minorities, shouldn't have to feel insignificant or not welcome simply because they might make the ignorant feel a bit uncomfortable. When you boil it down, it's just the opinion of one person who simply doesn't understand what you are about or where you've come from. One racist person is not a representation of everyone, and one bad gay or black person isn't either. The real extremists and racist people are stuck in their ways, and that's what they've always known. I feel sorry for them, because I guess they will never get to know about my culture or my upbringing. I'd like to think I'm pretty funny, and they'll never get to hear my funny jokes. My parents are two of the kindest people you could ever meet, and they'll never get to meet them. My brothers and sisters are all amazing people, and they'll never get to know them. They're the ones missing out – not us – and I feel sorry for them for that reason.

The recent Black Lives Matter movement has achieved a lot here in Australia because, in the past, it was mainly black people fighting against racism and social injustice, or people being mistreated or killed by police. But now the movement is so big that we've got white people also fighting for our cause, and really doing something about it. While I couldn't attend the protest in Melbourne in 2020 because of the AFL's COVID-19 restrictions, I was buoyed by the number of friends, both black and white, who went along and sent me videos and photos showing what they were doing. My white friends made it clear that they went to the rally because they love me. It was pretty powerful, amazing, and it gives me hope, to be honest. The best thing about it is that it hasn't stopped, and it's just going to keep going until there is meaningful change.

10

Thiäär

I woke up and my knee was aching. I pulled the bedsheets aside, looked down at my leg and saw that it was badly swollen. It was the final day of our mini-break in February 2012 – a pre-season breather for all the teams in the AFL that consists of four days off in a row – and Emily and I had gone down to her family's beach house on Phillip Island for a little getaway. I was in rehab, and had been since Christmas, after injuring my knee and undergoing a minor arthroscopy and clean-out.

Prior to heading down to the southern coast for a few days away, I had trained with the other players in rehab and had gone out on the Friday night with some of the younger boys to various nightclubs, which was against club rules for someone with an injury concern. The club had strict rules for players coming back from injury, which included lots of rest and staying off your feet as much as possible, and no alcohol – no matter what the occasion. I'd known it was wrong to be out drinking and on my feet for an extended period of time, but I'd gone along anyway.

I'd felt somewhat pressured into heading out with the boys, but I can't blame them for making the decision to go – that was solely on me.

With my knee swollen and not feeling great at all, I tried everything to remedy it, including ice baths, salt crystals and massage, but it remained severely inflamed and full of fluid. I knew I'd have some explaining to do to the medical staff at the club on my return, and I started to panic. When I got back to Arden Street after the mini-break, I headed in to see the physiotherapists, and they were horrified to see how bad my knee had become.

'What the fuck happened, Maj?' one of them asked me as he prodded around to see what the damage was.

I lied without even thinking: 'I don't know. I just woke up one morning and it was swollen.'

'Did you drink over the weekend?' he asked.

'No, I didn't drink.' Hindsight is a great thing, and looking back, I should have been honest from the start, but I had dug a hole for myself and I doubled down.

'Maj. This can't have "just happened". You had to have done something to reinjure your knee and make it worse,' the physio continued.

'No, I didn't. I didn't do anything.'

My knee was really sensitive and I could barely withstand the physio's physical examination of it. The medical staff had reported my condition to the coaches, and then senior assistant coach Darren Crocker sought me out to quiz me some more. 'Maj, this looks really suss, mate. Were you out drinking over the weekend at all?'

I stuck to my story. 'No, I didn't. Not at all,' I replied. I had more than a few opportunities to tell the truth, but I was just scared of the consequences. After my conversation with Darren, I had hoped that the ordeal was over and that I had avoided getting into any trouble, but I was delusional and, as it also turned out, naïve, stupid and too trusting. Someone had clearly dobbed me in, but I refused to even consider that as a possibility.

Just when I thought it was all done and dusted, North Melbourne's head of footy, Donald McDonald, told me the coach, Brad Scott, wanted to see me in his office. That situation is like being back at school and being summoned to the principal's office – it's never a good thing and makes most players extremely nervous. What had happened in the lead-up to my meeting, but was unknown to me at the time, was that Brad had spoken to all the other players I was drinking and clubbing with on Friday night, and asked them if I was out with them. Knowing their careers would be in jeopardy if they lied to protect me, each and every one of them would have told him the truth.

This was my time to come clean, too, but for some reason I didn't. I sat across from Brad and he asked me whether I had been out drinking, against team rules. I should tell you, Brad is a very intimidating person but he has a softer side too. Initially, I got the 'softer' Brad, who invited me to tell the truth. He said words to the effect of, 'Maj, if you've lied up until this point, that's okay, I get that you may have acted in the moment, but now is your chance to tell me what really happened. Were you out with

the boys on Friday night, drinking? Just be honest with me.'
I've learnt that going forward, if I fuck up the best thing
to do is just to be honest straight away, because otherwise
you can make mountains out of molehills. Unfortunately,
I learnt this the hard way by making a massive volcano.

'No, I wasn't out drinking or anything like that,'
I lied straight to his face. 'I know some of the boys went
out because they invited me, but I didn't go because of my
knee.' He had given me the chance to be honest, a second chance, but I was just so adamant that he wouldn't
or couldn't have known that I went out. I was blind to the
fact that the other players had given me up, but it wasn't
long before the not-so-soft Brad let me know. It was the
moment that our relationship really fractured, and probably never recovered, if I'm going to be honest. One of the
worst things you can do as a player is betray the trust of
your coach or teammates and lose their respect. It takes a
hell of a long time to win it back – I know that only too
well. Brad roared words to the effect of, 'C'mon, Maj! Do
you think I'm stupid? Are you really gonna sit there, look
me in the eye and lie to my face, mate? I'm bitterly disappointed in you, Maj.' The gig was up, I'd been outed and
there was nowhere for me to hide. Brad told me the club
would issue a punishment after consulting with the leadership group. As soon as he said that, I knew it wasn't going
to be a good outcome for me, because I was already out of
favour with several senior players.

Several months before my indiscretion, I had started
seeing a girl named Emily McKay who I had met at a few

social gatherings. We immediately hit it off and went on a few dates before I found out that she had previously dated a then teammate of mine. I was initially reluctant to continue dating her, as I didn't want to jeopardise my relationship with that player or anyone else, but Emily assured me that it was all okay, as they had well and truly broken up around a year earlier and had been seeing other people in between. Despite Emily's belief that it would be okay, it wasn't, and the shit hit the fan in a big way. Being a senior player, Emily's ex and his closest mates at the club didn't take too kindly to me dating her and let me know it. It split the playing group down the middle and caused huge amounts of tension. A lot of the younger boys sided with me, while the more senior players sided with him.

That's why I knew when it was time for the leadership group to punish me for lying to the coach and going out while in rehab, it was going to be a heavy-handed sanction. I was suspended indefinitely from the club and banished to the VFL. I was told to do all my weights and running in the morning, before any of the other players arrived at the club, and I was made to work a full-time job as a primary school teacher's aide. If I didn't finish my weights or running in the morning, I had to come back at night after work and complete it. It meant many of my days would start at 6.30 a.m. and wouldn't finish until after 8 p.m. It was rough, but I considered it fair, given what I had done and the decisions I had made. In the end, you can't lie to the coach and get a slap on the wrist.

What was supposed to be an 'in house' issue and sanction was quickly leaked to the media – and I don't think that was an accident, but rather, retribution. It was also leaked that I 'owed' some teammates money, which was true, but it was reported out of context and came across as if I had stolen money from them. The fact of the matter was that being a rookie, I hadn't been able to afford to go on the previous year's end-of-season players' trip to Bali. Gavin Urquhart had generously offered to pay for me, and I was in the process of paying him back. Although I was only a rookie, and hadn't even played a game in the AFL yet, news of my suspension, relationship status and financial situation was splashed across the front page of the *Herald Sun* – yes, the front page of the city's main newspaper. It was completely overblown, and all perspective had been lost. No other rookie at that time would have received that sort of attention or treatment – it was confusing to me and completely unfair.

The leak forced the club to come out and explain what had happened and clear up some mistruths. CEO Eugene Arocca moved to give some perspective and told the media, 'I've seen some absolute superstars of the game be able to do things and be in public in a way that is not as confronting as when Majak walks down the street,' he said. 'I think we would struggle to understand what he has been through and what he is going through, and I guess to some degree the quicker he plays his first AFL game, the better it may be. There's this enormous expectation from everyone – from the AFL to the Sudanese community to world media.

[Everyone] has this enormous expectation of this young man.' Although I had lied to him, Brad also defended me and told the *Herald Sun* that the other issues had no bearing on my suspension. 'Wholly and solely he was suspended for two reasons,' Brad said. 'One, he breached rehab protocol in that he went out. There was talk about it and I confronted him and asked him specifically if that was the case, and he denied it. Subsequently, I found that not to be true.' Regarding the other issues that were reported, Brad said, 'Maj's conduct is completely above board.'

The snowball effect of my lie was unimaginable. I had not only brought unnecessary pressure and attention on myself, but I had embroiled Emily and my teammates in something that didn't need to be in the public domain. It was a pretty harsh lesson, looking back, but also it was necessary for me to learn that I couldn't just lie and think I'd get away with it. It affected how my teammates perceived me, my whole family was really disappointed in me, and the attention Emily copped was unfair.

Growing up in Sudan, family was everything. I was always surrounded by a lot of people.
TOP: My grandmother Nyluke's baptism, in Khartoum.
BOTTOM: Building a school, using mud bricks and sand mixed with glue.

TOP: I'm one of nine siblings. This photo is outside our first home in Omdurman, in Sudan. Peter is holding Teresa, and on the left are me and Augustino.

INSET: My parents, William and Elizabeth, wanted a better life for all of us, but before we moved to Australia we spent three difficult years in Egypt. This is the only photo of us, as a family, from that time.

BOTTOM: Anthony and me enjoying a happier moment while in Egypt.

Our very first house in Australia, in Footscray. This is Mum with (from the left) Sarah, Mary, Angelina and Anthony.

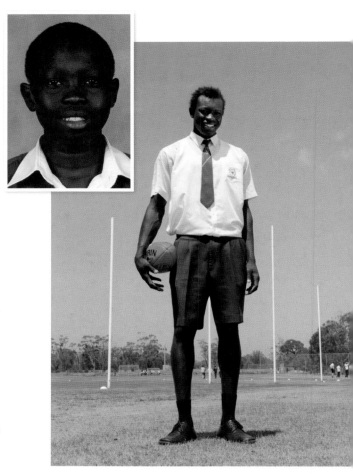

INSET: Photo day at Catholic Regional College, a few years after arriving in Australia.

RIGHT: Me in the MacKillop College uniform. Being invited to join a game of kick to kick at lunchtime revealed a talent and passion for footy, but it also opened a lot of doors for me socially. *(Vince Caligiuri/Fairfax)*

BELOW: (From the left) Joey, Dion, Jack and Jesse, all part of the MacKillop College football team. Joey went above and beyond to welcome me, and he's still one of my best mates.

(Craig Sillitoe/Fairfax)

TOP: The Western Jets team from 2007. Playing in the TAC Cup was a massive step up. I could compete physically, but it made me realise I had a long way to go with my skills.
BOTTOM: In my Western Jets jersey, with Mum and Dad. They were both hesitant about me playing Aussie Rules, but they supported me nonetheless, and are very proud of what I've achieved.

Being drafted by North Melbourne in 2009 will always be one of my most cherished memories. This is me with my youngest brother, Ajak, not long after joining North.

(Joe Armao/Fairfax)

LEFT: Media day in 2009. The intensity of training with the Kangaroos was like nothing I'd experienced before. Only four years earlier I'd never even played the sport! There was a lot of work ahead before I could become a regular in the AFL side.
(Lachlan Cunningham/AFL Media)

BOTTOM: Brad Scott and me, in 2010. Brad always believed in me, working hard to help me develop my skills and become a more rounded player. But it wasn't easy for him, or me, because I was coming from such a long way back.
(Lachlan Cunningham/AFL Media)

In 2011 I played my first AFL
pre-season games, at Skilled
Stadium, with the pool format
seeing us play both the Western
Bulldogs and Geelong on the
same day.
(Darrian Traynor/AFL Media;
Lachlan Cunningham/AFL Media)

Injuries and mistakes off the field cost me opportunities, and in 2012 I was dropped down to the Werribee Tigers VFL side indefinitely. I still hadn't made my AFL debut.
TOP: Playing for Werribee in the 2012 Foxtel Cup grand final. *(Will Russell/AFL Media)*
BOTTOM: Until my chance came, all I could do was train relentlessly. *(Michael Willson/AFL Media)*

TOP LEFT: The jumper presentation before my AFL debut in Round 4, 2013, against the Brisbane Lions at Docklands.

TOP RIGHT: I played well, and even managed to kick an early goal.

BOTTOM: Unfortunately, I was knocked out in the first quarter, after a clash of heads. My mum said, 'I told him not to play this sport!' *(Lachlan Cunningham/AFL Media)*

Round 5, 2013, in the ruck against Nic Naitanui in my second ever AFL game – an awesome and unforgettable experience.

(Will Russell/AFL Media)

TOP: While I was found not guilty, the stress and media attention of a 2015 court case was a long and painful ordeal. I think this is when I became good at hiding my feelings from those around me, without realising the toll it was taking.

(Adam Trafford/AFL Media)

RIGHT: By 2016 I was playing in the AFL side a little more regularly. This screamer against Collingwood in Round 18 won me mark of the year.

(Michael Willson/AFL Media)

A positional change saw me playing eighteen games in 2018, a breakout season for me. This is Round 19, a win against West Coast, the eventual premiers. *(Michael Willson/AFL Media)*

Speaking at The Huddle in 2018. It's an initiative by North Melbourne Football Club to help migrants and refugees, using sport to break down barriers. It's a cause very close to my heart, and I love every opportunity to be involved and make a difference. *(Michael Dodge/Getty Images)*

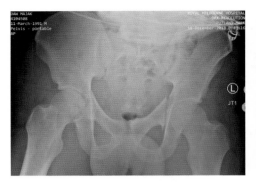
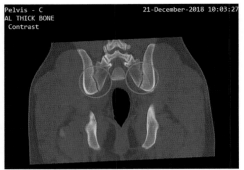

TOP: Following my fall from the Bolte Bridge, there was genuine concern I would never walk again – I had obliterated my hips and pelvis. The rehab was excruciating, but I was determined to play footy again. MIDDLE & BOTTOM: My VFL comeback game, in Round 14, 2019, against Sandringham. I think the smile says it all. *(Graham Denholm/AFL Media)*

Playing in the Queensland bubble in 2020 was a challenge, but nothing could take the shine off coming back to play top-level footy. A lot of people thought it would be impossible, but nothing was going to stop me.

TOP: Celebrating my first goal back with the boys, against Adelaide in Round 9.
BOTTOM: The only thing better than kicking that goal was celebrating the win.

(Chris Hyde/AFL Media)

ABOVE: Getting delisted by North Melbourne hurt, and at times I found it hard to know what to do with myself. When the opportunity came to join Melbourne, I grabbed it with both hands. *(Robert Cianflone/AFL Media)* INSET: My son Hendrix is the reason I'll never stop working hard for my dreams. He's my purpose and my inspiration.

REFLECTIONS

Brad Scott, Shane Casley

Brad Scott was one of the most supportive people of me at North Melbourne and gave me the chance to be the best version of myself. He taught me a lot about not only football, but about being an adult and a professional athlete away from the football field. While I regret lying to him all those years ago, I look back on it as a time that helped shape who I am today. Here, he explains his side of the story of how it all went down.

When the news got out that Maj had lied to me, I remember News Limited had gleaned all this other peripheral information completely unrelated to the issue at hand – that Maj had lied to me, the coach, and was in trouble for that. I remember sitting in the office of the CEO, Eugene Arocca, with our GM Media, Heath O'Loughlin, and we called the editor of the paper to clarify some things and set the record straight. We told News Limited the absolute truth and said, 'Here is everything about the story and the issue at hand as far as we're concerned, and it is very simple: Maj told me and others some porky-pies [lies], and that's it.'

The thing that really made me angry was that News Limited were given the full story and context by us, and then ran the salacious front-page story anyway, and included stuff about Maj's private life that wasn't a concern of the club's, nor was it in any way relevant to his suspension. We did a hell of a lot of work in the background, to try to protect Maj – not to cover anything up, but to tell the truth and look after him as much as we could.

The other issues weren't a big deal for us. He owed a couple of teammates a bit of cash, and it's not the first time and won't be the last time that a player was dating another player's ex-girlfriend. So, I spoke at length to the editor and even spoke to the journalist who was writing the story and both of them said to me in separate conversations, 'I understand,' but then they ran it anyway with all the juicy stuff and we were like, *Oh God! You guys just lied*. It certainly didn't warrant a front-page story, or anything of that magnitude, and if it was any other player, it wouldn't have made it anywhere near the front of the paper.

In terms of what Majak did, it was an extremely minor thing that most young footballers will do at some point. They will go out when they're not supposed to and they will make some mistakes. It's the lying that I had the biggest issue with, because as the senior coach, it's very hard to build a relationship and go forward when someone isn't being honest with you. I was trying to build a relationship with Maj, where he could tell me anything, and he'd feel comfortable to tell me anything. The reality is, and he knows this now, if he'd told me the truth, it would have been,

'Okay Maj, you shouldn't have done it, so don't do it again, let's get on with it.' And it would have been as simple as that. We did everything we could to look after Majak, knowing he would be crucified by the media.

To punish Maj for lying to me may have seemed like an over-the-top reaction, but the relationship between player and coach is similar to that of a parent and child. When your child lies to you, you have to make sure they know that it's not acceptable, and it's hard to trust them after that. From my end, with Maj, the straining of the relationship was more just, *Oh, shit. How am I going to build back a decent level of trust with him?* My angle was, *Okay, now I've got to somehow show him that despite what had happened, he can still tell me anything.* He's petrified about the consequences and I needed to show him that he shouldn't be petrified about the consequences, he should be petrified about lying.

I think that any young draftee can get caught up in all the trappings of being an AFL footballer because, all of a sudden, there are all these people taking an interest in you. Maj had that magnified at least tenfold, because he was just so recognisable. There were so many people who wanted a piece of him, and he had a bigger social media following than our best and most accomplished players. He'd go to a nightclub and the security guards would walk him to the front of the line and let him straight in. In fact, some of our senior players would want to go to a nightclub with Maj, because Maj would be the one who could get them in. So, I was really concerned that he was just going to get caught up in this false AFL world. I was worried, and those at North Melbourne were worried, that his career was going to be over before it began, because he may have thought, *This is all fantastic.* We needed him to focus on the hard work, because he had a hell of a long way to go as a footballer, and if he didn't get the football bit right, he'd be straight out of the system and back at the end of the nightclub queue.

The funny thing is, I think, over his career, North Melbourne did the least off-field stuff with Majak of anyone, because the club wanted to protect him and ensure that he had the chance to focus on his footy. As much as he could have been overly used as a poster boy for the club's multicultural arm, The Huddle, he only did external things he was comfortable with and wanted to do. The club never pushed him in that respect and always saw him as a player first, which can't be said for everyone Maj was dealing with.

That wasn't the only awkward conversation I had to have with Brad. My manager, Shane Casley, recalls the time we had to tell Brad that another team was interested in signing me and that I would consider a move unless I started getting some playing time at North.

A few years into his AFL career, Maj was getting frustrated at not being able to break into the senior side for a game. He was playing all sorts of roles in the VFL with Werribee – he'd be playing in the ruck one week, down back another week, and even up forward – he was just all over the place. After Maj had a couple of years on the rookie list, Collingwood showed some interest in getting him on their senior list with intentions to play him. I remember sitting there with Maj, chatting about his future, saying, 'Well, where are we going here? Where are we going at North Melbourne? We can't crack it for a game. You've shown enough at Werribee to deserve a game at some point, but it's not happening.'

At the end of the season, Majak and I sat down with Brad Scott and I just said, 'Brad, Maj is very, very frustrated. He wants to play AFL footy. He's keen to play AFL footy. We haven't had an opportunity, and I want him to tell you about his frustrations, and I want him to tell you why he wants to play footy, and maybe even about where he should be playing.'

To Maj's credit, as a 20-year-old kid, to get up in front of a fairly hardened football person like Brad took some courage, and he was magnificent in the way he spoke. He was very respectful to Brad, but he was firm with his views and with what he wanted. I backed Maj up and said to Brad, 'We need to find Maj a spot . . . We have to find him a spot.'

Brad got very angry at that chat. When we told him there were other suitors for Maj, Brad wasn't impressed, which was to be expected. 'If you don't want to be here, that's very disappointing, because as a club, we are invested in you and we are committed to playing you, but not before you are ready.' It was that sort of response we got from Brad.

Again, to Maj's credit, he responded with respect, he responded firmly, and we stayed at North Melbourne. 'No, I want to be here,' Majak said. 'But I want to play AFL footy. Let's work out how I get into the team, because that's what I want to do.' He is a very loyal guy, Maj, and there are a lot of footballers who aren't. In those early days, the frustrating part for Maj was that he was always a fill-in or backup player. It wasn't until he got that opportunity to play down back in 2018 that he really established himself as a regular player, and an elite regular player.

11

Thiär ku tök

My head was pounding. I opened my eyes slightly and had no idea where I was or how I had gotten there. My vision was very blurred, and the room was too bright for me to see clearly – everything was blown-out and stark white. It felt like a giant spotlight was aimed right at my face. My eyes were so sensitive to the light, I had to keep closing them to allow myself to adjust to the intensity of it. I heard voices but couldn't make sense of what they were saying at first – everything was so confusing. It felt like I had just woken from a deep, deep sleep but couldn't get my bearings or make sense of what was happening around me. Slowly, as I started to come to, I began to catch on to words and sentences and was able to respond.

'Majak, can you hear me?' one male voice said.

'Y-y-yeah,' I replied with a stammer.

'Do you know where you are?'

'Um, no. Hang on . . .' I tried to open my eyes fully and identify something about my surroundings that would help me make some sense of what was happening. I couldn't turn my head and knew I was flat on my back. I looked down towards my feet and saw my football boots, then scanned up and saw that I was wearing my North Melbourne playing shorts and jumper. My brain was in overdrive trying to put the pieces of the puzzle together. Through what I could see, I guessed I was in uniform to play footy, but I couldn't understand why I was lying down and felt so groggy.

'Majak? Do you know where you are?' the male voice prompted. He was Irish or Scottish and that gave me another clue.

'Am I at the footy?' I replied as I opened my eyes again and took a better look at the room. Each time I opened my eyes, they became less sensitive to the light and I could make out more objects around me.

'Am I in a doctor's medical room?' I asked. It was at about that time I had some flashbacks. I knew it was game day, and I could remember driving to the ground and warming up with the rest of the players. I remembered our coach, Brad Scott, handing me my jumper. I had visions of running out through the cheer-squad banner and the crowd cheering. 'Am I at Etihad Stadium?' I asked.

'Yes,' the man replied. He had that thick accent, so I figured it was our club doctor, Andy McMahon. 'How are you feeling? Can you wiggle your toes and fingers for me?' I did as I was instructed and figured I must have been knocked out, but I had no idea how or when it had happened.

It was such a long wait leading up to my first game in the AFL in 2013. I was sweating in between each game I played in the VFL, as the coaches, especially Brad, didn't really give me much indication of where I was at. I was named as an AFL emergency player for a third consecutive week, and this time it was for a game against Sydney in Hobart, which gave me a taste of just how hard being on the cusp of the senior side was. I had to fly down to Tasmania with the team on Friday afternoon, and was on standby in case one of the named players in the 22 got injured or fell ill. However, I was told that if I wasn't required to play that day, I'd have to fly back to Melbourne and play for Werribee in the VFL later that night. It was a difficult proposition to get my head around, but – as players must do so often throughout their careers – I just agreed and trusted that the staff members at the club would help ensure that I got on the right flight and could physically do what was asked of me.

The night before the game in Hobart was a strange one for me. We all gathered at our accommodation, had a team meeting and sat down for a group dinner before heading back to our rooms for an early night. I couldn't really get settled or stop my mind from racing, and I kept wondering about what might play out the next day should one of the players be unable to take the field. In one respect, it could have been a good thing to be suddenly activated and thrown in the deep end and make my debut, but the anticipation of the unknown was a lot to deal with.

After a restless night I arrived at Blundstone Arena in Bellerive on the team bus just before lunchtime for a 1.45 p.m. game. As an emergency, you don't really do a lot in the lead-up. You just wait and watch, but sort of stay

ready and alert in case something untoward happens, and
you are suddenly required to 'suit up'. With all the players getting through the two warm-up sessions before the
first bounce, my chances of being called on to play as a
late inclusion faded fast. Before long, the boys were in full
uniform and were running out through the banner, ready
to fight it out against the Sydney Swans. When the umpire
threw the ball down and the clock started, I was officially off the hook and was quickly loaded into a taxi and
sent off to the airport to catch a 3.30 p.m. flight back to
Melbourne.

I touched down at Tullamarine Airport in Melbourne
at 4.45 p.m. and headed straight to Werribee for a 7 p.m.
game against Collingwood. I arrived at the ground at about
6 p.m. and quickly got changed and warmed up. To my
surprise, I actually played quite well considering the day
I'd had. I managed to clunk a few marks and kick some
goals. Also going in my favour was the fact that the boys in
Tasmania went down badly to the Swans, meaning there'd
be a chance that Brad Scott and the match committee members would make some changes to the team in order to
find a winning formula. I knew the way that the game had
ended in Hobart would make it hard for the match committee to back in the same 22 players. North had led by
14 points at half-time but allowed the then reigning premiers to pile on 11 goals in the third quarter. What had been
a tight tussle up until the main break became a blow-out
and one-sided affair. The boys found themselves trailing
by 47 points with a quarter to play and ended up losing by

39 points. It was our third loss for the year from three games, so the pressure was on everyone early.

I put my head down throughout the week at training, knowing I was a real chance of being selected and making my debut. Key position player Robbie Tarrant was in doubt, with an injury cloud hanging over him, and if he missed out, a spot would open up for me. I trained well, and at the end of the main session I was having some shots at goal and saw, out of the corner of my eye, Brad making his way towards me. I pretended I didn't notice and concentrated on my goal-kicking routine. I thought that if he was watching, I'd better put one through the middle. I slotted one from about 40 metres out, and as I turned to head back to the 50-metre line, Brad was standing right there. 'How are you feeling, mate?' he asked – a generic question like that is something all coaches ask their players, to see if there are any injury niggles or concerns.

'I feel great,' I replied. 'My body is good and I think I've been playing some good footy with Werribee.' Brad agreed and said he was really happy with how I was going of late. He put his hand on my shoulder and said, 'Mate, we're going to go with you this week. You'll make your debut against Brisbane.' I thanked him about 20 times and felt a surge of adrenaline rush through my body. I couldn't believe it – after three years on the North Melbourne playing list, I was finally getting my chance to wear the royal blue and white striped jumper!

The rest of the afternoon was a blur. Before I knew it, I was doing a media conference alongside Brad to announce

that I'd be playing my first game for the club. It was unusual for a rookie-listed player to get a media conference
for a debut game, but I fully understood that my story
was very different and garnered a lot of attention and public interest. The turnout was enormous. There were about
15 cameras pointed at me, bright lights blazing and a room
full of journalists poised to ask questions.

While I could tell you about all the reasons I was picked
to play, it's probably best to tell you what Brad said to the
media instead: 'I think it's a great news story . . . you know
Majak has been really pushing hard for this opportunity
for a long time, and he's been held out by some pretty good
players who have been doing the job for us. A little mishap for Robbie Tarrant, who has been carrying a slight
knock for a couple of weeks now and hasn't been able
to train fully for three weeks, and we think pushing it into
a fourth week is just not fair on him. So, he hasn't quite
come up and now the opportunity has come up for Majak
to make his debut, which we're obviously really excited
about. He's been marking the ball really strongly and he's
worked extremely hard for this opportunity . . . now he
gets the opportunity to play and so his challenge is to take
that opportunity and make the most of it. I think that
the thing about Majak is that he gives us great flexibility . . . he's a very effective ruckman, very, very difficult for
opposition ruckmen to counter because of his agility, and
his leap and speed. But we know he can also mark the ball
really strongly, so we think we can use him in a variety of
roles, and he adds another dimension to our midfield and

our forward line . . . It's Majak's opportunity this week and I'm confident he'll acquit himself really well.'

Brad also addressed the hype surrounding my debut and said the club was happy to embrace it. 'My responsibility is to the club, and to Majak, and to make sure that Majak is ready to play. We know we can't control the external hype, I understand that, though. And, you know, in a way, we welcome it, because Maj has been through some tough times and you know that there is going to be pressure on him to perform. Now, all we expect Majak to do on the weekend is play the way we want him to play – don't hesitate, go out and just attack the game – and if he does that, I'm sure his preparation to this point will hold him in really good stead, but we know it is a great news story and I don't want to keep a lid on that. I think it is fantastic for the football club, it's fantastic for Majak, it's fantastic for our game in general that we've got someone from Maj's background playing our game and playing it at the level that he'll produce on Sunday. So, up until now, my job has been to make sure that he's prepared for this moment, and I'm really confident that he is.'

The club made the most of the opportunity too and coined the hashtag #MajakHappens to be used on social media throughout the week. They even had posters made up with the hashtag on them so people could celebrate the occasion with us all. As the news spread to my extended family and friends, the ticket requests came flooding through. I initially asked for 20 from the club, then had to go back to the club and ask for 40, then 60 and finally 68.

I felt bad for asking for that many freebies, but the club was fantastic and told me that it was fine. Being the first Sudanese-born person to play in the AFL was a big deal not only for me, but also for my community and the sport itself. So many of my family friends and their friends wanted to be a part of the occasion, rightly seeing it as a big win for our people and a real example to other young African kids that they can aim high and make their dreams come true. The symbolism of me playing professionally in a home-grown Australian sport was significant and broke down many barriers. A lot of people get picked to be on AFL club lists but never get the opportunity to play a game, so I wasn't going to let this opportunity slip.

Although I had been an emergency on many occasions in the lead-up to my debut game, I really didn't know what to expect when Sunday's game against Brisbane at Docklands Stadium rolled around. I had played in the VFL for so long and knew I could play well at that level, but I didn't know whether I was actually up to playing AFL footy. So while there was all this hype and expectation that I was going to come in and rip it up, in the back of my mind I was worried that I could be an absolute flop, one of those blokes who comes in for a few games and is then never seen again: chewed up and spat out, as they say. The pressure on me was enormous and I heard a lot of commentary in the media that week suggesting the hype around my selection was similar to what a number-one draft pick would experience before playing his first game. The fact that I was an elevated rookie-listed player made it an extreme case and set of circumstances. While I did my best to block out all of the external pressure, it was hard to ignore completely and it made me very nervous.

The change rooms before an AFL match are viewed as an inner sanctum, a VIP area, and access is heavily limited and policed by the club. Passes to get into the rooms to watch the players prepare for a game are highly sought after but very rare, and each week, players are asked to get some passes for friends, family members and even members and fans. I was lucky enough to have a select few made available for my family for my debut, so I had Mum, Dad and Anthony underneath the grandstands with me before I ran out. It was extra special for me because when I was drafted in 2009, Dad was overseas and never got to join in the celebrations. But this time around, he was front and centre and you couldn't wipe the smile off his face.

For anyone reading this who doesn't really know the culture and inner workings of a football club, I can't stress enough how special and significant a debut game is for not only the player running out onto the ground for the first time, but also for everyone at the club. It's like the birth of a child for those staff and fans who have had a heavy involvement with the player's development and ultimate selection. So many years are put into the development of younger players, and to get them to the point where they're ready to play is viewed as a special moment. The coaches, welfare officers, development teams and wider staff embrace players, sometimes from the age of 17, and the club then becomes a second home and second family to that player. The relationship between player and club is very tight, and as a general rule, a debut or milestone game is a moment in history that people associated with that player want to relish and celebrate. So, for my parents to witness what could be described as my club baptism, in a way, was super-special.

After the final warm-up, our captain, Andrew Swallow, called us in for a last-minute rev-up. This was also the time I was set to receive my jumper from the coach. 'Bring it in, nice and tight,' Brad ordered. We moved in closer and all stood shoulder-to-shoulder. 'Maj: 975th player to wear this jumper, mate, and I always say to our boys that when you put this jumper on great responsibility is expected. The other 21 players who represent this club today – you gotta support this bloke. You've worked extremely hard to get this opportunity and you deserve every second of it, Maj.'

Brad shook my hand and handed me my jumper with No. 38 on the back. It felt so good putting it on, like a suit of armour that made me feel invincible. We huddled up as a group with our arms around each other and Andrew asked us to give our all for the club out on the ground. 'C'mon, Dawsy! Give us a big contest!' defender and player favourite Nathan Grima yelled out. I made my way towards the players' race that led up to the playing arena and greeted my mum and dad on the way out with a quick hug. They were in unfamiliar territory and I could tell by the looks on their faces that they were very nervous and worried about me.

Marching up the race felt like a scene out of Russell Crowe's *Gladiator* movie. Crowds of people were hanging over the railings of the grandstands on both sides of us, yelling out well wishes to me and cheering on the team. The atmosphere was electric, and the stadium's PA system started belting out the club song to the delight of the fans. When my foot left the last piece of concrete and hit the grass on the oval, I sprinted towards the huge banner with the rest of the boys and broke through it with real purpose. I had been watching players break through those banners in the AFL since I was 12 years old and had always wanted to do it. The moment was everything I had imagined – it was electric.

In the forward pocket behind our end of the ground, a sea of people waved the 'Majak Happens' posters, and it was a brilliant sight to see. I spotted so many familiar faces in the crowd and saw just how many people had made the time and effort to come out and support me. I was lucky enough to start the game on the ground and got a huge surprise when I saw that in-form Lions defender Daniel Merrett came my way. Merrett was a big boy, standing at 195 centimetres tall and weighing more than 100 kilos – I knew I wasn't going to be able to push him around. I had to be smart and use my agility and speed against him. But then, to my surprise and relief, he switched with another defender, Niall McKeever, and instead Merrett went to play on Drew Petrie. That happens often in footy – players will pretend to line up on you and then make a quick change to throw you off and unsettle you.

The siren sounded and with it came a wave of energy through my body. The umpire blew his whistle, slammed the ball into the turf and the game was under-way. Daniel Wells got the ball from about 75 metres out and bombed it in long with his raking right foot. I quickly identified where the ball was going to drop and found some space behind my opponent. He, too, had run to the drop of the ball but had gone too far underneath it, leaving me a great run and jump at it. I saw Merrett running back with the flight of the incoming footy and knew I had to launch at it. I jumped high over the back of McKeever and marked it, sending him and Merrett crash-ing to the ground.

The crowd went berserk. It was a sound I had never experienced before in that way, knowing they were all screaming and shouting for me. Drew Petrie came straight to me and tried to calm my nerves, telling me to breathe deep and take my shot. As I walked back to take my kick the captain, Andrew Swallow, came over and gave me a pat on the bum and told me to block out the noise and go through my practised kicking routine. As I ran in, it was supposed to be about a 30-metre kick, but I stopped so short, because I didn't want to kick the footy into the man on the mark, I ended up booting it from about 45 metres. Despite my miscalculation, it went dead straight and sailed right through the middle of the goals.

Lindsay Thomas came hurtling towards me with a look of pure delight on his face and jumped into my arms to celebrate my first goal. In fact, every North player from all over the ground came to congratulate me. I looked up at the scoreboard, took a sneaky look at the replay and realised it had all happened within 20 seconds of the opening bounce. It really was the perfect start to my AFL career.

Before long, Merrett came to play on me and I was fortunate enough to take another mark in the pocket on him. The ball fell into my lap and I was stuck on an extremely tight angle – about 15 metres from goal. Although I was very close, there was a problem: I didn't know how to kick the ball around corners or execute what we call a 'snap' or 'banana' kick. I know it sounds silly to say after playing the game for so long, but snaps and bananas were never really the types of kicks that I'd practised. At this moment, I wished I had! I did my best, but couldn't bend the ball around far enough and missed badly.

With Todd Goldstein's hands full in the ruck, I was asked to go third-man-up in a ruck contest in the forward half, and my first ever hit-out was one to remember. Goldy had pinned his man, Stefan Martin, down, allowing me a clear jump to the ball. I leapt onto Martin's shoulders and tapped the ball down to one of my teammates, to the delight of the crowd. 'When was the last time you heard the crowd get off their feet and roar for a ruck contest?' Fox Footy's Dwayne Russell asked his fellow commentators during the coverage. 'A long time ago, but that was a spectacular one!' Gerard Healy replied.

I was having the time of my life out there, and while I was pretty exhausted, I didn't want it to end. Unfortunately, it ended a lot earlier than I had planned. With eight minutes left in the first quarter, I ran onto the ball and fumbled it as Merrett tackled me around the waist. The ball spilt free of my possession, I threw my arms into the air to plead to the umpire for a free kick for holding the man, and that was the last thing I remembered before waking up in the medical room.

Lying there in the room, strapped to a stretcher, I could hear the faint sounds of crowds cheering and clapping. 'Maj? Do you know where you are?' the club doctor, Andy McMahon, asked.

'Huh,' I replied.

'Do you know what day it is? Do you know who we are playing?' McMahon continued.

'What happened?' I asked. The doc went on to explain to me that I had been knocked out. Merrett had accidentally slung me off the ball and into Ben Cunnington, who was trying to grab the footy. Our heads had clashed and it was lights out for me. My parents came down to the rooms to see if I was okay, and despite having a whopping headache, I was allowed to sit on the bench for the rest of the game and watch as we went on to win by 63 points. To celebrate the win, I was allowed to join the club song and was drenched with sports drink – a tradition for debut players on their first win.

I recovered well enough from my concussion to play the next week against the Hawks and had a much tougher time of it. How we'd played against Brisbane had really suited me, but Hawthorn was a different beast and paid a lot more attention to me and Drew, up forward. While I had a few shots at goal, I couldn't convert my opportunities and finished the day with three behinds and no goals.

Seeing that I was getting chances to score, Brad Scott told me, 'Keep putting yourself in the right position and keep flying for your marks, and the goals will come.'

The following week, we played Port Adelaide and I booted one goal, but for game number three we faced the Western Bulldogs, and I was matched up on a slightly under-sized defender in Tom Young. I mean, he wasn't that small at 191 centimetres, but it gave me a 4-centimetre height advantage, and in the AFL, you take whatever you can get. I was getting some great opportunities to mark the ball in the first quarter and was able to kick three goals in the first half. I remember being completely gassed throughout that game. I kept asking our runner, Jona Segal, if I could come to the bench and have a break, but he kept telling me to push through and stay on the field. As the game wore on, all my marks were sticking, and I kicked another two goals in the third quarter. My sixth goal came late in the final term, and we managed to win by 54. My final statistics line read 6 goals, 8 marks and 18 possessions – by far my best game of football.

When I got home that night, I was stuffed; I was abso-lutely cooked. It really showed me how hard I had to work at that level to be successful. You see some of the great for-wards in the competition and they make the game look so easy, but it's not. I mean, someone like Tom Hawkins, who can turn a game on its head, or someone like Drew Petrie, who kicked five goals in 20 minutes once, are incredible, because they do it week after week. But I will admit, after kicking six goals in my fourth game, I thought that would be the norm for me and that I'd be able to replicate the performance every week thereafter. However, the amount of hype surrounding my career-best game took me by surprise and it resulted in opposing teams putting more time into figuring out how to play me and negate my influence. Brad Scott knew what was coming for me and warned me that defenders don't take lightly to forwards playing good games.

Game five was against the West Coast Eagles, and they were built for a physical game. I was matched up on Will Schofield, a very versatile defender with good speed. I quickly found out what Brad was talking about. He put that much work into me; he was pushing me under the ball, whacking me behind the play – nothing untoward but enough to really agitate me. I felt like a boy playing against a man. Everywhere I went, Schofield was right behind me and wasn't allowing me to have any space at all. He was pretty quick and very athletic; the perfect match-up for me.

After a solid stint up forward, I was called on to go into the ruck, and one of the highlights of my career unfolded there. As I trudged up to the centre circle for the next bounce-down from the umpire after a goal, I saw that waiting for me on the other side of the centre circle was Nic Naitanui. It didn't feel so long ago that I had been watching him in the TAC Cup at Docklands Stadium during my work-experience stint with the *Herald Sun*. Even after I'd been drafted, I still watched him closely and considered him somewhat of a hero – someone I looked up to and wanted to emulate. In the past few weeks, commentators and media were comparing me to him, which I thought was very pre-mature but flattering at the same time. As I walked up to him in the middle, I couldn't get over how huge he was. He stood 201 centimetres tall and weighed about 110 kilo-grams; an absolute man-mountain who moved like a gazelle.

The umpire stepped into the middle and threw the ball down into the turf. The bounce was really poor, and the ball landed on its left point and bounced my way.

That might sound like a good thing, but it's not at all in a ruck contest, because it meant it was going to land on my head and I didn't have the opportunity to get a run and jump at it. Nic, on the other hand, had a clear run and jump at it. I could see him charging towards me, and he leapt off one leg into the air. I could only manage a jump of my two planted feet, meaning I shouldn't have been able to get as high as him but, somehow, I did. 'He just got his hand higher,' commentator and former champion player and coach Leigh Matthews said on the Channel 7 commen-tary. 'We don't see that very often against Naitanui, do we? To have someone who can jump higher than big Nic.' It was only a matter of millimetres, but I managed to out-jump Nic and win the hit-out, and was able to tap it down to the feet of Andrew Swallow. That ruck contest was perfectly captured by one of the photographers at the ground, and it became an iconic photo depicting the cultural diversity of the game. It was probably the highest point that any ruckmen had ever contested a hit-out up until that point.

In those early days, as I was a new player on the scene in the AFL with a lot of media focus, defenders would try all sorts of tactics to unnerve me. Some, like Hawthorn's Josh Gibson, who was a former North player, would act like my best friend on the field, probably to lower my level of aggression against him. Others, like Daniel Merrett from the Lions, wanted to see if I could play the physical game, so he'd rough me up and wrestle with me to exhaust me. For years and years, Brad Scott had been telling me to be more aggressive, but I don't think I really understood what he meant. What he was saying was more about crashing packs and bringing the ball to ground if I couldn't mark it, tackling defenders inside our forward 50, and using my big body to create space. It wasn't about getting sucked into a push and shove contest, or a wrestle or fight. I quickly learnt that wrestling, fighting, pushing and shoving would wear me out, and I was never built for endurance. I'm more of an explosive athlete, and the way I play football relies on bursts of speed, sprinting and jumping.

The way the fitness guys explained it to me, the more muscle you have on your body, the more oxygen you need in your system to keep the muscles going. More than anything, football has become an endurance sport, and the biggest change for forwards was having to get all the way down to the other end of the ground to defend, and then sprint back to the forward line to become a target in front of goal. So, I really had to adapt the way I lived, trained and played to mould my body for the game, and try to strip off some muscle, or at least not put any more on. I also had to learn to play the game smarter and identify when to go at 100 per cent capacity, or 80 per cent to save some energy for the next contest. Because I can build muscle so fast, some of the club's strength and conditioning coaches banned me from lifting heavy weights in the gym. I was prescribed more strength work and injury-prevention exercises. To lose the muscle, I had to fast a lot in the mornings and not eat anything until lunchtime. That's called intermittent fasting, and it's easy to do in season, but it's much harder to do in the off-season when we are training a lot more.

The level of physical punishment you go through in a game is incredible. Even after spending so much time in the league, I still shake my head at what we have to endure. It's such a battle of attrition out there; the weakest fall away and are left behind, while the strongest rise to the top. No one likes to feel pain, but that's what you sign up for when you play AFL. Your legs are aching, your lungs are burning and every part of you wants to stop, but you have to find a way to keep going. You have to push through pain barriers you never knew existed. When you are out on your feet and the ball comes your way, you've got to go and get it. It might be a 30-second effort or it might be a 10-second effort, but it could swing a game your team's way. You just have to hang in there for as long as you can before you're able to get to the bench for a break, or there's a boundary throw-in or a break in play. That's the hardest thing to try to explain to people: when the game is on the line, it comes down to which players are willing to grit their teeth, grind it out and go the extra mile.

Someone I really admired at the North Melbourne Football Club was Robbie Tarrant, because no matter the situation or how much time was left on the clock, he would always be able to muster up enough energy to contest a mark or spoil the football. He always managed to find a way to keep going. 'Taz', as we called him, was someone I modelled my game on when I made the switch to become a defender, and it's partly because of him that I was able to turn myself into one of the best defenders in the game.

REFLECTIONS

Scott Thompson

A teammate I absolutely loved playing with and looked up to was Scott Thompson. 'Scooter' or 'Turbo', as we called him, was an absolute warrior and would never, ever admit defeat. I credit him and Robbie Tarrant with helping me become a decent defender. I wanted so badly to get back on the field and to play with them again, because in 2018 we were a formidable back trio. Scooter also loved playing with me, which meant a lot.

When Robbie Tarrant and I were playing on Majak when he was a forward, on his day he was really hard to beat. So, I thought a move to defence would be really good for him because of the way he plays – he can just follow someone around, they'd bring him to the ball and then he'd do his thing. His athleticism, speed and jump was just so good that we loved it. When he first came down back and started training with us, Robbie and I were really, really happy for him to come back.

Robbie and I had played together for so long, so we knew each other's games really well. Training with Maj took a little bit of time to get used to, but he definitely earned the trust and ended up changing our games on an individual level. Our roles changed to enable Maj to come off his man and do his thing. It was nice to have someone in the backline who could have such a big impact when the ball was in the air. Robbie and I would just hold our opponent down in a contest and wait for Maj to come off his man and mark or spoil it. With his athleticism, he would get across the pack, no matter how far away he was, and he earned our trust by doing it time and time again. He would do everything he could to make it over to the contest and help you out.

There was a pre-season game against Melbourne down in Hobart, and Jesse Hogan and Christian Petracca gave him a bath. It wasn't good at all. He got touched up, but Melbourne did move the ball pretty well that day, and Maj was just starting down back and learning the role. He was also in the position he played the season in. He was isolated deep in that game, which didn't play to his strengths. Once he found his spot as that third defender coming across, it really clicked. I'm sure he would have been a little bit worried about his position in the team after that game. It's a hard gig after you get touched up, in your first game as a defender, too, but he adapted well to his role and he was sensational for the rest of the year.

Maj had an outstanding 2018 and I think he also won mark of the year. I don't know how you beat him. Probably you try to turn him around in circles, but he's hard to beat. We did a heap of one-on-one work with him. I would like to think I gave him a lot of information on one-on-ones, because he's pretty strong, but his main attribute is leap. So, we worked to try to make sure he didn't allow his opponent to hold him down or make him wrestle. We taught him to stay one step off, because that gap would allow him to leap. He fit into our team really well, and it was unlucky and disappointing that we only had one year with him in the backline. He improved so much throughout that year that I could see him being a stalwart in the backline. He should've been there probably a long time ago. He hit the gym pretty hard that year as well, so he was really strong.

12

Thiär ku rou

Melbourne is being 'overrun' by African gangs. There's a 'new menace' out there and it's big, black, nasty and unstoppable, no matter what we do. We're facing an 'African gang crisis'. In this 'state of fear', looting, car jackings, violent home raids, bashings, theft, robberies and armed offences committed by black people are on the rise and they're 'out of control'. Prime Minister Malcolm Turnbull told a prominent radio station there was 'real concern about Sudanese gangs' in Melbourne.

These headlines, commentaries, supposedly informed opinions, and narratives were a media constant back in 2016, 2017 and 2018, and were being run, pushed and promoted by just about every major outlet in the state of Victoria, and across Australia on some occasions. Images of young Africans wielding weapons, brawling and causing havoc made front-page news and fuelled anger towards all people of colour. But it was far from what the truth actually was, and it brought about one of the most disappointing times I've had in Australia, because of the damage that was done to race relations and social cohesion here. All the hard work and effort so many people had put in for years and years was systematically destroyed by irresponsible reporting and, let's be honest, widespread racism. At the height of the issue, there were constant calls to 'stop immigration' by some increasingly fearful members of the community.

I want to be clear: I am in no way condoning the unlawful actions of those who committed such terrible crimes. They all deserved to be caught, prosecuted and punished just like any other criminal – black or white. I also acknowledge that the increase in crimes being committed by Sudanese people, particularly Sudanese youth, was an issue that needed to be addressed and confronted.

A look at the statistics from that time in 2017 shows crimes committed by South Sudanese people made up around 1 per cent of crimes in Victoria. The overwhelming majority of crimes were actually committed by Australian- or New Zealand-born people – not Africans or African 'gang' members. Adding to this, population statistics at the time showed Australian- and New Zealand-born people made up 64.8 per cent and 1.6 per cent respectively of the state's population, while people born in Sudan and South Sudan made up just 0.14 per cent of the population. But if you regularly consumed what the mainstream media had to offer, you'd be forgiven for thinking it was the other way around, such was the hysteria and level of panic.

Basically the 'African gang' crisis was a myth, but it was heavily promoted by various media to drum up unprecedented fear, hatred and anger – and most probably to sell papers and increase TV news ratings.

Being in the position that I was in, people looked straight to me when the African 'gang' situation flared up in Melbourne. Other high-profile Africans were also looked to for a reaction, but with the AFL leading the way in a lot of social and political areas, I felt enormous pressure to come out and fight for my community and people, and try to give some context and balance to what was actually happening out there.

The first thing that stood out to me was the nature of the media reporting and how irresponsible it was. Being of African heritage myself, as are many people close to me, I couldn't get away from it. It was splashed across the front page of the major papers for months, all over the radio on just about every station I tuned into, visible on every TV channel in every bulletin and on all my social media feeds. As well as that, my family, friends and other people I knew wanted to talk to me about what was going on, all of the time.

For me, social media was perhaps the hardest to stomach, because I was targeted with some truly vicious comments and abuse simply because I was African. Things like, *You should all go back to where you came from! Get back on the boat and fuck off home! We should lock you all up and throw away the key!* But I considered myself relatively sheltered from the worst of it. I know many of those closest to me, including my parents, brothers and sisters, copped a hell of a lot worse than me because they had to catch public transport every day to get to work, school or university, whereas I had the comfort of my own car and the protection of the North Melbourne Football Club. When I went out and about, I was usually with a whole group of big white guys from the club, so, in a way, being with them was like a shield or some sort of endorsement, which prevented me from being attacked verbally or physically. I mean, if someone had've had a crack at me in public, I would have gone back at them and so would have the other players I was constantly with, such as Luke McDonald, Taylor Garner and Ben Jacobs.

With the media and police painting a pretty ugly picture of African people or those of colour, I couldn't just sit back and say, 'Well if it doesn't affect me personally, I should just stay out of it.' In some ways, I had every right to just sit back and do nothing, but I guess when we don't have enough people with my skin colour in the media, entertainment or sports, I felt like I had to be a voice for all by standing up and speaking out. It was just the right thing to do. Even the then Race Discrimination Commissioner, Tim Soutphommasane, went on Twitter to criticise certain stories on the topic as 'fear-mongering and racial hysteria'. Melbourne-based lawyer, activist and Sudanese-Australian Nyadol Nyuon said, 'When the voting is done, and political careers are secured or lost, when the journalists put down their "pens" and head to their families or bed, and when the publishers are onto the next story, the resultant scars from this episode of moral panic will still be carved into our lives. And they will still be there, weakening the ties that bind us into a shared identity as Victorians.'

I knew I needed to find a way to add some balance to the issue and try to explain to people out there why crimes were being committed by such young African teens. I thought if I could help people understand the cause, they could go about finding a solution that wasn't just a band-aid approach. It's a fact that young people are more inclined to commit crime than older people – that's the case the world over – and the highest number of alleged Sudanese offenders in the state were aged between 16 and 24. This isn't surprising, given a massive 42 per cent of the South Sudanese population in Victoria at the time were under 25. With this in mind, I was keen to find out what the root causes were for so many young African kids to be turning away from their education towards crime.

I believe that to properly identify these reasons, you have to understand the culture, dynamic in an individual's home and other circumstances in which many of these young people lived. Not only was I directly connected through my skin colour, heritage and background, but it just so happened that one of my mates was a police officer working in a task force specifically formed to combat African youth crime. I was able to get a very clear understanding of the issue through him.

Sitting somewhat on the periphery, I had the privilege of seeing the issue from both sides. I mean, I too could have been sleeping at night and been woken by someone breaking into my house or trying to steal my car. I know that would be pretty scary for me, and I'm six foot five and weigh 100 kilos! I feel for all the people and the families who went through such terrifying ordeals.

Having two parents is something I've never taken for granted, because I know it's quite rare for people in my community. Many of the kids who come to Australia from African countries come from really low socio-economic backgrounds. A large portion are being raised by a single mother. She might have five or six kids at home, and is required to work two jobs or do double shifts to earn enough money to support the family. When she's out working day and night, she has to rely on her children to do the right thing and trust that they will go to school every day, come home straight after, do their homework, and generally behave and stay out of trouble.

Without a father figure there to help out, because he's either separated from the mother, still working overseas and sending money back, unable to make it to Australia for various reasons, or even dead because of the civil war, it's extremely tough for a single mum to keep tabs on her kids' whereabouts. There's also no help to discipline them if they've done something wrong, and no family structure to keep them in check. As kids do, they constantly push the envelope and try to see where the line between right and wrong is. When there is no clear line, due to no adult or guardian showing it to them or enforcing it, it's easy to step over it.

I could have easily been one of those kids, had it not been for my parents being able to stay together despite some really tough and testing times. When I was young and living at home, if I was playing outside past six o'clock, I'd have my mum or dad telling me to come inside. If I was at a friend's place, I'd have to call them to tell them that I was either on my way home, needed a lift or was staying the night – always with their approval, of course. Often was the case, they'd demand to speak to my friend's parents to ensure I wasn't fibbing or trying to pull the wool over their eyes.

Many of the kids who get into trouble don't have someone watching over them 24/7 and are easily led astray. Typically, as my mate explained to me, they'd start to hang out with the wrong crowd, and there'd be no one to tell them to pull their heads in or dissuade them from connecting with the wrong people. From there, it just becomes a ripple effect: they'd get pressured into hanging out with groups of kids who would start stealing small items from the local milk bar, and then they'd start skipping school, and from then on it leads to bigger stuff. It's pretty easy to influence young kids, particularly when there's quick, easy money to be made.

These kids might know what's right from wrong, but when they're in a group setting, they get influenced and tempted. In that environment, they can tend to just go with the flow, and when they keep getting away with bad behaviour or committing crimes, they become a repeat offender. Many of these kids could skip school and not come home until very late at night, and their single parent would be none the wiser, because they'd be out working. When I got up in the morning, Mum would send me off to school with a packed lunch, and she was always there when I got home, asking how my day was, what I did and what I learnt. Kids without that can figure it out very quickly: if there's no one waiting for them at home, they can get away with just about anything. They see their friends skipping school and pocketing hundreds of dollars a week from stealing, or getting around in brand-new shoes and clothes, and they think, *Why am I wasting my time at school when I could be earning big money like them?* They know their parents can't afford that type of stuff and the only way to get it is by taking it for themselves. If a lot of kids from a particular area are all doing the same thing, like stealing phones, selling them for quick cash and buying things they've only ever dreamed of owning, then others will be tempted to take the same risks and join in. It's a vicious cycle and a sad one – but when you understand the circumstances, you can understand why so many might go down that path.

Making matters even worse, people involved in organised crime saw an opportunity to prey on these young, vulnerable kids and get them to act as foot soldiers, committing more serious crimes on behalf of others. Soon, it wasn't just small items at a milk bar or mobile phones being stolen; cars were pinched and their parts sold, homes were broken into and people were threatened and, in some instances, bashed. Instead of earning hundreds, some kids were now lining their pockets with thousands of dollars in cash every week.

The damage created by the 'African gang crisis' was widespread: it divided people and painted all African people, and Sudanese people in particular, as thugs, criminals and untrustworthy. Cast to the side and unfairly tainted were all the other African and Sudanese people who were really working hard and trying to make a better life for themselves and their families. I heard many stories from friends who applied for jobs but were knocked back, despite being over-qualified, because of their skin colour and background. A lot of law-abiding African citizens suffered tremendously off the back of the actions of a few.

With my friend, the police officer, as close to the situation as anyone, being in the special police task force, he reached out to me for help. He told me that so many Sudanese youths were reoffending despite spending time in juvenile detention, and he was desperate to find a circuit-breaker for them. He asked if I could spend some time with one young man in particular to see if I could somehow save him from a life of crime and the inside of a prison cell.

My old club, the Western Jets, had a young gun on their hands. He was 16 years old and super-talented, and had all the attributes required to play in the AFL. From the very first training session I attended, I could see that if he stuck at football and didn't go down the wrong path, he definitely could put himself into a position to get drafted like me and make it big. But he was distracted and being pulled in the wrong direction by some bad influences. This kid was one of those from a low socio-economic area in western Melbourne, with a mum who was battling hard to make ends meet, with no less than five mouths to feed, look after and put through school.

There were red flags everywhere for this kid, including, as Joey had told me, that he had been spending a lot of time with the wrong crowd. With footy a common interest between us, I quickly formed a relationship with the young man and did my best to bring a positive influence into his life and guide him in the right direction. I met him at training once a week, caught up with him for coffees, checked in with his mum and teachers to see how he was going and just showed genuine care for his wellbeing and future. I tried to ensure he was getting the extra support he needed and even gave him driving lessons.

For a time, it seemed things were going well, but he was actually living two lives and hiding the ugly truth from me and all those who were trying to help him. My friend in the police force suspected he was committing some crimes and would again come to police attention. Sensing we were a real chance to lose him, we upped the ante and poured even more time and effort into him, but to no avail. It soon became abundantly clear to us that he was more interested in what his mates were doing and the money that was on offer – we simply couldn't pry him away from their grip. We found out he was stealing BMWs and other luxury cars and was being paid in excess of $2000 cash per vehicle. His bosses, for want of a better term, would put him and other kids up in plush hotels or Airbnb accommodation and also supply them with copious amounts of alcohol and drugs as extra rewards.

The inevitable happened, and one day, we found out he'd been arrested for a whole raft of different crimes and locked up in a detention centre while he waited for a court date. I was shattered when I was told, and felt like I had failed him. Looking back, I don't know what else

I could have done, but it still weighed heavily on my mind. Unwilling to give up on him, I visited him in the detention centre.

It was one of the saddest things I've ever experienced. So many young kids just like him were in there, all with their futures on the verge of being snatched away from them. It was one of the few times I've felt like an outsider among those from a similar background to me. I say that because I could feel that these kids were looking at me and they weren't able to identify with me. Maybe it was because they considered me as someone who had 'made it', or that I represented some sort of social privilege because of what I did for a living and what was afforded to me as a result. It's widely known that AFL players get paid very well, regardless of age and experience, but what they needed to realise, and what I was quick to explain to them when I got the chance, was that I'd had to work extremely hard for everything I had – nothing was ever given to me. I had to try to break down the barriers, because all that these kids could see standing in front of them was Majak Daw, the North Melbourne Football Club player who was on TV, in all the papers and spoken about on radio. They couldn't see my background, history or what I'd been through to get to where I was. They had no idea about my family and what we'd all endured and how similar we were. I was as foreign to them as the guards on the doors of their cells.

I asked if I could speak to all of the kids and was given the opportunity to enlighten them about my past and the times when I had to rely on clothing hand-me-downs and used shoes from my older brothers. I told them about working full-time in Egypt at the age of nine. When I shared one room with ten other children and couldn't afford a pair of football boots. I told them my life had never been easy, and still wasn't easy. I told them that even as an AFL player, I had to go to work every day and compete for my spot in the side or risk being delisted and left on the scrapheap without a job. I told them I wasn't guaranteed anything and there was no easy way to get what I wanted.

It took some time, but I eventually broke through their defensive walls and saw these 'tough' young criminals become little boys, right before my eyes. It was heartbreaking. From not wanting a bar of me to asking me endless questions about my journey to the AFL and through life – these children dropped their guard and showed their innocence and naïvete. They tried to be tough, but they weren't tough. They were just little kids. I was a wreck when I left and had so many mixed emotions. They'd committed some serious crimes but probably didn't realise what they were doing or how it would ruin the rest of their lives. There was an inability to see the consequences of their actions. They were lured by the short-term grab for money, and the people offering them that money were just exploiting the shit out of them, knowing they didn't have anything else.

I just wish people had more compassion or were provided with more measured information and context from the media about the situation and those involved. It was a shame that some jumped to conclusions and labelled all

Africans or Sudanese as thugs or criminals. We need to be better as a society and provide all kids, regardless of their skin colour, with the same opportunities and level of understanding. The way I look at it, I have experienced a lot of racism, and many white men in particular have said terrible things to me, but I don't consider all white people racist as a result of those experiences – that would be unfair. Despite the things I've gone through, I still have so much love for everyone. We shouldn't just judge a situation when we don't understand a culture or know anything about a person.

I hope any young kid who is unsure about what path they're going to take reads this and realises that life is not easy – for anyone. On most occasions, if it seems too good to be true, then it probably is. You have to work hard to be rewarded and get what you want, and the easy option isn't always the one that will serve you best in the long run. I know opportunities can sometimes appear limited, but stay in school, finish university and get a degree, or find a nine-to-five job and things will open up for you. I'd also encourage anyone feeling like they don't quite belong to play a team or organised sport, or engage in a social hobby of some description, to open up your networks and meet new people. From my experiences, by doing this you learn about other people's cultures, how they interact and how they carry themselves.

13

Thiär ku dïäk

I don't know the exact moment that my mental health declined to a point that it became a significant issue, but I can pinpoint the events that led to it. I know it was a number of things that built up over time and brought me to a breaking point, rather than one particular thing. In hindsight, there were red flags everywhere, but I just couldn't see any of them, because I didn't know what to look for. If I think back, I've come to realise that one significant event probably had more of a negative impact on me than any other.

In 2014, I was charged by police with three counts of rape. The things levelled against me absolutely stunned me and came as a shock. The allegations dated back to seven years earlier, when in 2007, I attended a party with many students from my high school. My accuser was also a student at my former high school, and at the time of the alleged incident, I was 16 years old and she was 15. I vehemently denied all the charges brought against me and was found not guilty by a jury made up of my peers in the County Court, but the drawn-out ordeal, damage to my reputation and the overall experience affected me immensely. While the not-guilty outcome of the court case – which began a year and a half after the charges were laid – was the right one, I still paid an incredibly heavy price for it – one that almost cost me my life.

I had a lot of support around me during my trial from family, friends, the North Melbourne Football Club and my management – everyone stood by my side and never wavered in their love, care and loyalty. I needed all the comfort and support I could get, because with the charges came an unprecedented amount of scrutiny, media attention, speculation and negative publicity. I was front-page news most days. When I made the short walk from my lawyer's offices to the County Court on William Street – only about a block and a half – a large throng of print journalists, camera operators and television reporters would be waiting to bombard me with questions. I always made sure I put on a brave face and held my head up high, because I was innocent, but deep down I was in a lot of pain and the negative attention was slowly eroding my strength and confidence.

To have bad, painful things said about you is never good, but to have such heinous things levelled against you and then splashed across every newspaper, news program on TV and in every radio news update is another thing all together. It's hard to keep positive and feel good about yourself when all that is happening. There was nowhere for me to hide, and while I had a large support network, at the same time, I also felt completely isolated and alone.

I think I had some level of social anxiety from an early age, but it was relatively minor and manageable. When I joined the North Melbourne Football Club and gained a significant public profile, I really didn't know how to deal with what had suddenly become a very public life. Even as a rookie-listed player who had barely played any games, it was easy for me to end up on the front page of the city's major newspaper, the *Herald Sun*, for no real reason. On one occasion my image took up the entire front page after a routine recovery ocean swim, simply because I was coming out of the water with my top off. The headline read, 'Majak Daw is fast becoming the most talked about body in AFL football'.

I was a relative nobody in terms of my playing record, yet the treatment and attention I received was akin to that of one of the game's best players. It was disproportionate to my achievements, that's for sure. To me it made little sense and with every picture, article or news item that was aired or published, the attention on me grew, and with it, the pressure on me to perform and live up to the expectations being placed on me continued to mount. It got to a point that even being out in public resulted in me being approached for a photo and an autograph. Complete strangers would come up to me for a chat at the shopping centre or local café, and I really didn't have the communication or social skills to deal with all the attention.

I had always been a shy kid and preferred to fly under the radar, but when I became an AFL footballer I was catapulted into the spotlight. I wasn't good at 'small talk' or making conversation with people I didn't know, and as a result, I'd become anxious about the prospect of going out in public and being noticed.

After each day of my trial, which began in November 2015, I was home alone. My then housemate and team-mate Taylor Garner was overseas on a training camp in Utah. I had hours to ponder what had unfolded in court that day and then hours to worry about what the next day would throw at me. On top of that, there was the prospect of being found guilty for something I hadn't done and the chance I'd be sent to an adult prison for a very long time. When I eventually got to bed each night, I'd wake up inter-mittently, covered in sweat. I mean, my clothes and sheets were absolutely drenched to the point that I had to change them. A strange numbness came over me as the trial con-tinued, and I began to feel nothing inside – just a strange emptiness and feeling of isolation.

On the ninth and final day of the trial, when the jury read out its finding, 'NOT GUILTY' on all three counts, I was of course overjoyed and overwhelmed with emo-tion, but it was far from a celebration for me. My name had been dragged through the mud for the best part of two years, and regardless of the jury's decision that day, I knew some people would never view me the same way again. I put on that familiar brave face to address the wait-ing media outside court and told them I was relieved. 'It's been a tough time,' I said. 'A tough nine days. I just want to thank all my family and friends for being here for me. I've been through this, I can get through anything in life.'

Looking back, I know I should have taken some time off after the trial and had a well-deserved holiday, but with the football club having taken a big risk by giving me a new contract despite my running trial, I wanted to repay the faith and get back to training as soon as possible. I thought that diving back into footy would help take my mind off everything that had happened, but it was a big mistake. I became accustomed to functioning at a really high stress level, and of course it turned out to be unsustainable. The trial, the pressures of playing AFL football, trying to cement a spot in the senior side and never feeling like I was safe from being dropped, trying to help my family and the financial strains I was experiencing were a lot to bear. At times I really felt like I was wasting my talent and unable to make the most of the opportunity I had at North Melbourne. While I thought I could deal with those letdowns and disappointments, I was probably just pushing things to the side or burying them deep down and wasn't dealing with anything properly.

As I've already mentioned, I had my best season in 2018 as a key defender despite playing the majority of the year with a pretty serious injury. While the medical team expected the bone in my foot to crack all the way through, it didn't, and they put it down to my genes and abnormal bone strength. At the end of the season, however, I had to have surgery to repair the fracture, so while I should have been enjoying the off-season, having had one of the best seasons of my career, instead I found myself back in rehab and again having to prove to the coaches that I would be okay to play the following year as a member of the club's best 22.

At this time in my private life, my relationship with Emily was shaky. We were constantly fighting, and I started drinking alcohol quite heavily as a way to deal with everything that was happening to me. I didn't seek any help or reach out to any family or friends to tell them what was going on. I actually don't think I knew what was going on, but there were warning signs everywhere that my life was spiralling out of control.

Emily and I attended a party in October, and an incident occurred that really tipped me over the edge. If I look back at what was happening in my life at the time, and the previous emotional trauma I had buried deep down, then I would call this moment the straw that broke the camel's back. I'd had a fair bit to drink on this night and, for no reason whatsoever, a guy who was well known to Emily's family started abusing me and saying inappropriate stuff about Emily, which was extremely hurtful. I couldn't believe the things that were coming out of his mouth – he was supposed to be a family friend of hers, but he was speaking disrespectfully.

I walked away, found Emily among the crowd of guests and told her what had happened, explaining that this bloke was clearly trying to bait me into doing something I'd regret. As happened a lot in my life, people would try to push me, knowing that I couldn't do anything to retaliate because of my public profile and what I had to lose. I really wanted to deck the guy, but I knew it would only come back to hurt me in the long run and cost me my playing contract with North Melbourne. I was so worked up and angry and couldn't get over what he'd said to me. Making matters worse, Emily and I then had an argument, where she suggested that I was overreacting. Tensions were high and the incident was becoming known to everyone at the party, so I decided to release the pressure and leave. I called for an Uber and had assumed Emily would follow me out the door, but she wanted to stay with her sister and family, which was fair enough.

When I got home, I was still furious, so I kept drinking to numb the pain and frustration. I found some red wine in the cupboard at home and ripped into a few bottles. I was really intoxicated and started having some extremely negative thoughts. I somehow reached a dangerous level of numbness and decided I wanted to take my life. I found some sleeping tablets in my bedside table drawer and took them all – I can't remember exactly how many I swallowed, but it was a lot.

Luckily, I woke up the next day, but I felt terrible. I was hungover and down in the dumps like never before. I called Joey, and I rang my other best mate from school, Rory, and asked them both to come around to see me. I also called the footy club doctor, Peter Baquie, and told him I was in a really bad way and needed urgent help. They all came over, and I told them that I had succumbed to depression. I also said that I had come to terms with the fact that I had some severe mental-health issues that I needed to address and deal with head-on. Talking about my issues came as a great relief, and I felt like a huge weight had been lifted off my chest. Pete arranged for me to see a psychiatrist and also urged me to call Emily and tell her what was going on, but I was reluctant to do so. Even though she was my partner and knew me better than most people, I was still feeling a bit upset about the fight we'd had the previous night, and I worried about what her reaction would be. I also think given the stigma attached to men's mental-health problems at that time, admitting them to someone – especially my girlfriend – felt like a sign of weakness, and it would have made me feel less of a man. Pete stayed on me about it, though, and I eventually called Emily and asked her to come over. I really wasn't sure how she'd react. It was different with Joey and Rory, because they'd been there for me ever since I'd arrived in Australia, and I felt so confident speaking to them. I knew they wouldn't judge me or think any less of me.

I sat in the living room and broke down while explaining to Emily what I was thinking and what I was going through. I cried and cried, uncontrollably. The tears flowed like never before. Pete checked in on me again and told me to take a few days off at least, and to avoid coming into the club until I felt up to it. I stayed home that day and Rory took a day off work to be with me, sensing I was pretty vulnerable. I think I slept most of the day, as I was exhausted both physically and mentally.

Throughout the next week I caught up with Rory and Joey frequently, having breakfast and coffee with them before I went to training. I explained to them that I couldn't really make sense of everything that was happening to me, and that I felt numb and was in a bit of a daze. Through speaking to them, though, we were able to break down the past few years of my life and could look at everything that had happened to me, identifying all the huge events that had compounded over time; things I hadn't dealt with well, like the emotional toll on me from the trial and the pressures of being an AFL footballer.

I continued to speak to Pete, and he told me to consider opening up to my then coach, Brad Scott, and telling him what was going on. I thought long and hard about doing that – and this is not a reflection on Brad, because he was always incredibly supportive of me throughout our time together at North Melbourne – but again, looking at mental health at the time with a man's attitude, and especially being in a sport like AFL football, I was deterred because of the bad stigma attached. I felt, whether rightly or wrongly, that if I told Brad and the coaches about my mental-health issues, it could get in the way of me being selected in the team. I was still coming back from rehab and had a lot to prove to them, so I didn't need anything else to go against me. I was worried that Brad might be compelled to tell me to take some time off footy, and that was the last thing I wanted to do. I was also in discussions with the club at the time about a new multi-year deal, and the contract we were discussing would have set me up nicely for a few years.

The only person at the club I decided to tell apart from Pete was Jona Segal, our strength and conditioning coach. He had been at the club for a very long time and was heavily invested in and close to all of the players. I knew I could trust Jona and knew he wouldn't judge me. I was adamant with Pete that he was not to tell anyone, and he explained that he was bound by patient–doctor confidentiality. I didn't even tell my parents or my brothers and sisters, because I didn't fully understand what I was going through, and I didn't know how to explain it to anyone else except Pete, Joey, Rory, Jona and Emily. I was worried that anyone outside of that group might ask me questions I didn't want to, or couldn't, answer.

I started seeing the club's former sports psychologist, Michael Inglis, who had his own private practice and also worked with the AFL Players Association psychologists. Throughout those initial sessions with Michael, I was pretty vague about it all. I mean, I was honest with him, but I probably didn't tell him absolutely everything that was going on in my life and head, and I left little bits of important information out because I was too ashamed to tell him about certain things. One of the things Michael identified as a big problem was my excessive use of alcohol, so we decided I would try to cut it down and avoid social settings where I might be expected or tempted to drink. I needed to avoid these situations because I loved socialising with my friends and teammates, so if I went out with them and told them I wasn't drinking, they'd know something was up with me and start asking questions.

I found it really tough living with the realisation that something in me was broken and that I was keeping a secret from the majority of my family and friends. As a result, I started to withdraw from everyone, even avoiding my teammates. I was in rehab following my foot surgery, and rehab is a lonely place at the best of times, because you have to do your training program away from the main group of players. I used being in rehab to pull away from interactions with staff and players at the club. When I had conversations with people, I would avoid eye contact with them, and I knew my anxiety was starting to take hold. I was petrified people would ask me things like, 'What have you been up to?' or 'What did you do on your day off?' I didn't want them to know the truth, that I spent two hours with Michael Inglis at a psychologist's clinic twice a week, but I didn't want to have to lie to anyone either.

As the weeks wore on, I was showing some signs of improvement with my therapy, and my appointments with Michael were reduced from two times a week to once a week, and then down to once a month. I know I should have been more forthright with Michael at the time, because I was still experiencing some red flags. I still felt emotionless about a lot of the things I used to enjoy. For example, I found it really hard to get enthusiastic about catching up with my friends or going to training, and I had started avoiding answering any phone calls, resorting to text messages only.

I knew I needed a circuit-breaker, and the opportunity came up for me to take some time away in late October. Emily's mum was turning 60 and she had decided to have her big birthday celebration in Bali. Although Emily and I were still on shaky ground, we saw a trip away as an opportunity to not only help mark her mum's milestone birthday, but to also get out of the rut that we were in back in Melbourne, to have some time to ourselves and work on some areas of our relationship.

I bought my plane ticket and we were all set to go when Emily realised something was amiss. She'd missed her last period and suspected she might be pregnant. We went to the chemist and bought an at-home pregnancy test and it came back positive. Emily was excited, as we'd had a few previous pregnancies that hadn't worked out for us. This time, I feigned happiness and told her I was excited to be a father. Really, though, I was deeply confused about whether it was the right thing, given the state I was in, to become a father. On the surface, I was coming off my best year of football and had a lucrative contract on the table from North Melbourne, so I was well set up in that sense to support a child and Emily; but emotionally and mentally, I wasn't good at all. We called Pete, who ordered some blood tests for Emily to confirm the DIY pregnancy test, and we received a confirmation via text message from him as we were boarding the plane to Bali that said, *Congratulations to you both. You're six weeks pregnant!*

Because I had bought my ticket to Bali at the last minute, as I was unsure if I'd go until late in the piece, Emily and I were seated at opposite ends of the plane. It was a bizarre time for both of us. We had a six-hour flight ahead of us, having just learnt that we were pregnant, and couldn't sit together to discuss our feelings, thoughts or plans for the future. With my mental state and anxiety levels, I really didn't need that amount of time alone with my thoughts about a future that would come with so many unknowns, responsibilities, expectations and immense pressures. I was worried about telling her parents and family that we were expecting, and I was really nervous about telling mine. I was concerned about how my parents, in particular, would react, because Emily and I weren't married or even engaged, we didn't have a house together or any formal commitment to each other. I couldn't stop asking myself, *Am I ready to become a father?*

All these things were playing on my mind, causing me a great deal of stress, and I just wanted to get off the plane and go home. The whole situation was so unusual, and I'd never thought it would be the way I'd bring a child into the world. I suppose like everyone growing up, I had the idea that I would follow the conventional path in that I'd meet someone, get engaged then married, buy a house and live together for a while, then start a family. But as most people know, and I was finding out for myself, life is full of surprises and things rarely pan out the way you envisage.

The plane touched down at the Denpasar International Airport in Bali, and we made our way to the popular tourist spot of Seminyak. On the way to our villa, Emily and I discussed our options and agreed to tell her family our baby news. Because it was a family holiday and a big celebration for her mum, everyone would be in 'party mode', with the expectation that they would have a drink and really relax, so we decided that we needed to announce the news right away to avoid any awkwardness about why Emily and I weren't drinking.

At dinner on the first night, we gathered together: all of Emily's family, including her mum, sisters, brother and all their kids. Emily's sister was really keen for everyone to have a drink to celebrate with her mum and had organised the first round of cocktails to be delivered to the table. She saw that Emily hadn't touched her drink, though, and immediately asked her why, knowing it was strange behaviour given the occasion. 'I don't really feel like it tonight,' Emily replied to her. Understandably confused, her sister pulled Emily to the side to quiz her some more and soon found out the truth as to why she wasn't drinking. With the cat out of the bag, Emily urged me to make an announcement to the family. 'I think you're going to have to say something soon. You have to tell everyone because they all know something is up with us both not drinking,' she said to me.

Although apprehensive and not prepared to deliver such a heavy speech at all, I knew it had to be done. I asked for everyone's attention and stood up at the table. I can't remember exactly what I said, but it was something along the lines of, 'I know we're all here for Vick's 60th, and Emily and I don't want to steal her thunder and take any attention away from her at all, but Emily and I feel like it's the right time to share some exciting news with you all . . . we've just found out that we are pregnant and we are going to have a baby.' There was a mix of emotions around the table: cheers, tears and awkward looks. Emily's mum started crying, but it was hard to know if her tears were because she was thrilled or upset. The others around the table didn't quite know how to react, either. They all knew that Emily and I were far from being on the same page in our relationship, so I think there was genuine concern about us having a baby together. After the initial shock, however, they all did their best to show their support and act happy for us, and I completely understand how awkward it all was for them.

Despite Emily's family being in the loop, I didn't tell my parents for about three or four more days, because I was still battling my insecurities about becoming a father, and was still worried they wouldn't take the news well. To test the water with my family, I sent a text message to my cousin Bol, and he was pretty happy for me and suggested my family would be fine. That eased my anxiety somewhat, and I felt better about making the call home to break the news to my parents, but as it turned out, I never had to.

The dreaded Bali belly, a bug that is notorious for making travellers to the island extremely sick, swept through Emily's family in a bad way soon after we arrived. The bouts of illness put a sudden stop to the celebrations, and Emily copped it the worst of everyone. At about eight o'clock one morning, she started vomiting constantly and had severe diarrhea, which put a lot of stress on her body. Dehydrated and in a lot of discomfort and pain, she also started to bleed. It was one of the scariest things I've ever been through, and I actually thought she was going to die at one stage. We called for an ambulance and she was taken to hospital, but with bad traffic causing huge delays, the ambulance took more than two hours to get to the hospital, which was a terrible ordeal for Emily, who was in an enormous amount of unease.

When we finally arrived at the hospital, Emily was placed on a drip and had some medication to stop her losing fluid. When things settled, she had an ultrasound that confirmed our fears: the baby had been lost. Emily had to have a little procedure to clean everything up and to make sure no further damage had been caused. The obstetrician came to see us and tried to reassure us, saying, 'There's nothing either of you could have done differently to change this outcome. It's a matter of natural selection and you've done nothing wrong.' Emily was discharged later that night and we headed back to the villa.

No one could quite believe what had just happened, and we were all emotionally wrecked. The days that followed were strange, to say the least. We were obviously keen to try not to impact the mood of the party, but we also realised that would be near impossible. Everyone gave us a fair bit of space to allow us to deal with everything. Emily was shattered and really down in the dumps. Not only did she have to come to terms with the loss of the baby, but her body had taken a real battering and she was low on energy and in poor health. At the age of 32, she really wanted to have a baby. Her sister had a little daughter and her brother had two children, and she wanted to have a child so the cousins could all grow up together. A lot of her close friends also had kids and she felt she was more than ready to be a mother. We kept to ourselves for the rest of the holiday and comforted each other as much as we could.

After what can only be described as our 'week from hell', Emily's mum's actual birthday was only days away, and the big party was about to kick off. We both did our best not to dampen the spirits and mood of everyone and joined in the celebrations as best we could. Emily had some drinks to try to relax and unwind after a torrid time.

The Bali experience had a bad impact on me, and my mental health started to deteriorate again as soon as we arrived back in Melbourne. The loss of the baby and the stress that went along with that lingered, and Emily and I started to fight incessantly about the smallest and most trivial things. We'd argue and then patch things up before something else would inevitably spark a rift between us, and we'd go at each other's throats again. Somewhere along the line, we'd somehow agreed that if she was to fall pregnant again, we'd both embrace the opportunity to become parents and we'd go into it much better prepared than last time. I don't know why I had agreed to that, because I knew I wasn't in a good place at all, and nothing had really changed for the better from the last time she'd been pregnant.

Things were far from good in my life, and I ignored all the professional advice I had received and I started drinking heavily again. During this time, I saw Michael, my psychologist, and again I chose to hide things from him, particularly the drinking. I did tell him that I was finding it increasingly hard to find the motivation to train and complete my rehab program.

It was now November, and as it does every year at this time, the city burst to life with the Melbourne Spring

Racing Carnival: a huge event on the social calendar, particularly for AFL players and socialites. I received a number of invites to various race days, events around the city and some trackside VIP marquees, including the famous 'Bird Cage' at Flemington for the Melbourne Cup. I knew the alcohol would be flowing and that I'd be exposed to social chit-chat and small talk, but Emily was really keen to go and have a good time, so I accepted the invitations. Deep down, I knew it wasn't the right environment for me to put myself in, and I knew I would turn to alcohol to get me through it and to calm my levels of anxiety.

The day before one of the big race days, Emily and I had another huge fight, and during the course of the argument, Emily revealed she was pregnant again. I had a near meltdown and told her I wasn't ready to be a father. We argued some more. Things turned nasty again, but despite it all, we went to the races together the next day – a Sunday. After a big afternoon of drinking and partying, I arrived home alone that night heavily intoxicated and received an invite from my neighbours to join them on the rooftop of our apartment complex for some more drinks and food. I accepted the invite and went up to meet them and kicked on fairly hard until the early hours of the morning.

Before I knew it, it was Monday morning, and my alarm went off at about six-thirty to allow me enough time to get ready and head to training. I was extremely hungover and not in the mood to go to the football club for an 8 a.m. start. I rang the doc, Pete, and told him I was feeling a bit off. I explained to him that I was in some physical pain, and had woken with something like the flu after coughing up all sorts of nasty stuff overnight. Mentally and physically, I was completely drained. A strange rash had broken out all over my body. Every part of me was struggling to function properly, and I was experiencing an aching like I'd never felt before – but it was beyond just a physical sensation and I knew it definitely wasn't something as common as the flu.

I wasn't seeing things straight, and I was wrapped up in my own world of darkness. I couldn't see anyone else's point of view and only considered how things impacted me. I thought about how Emily had told me she was pregnant again, reflecting on the way I'd reacted by telling her I didn't want to be a father. I was upset that she hadn't been more compassionate towards me and more understanding of my circumstances. In hindsight, I know that she would have been going through an incredibly rough time of her own, because she wanted the child, we'd agreed to have one together, and then I'd done this sudden backflip on her and changed my mind without any warning whatsoever. Having lost our last child in Bali, Emily wanted to go through with the pregnancy and was never going to consider terminating it.

I spent the day in bed and didn't improve at all. That night, Emily came over to my place again to continue the discussion about having the baby. I said, 'Look, I'm not going through this again. I just can't be a father. I'm in a pretty bad place right now and it's not a good idea.' We had another big argument about it and she left. I went straight to the kitchen, grabbed a bottle of wine and went pretty hard. I went through two bottles of red wine fairly quickly and some bad thoughts got the better of me. I was in so much emotional pain and I searched through the drawers around the house to find something sharp to cut myself with. I found a Stanley knife in the laundry, ran it across my left wrist and watched the blood run down my arm. I didn't really know what I was doing; everything was a blur and I was so numb to it all. It was like my body and mind had separated, and I was watching someone else do these silly things to my physical body, but I couldn't feel anything.

For whatever reason, I was unsuccessful with the Stanley knife, but my determination to end it all remained strong. I went to the cupboard in my bedroom and took the cord off my dressing gown. I tested the strength of it and took it to the bathroom. I tied the cord to an exposed pipe near the ceiling and placed the other end of it around my neck. I had so many opportunities to stop what I was doing and reconsider, but I couldn't see another way out of the misery I was experiencing. In my mind, the only option was to commit suicide. I put all my weight through the dressing-gown cord and neck, but the fabric wasn't strong enough to hold my body weight and it snapped, causing me to fall to the ground with a thud. My second attempt had failed.

I can't explain it, but I was on a mission to make sure of what I was trying to do. I grabbed my car keys, stumbled outside and got in the car. I thought of a way to end my life that would be more foolproof and drove to the Bolte Bridge, which wasn't that far away from where I was living. The whole way there, I wasn't thinking clearly at all. Something very dark had taken complete control of me. I pulled over to the side of the bridge, took my phone out of my pocket and sent a text message to Emily, telling her that I was sorry, but I couldn't stay around any longer. Soon after I hit send, I threw the phone back into the car. I didn't stall or wait for any cars to pull up and see if I was okay, I just ran to the edge of the bridge and jumped over.

Within a split second of making the decision to leap over the railing, my survival instincts kicked in and I changed my mind. I tried to twist and reach back to grab hold of the railing, but it was too late. My wrist slammed against the steel barrier and I was unable to stop myself from falling to my death. I hurtled towards the river below in a pin-drop position, and my feet crashed through the surface of the water. I remember the noise; it was an incredible sound that will always haunt me. I would describe it as an explosion of sorts and can only assume the noise was a combination of my body forcefully breaking through the surface of the water and my bones crunching and splitting on impact.

Everything went dark.

REFLECTIONS

Joey Halloran, Augustino Daw, Shane Casley

It gave me a great sense of guilt to find out what I put those closest to me through, but at the time, I was in a very dark place and couldn't see past all the issues that were consuming me. One person who could see it all from the outside and who knows me better than anyone is Joey. He was one of the first people on the scene after I jumped.

I tried to keep Majak as grounded as possible throughout the early years after he got drafted, because I could see it was going to be a tough slog to get himself up to AFL standard. It's a tough level to make, and I could see there were a few things he'd need to work on. When you go from being a nobody to a person with a public profile pretty much overnight, it's a lot to deal with, and I could see some red flags early on that Maj was getting swept up in it all.

We lived together for a short time after he was drafted, and I was constantly reminding him who he was and what was important to him. After a few years, we weren't able to spend as much time together, because we had different things going on in our lives, and I think I saw the first signs of him moving away from what his values were and what was important to him. I had lost the ability to help keep him grounded – not that it was my job completely, but I think that it had an effect. I think he always had that respect for me and it was the role I played for him in his life. When things weren't working for him before getting drafted, he would turn to me.

I became a dad in April 2018, and that meant my time was dedicated to home and work. It was also the same time Majak had his best year of footy and was a high-flyer in the league, and the future was looking pretty good for him. We'd catch up occasionally for coffee or he'd come and visit my daughter, but admittedly I didn't have much spare time and we'd drifted apart. I had no idea he was having a problem with alcohol nor any inkling things weren't great. He was very successful on the field, and he was always going to a lot of events and parties. I did as best as I could to keep tabs on him, but to learn how erratic his drinking and other things were was a bit of a shock. It all came to a head one morning when I received a call from him asking if I could come over for a chat. My wife and I were having trouble with our little one sleeping at that time, and I said, 'Can we make it later in the day?' And he said, 'No, I'd prefer it to be now.' I knew it wasn't going to be good, but I had no idea just how bad things had become.

When I got to Maj's house, I was bit shocked to see the scene. It was in the hours after he had taken a handful of sleeping pills, and he was pretty broken, just at a bit of a loss. At that point in time, he had to explain a lot of things to me and Rory, because his life was very different to ours. There were clearly some things he was hiding from us that he needed to explain in order for us to understand the full picture. That was hard for him to do. He was so different to what any other person in the world would've thought that he was at that time. He was down and out on the inside. He could've had a footy club appearance, clinic or a function the next day and would've bounced back up for it, but what he was showing on the outside wasn't what was really happening inside.

I felt sorry for him – not only was he going through it, but he had that obligation and inability to really fix it and deal with it, because it would be a huge bombshell for everyone else to learn. It was big enough Rory and I finding out, so for everyone else in the world to find out would be huge in his mind – and rightly so. We got help for him, which history shows wasn't enough, but we got help for him without it being the same episode, publicly, that it was a couple of weeks later.

A few weeks had passed and I'd kept in regular contact with Maj. He'd gone away for a bit to Bali, but Rory and I were constantly checking in on him. I was working late one night and I received a really vague message from Maj saying, *See you on the flip side*. So, with the history of the incident we'd witnessed a couple of weeks earlier, alarm bells started ringing. I tried to call him straight away. I was hoping it was like a cry for help, but when I couldn't get onto him, I started to really worry. I called Emily and she said they'd had a little fight during the night. I was going to leave work and go to his house initially, and then if he wasn't there, I was going to call the police, because he wasn't responding to any messages or phone calls. Emily told me she would also head to his house but from the south-east of the city. As I started making my way to his house, he sent me another message: *I'm done. I love you.* Shivers went down my spine and I felt sick in the pit of my stomach.

Emily called me. She was hysterical and told me she'd just gone over the Bolte Bridge and had seen Majak's car parked on the other side. I was in Sunshine at the time of her call and managed to get to the Bolte Bridge fairly quickly. Emily arrived first and went to the top of the bridge where there were emergency crews around Majak's car. Driving there, I was thinking he was dead. Because Emily was on the bridge, I went to the bottom and met the emergency crews and told them who I was. I told the first police officer I saw that I knew Majak and asked him for an honest response: 'How is he?'

The incident took a big toll on my family. Augustino was one of the first to come to the hospital to see me.

On that night, I was on the phone with Majak. We were chatting and it was kind of awkward because I had to go to work the next day. I told him, 'Mate, it's getting a bit late but I can come past your house if you want?' He replied,

'Oh. No, no. I'm just going to chill out with the boys.'
I didn't live that far away, and in the back of my mind I
knew something didn't sound quite right with him, but
I didn't want to overthink it.

I couldn't sleep for some reason and stayed up for
another hour or two. The phone rang and it was Joey.
'Joey, why are you calling me at such an hour?' I asked.

He answered, 'I need to tell you something.'

I knew straight away that something bad must have
happened to Maj. 'Ah, shit. Something is wrong. What is
it?' I asked.

He told me to head straight to the hospital.

I was like, 'Joey . . . Mate, don't fuck with me!'

'It's your brother,' he said. 'There's been an accident.'
I just got up, jumped into my car and went to the hospital.
When I arrived, it was quite shocking. I thought Maj was
dead, because they had covered him from head to toe with
a white sheet. Then he opened his eyes and I was relieved.
Even though he was out of it, I said to him, 'Man, you
should have told me!'

I had to call Mum and Dad and tell them what had happened. When my dad came, the whole blame game started.
Dad was saying things like, 'How could I witness one of
my sons dying before me? I should have been the first person who was told what had happened! No father deserves
to bury his own child! I should have been the first person!'

Joey confessed that he knew a lot more than us about
Majak's mental health and that only caused more angst.
I said, 'Joey, you're like a brother to me! We literally grew

up together. If Maj has told you this because you guys are mates, you should have picked up the phone to me and said, "Augustino, I think you need to go and talk to your brother." I could have talked him out of it.' I told Joey, 'You've let me down, and you've let my whole family down.' To me, family and brotherhood is something I hold very dear to my heart. 'Joey, I don't just eat with anyone off the same plate, but we ate from the same plate, right?'

Joey ended up breaking down, and then we found out from the club doctor and the psychologist that Majak had disclosed his issues to them as well. My family felt that we should have been told what was happening, so that we could have intervened and helped Maj. We felt let down as we know Majak better than anyone. We felt that patient–doctor privacy didn't matter because it was a matter of life and death. There was quite a lot of anger.

Shane Casley knows all too well the pressure I was under and the financial stress I endured.

We were doing really well with managing Maj's money and were able to put a lot of money away so he could buy a house or an apartment, and then the court case came. We had $150 000, or thereabouts, and it all just disappeared. He never recovered. That court case would have easily cost him a couple of hundred thousand dollars.

We were ready to go 'bang' and buy him a house or sign a new multi-year deal, but these setbacks kept coming – the court case, the bridge incident, injuries. His prime earning years of footy, where he should have been building his wealth and making the most of it, were taken away. Even in those first two, three or four years, there was always something that popped up and took his focus away from footy and his career. It was stressful for him always wondering what position he'd be in and never really having any financial security.

14

Thiär ku ŋuan

I opened my eyes and realised I was somehow still alive. I was underwater and began to panic, thrashing my arms to bring myself back to the surface so I could take a breath. It was freezing, icy. Adrenaline must have kicked in because I felt no pain, despite the fact my hips and pelvis had been almost obliterated when I collided with the water. Despite not having any movement, strength or ability to use my legs at all, I summoned all my energy and willpower to propel myself through the water using only my arms, and tried desperately to swim towards the riverbank. I thought I was going to drown, because the water was so cold, and it was so deep there, but I fought hard and eventually made it across to the side and to safety. I know now that if I had truly wanted to die, I would have just given up the struggle to swim and stay afloat. I would have stopped fighting and let myself drown.

That's all I can remember about the moments after my fall, but other people have filled me in on what happened. Apparently, several motorists had called the emergency services to notify them that a car had stopped on the side of the bridge and that they had seen a man out of the vehicle and near the edge.

Members of the State Emergency Service were the first responders, followed by the Metropolitan Fire Brigade. Some units went to the top of the bridge while others went to the riverbank below. The crews below found me unconscious, bogged waist-deep in thick mud. Apparently the emergency workers struggled to wrench me out by my arms – and I was told only recently by the co-writer of this book, Heath, that when they did pull me out, my pants and shoes were left behind, deeply cemented in the swampy embankment. When Heath told me this fact as we sat down to write this chapter of the book, it dawned on me that for the past year and half, I had been regularly searching my bedroom closet and other spare room cupboards for a particular pair of shoes and pants that I loved but could never find. Now I know exactly where they are – at the bottom of the Bolte Bridge, buried in mud.

Like I said earlier, I don't have any memories of what unfolded on the riverbank once I was found by the emergency service workers, but I am so thankful to all those who attended the scene and saved my life. I'm also thankful that I was unconscious, because I don't think I could have sustained the levels of pain required to free me from the thick mud with all the injuries I had suffered.

My next memory was waking up in hospital in a drug-induced fog. With my lower body badly smashed up, I was on an extremely high dose of painkillers that really didn't allow me to function properly. I had no idea what was going on or what day it was, let alone why I had jumped from the Bolte Bridge. At a time when I should have been allowed to recuperate, come to terms with my actions, life situation and circumstances, and also recover mentally and physically, I was instead inundated with hundreds of visitors and lost control of my surroundings. What should have been a quiet, private space in hospital had been turned into a visitor's centre with a virtual revolving door. The best way I can describe it was waking up in the middle of a shitstorm.

One of my first recollections was seeing my mum and dad in my room at the Royal Melbourne Hospital with my brothers and sisters by their side. It was a tiny room and could barely fit them all in. It was far from a private family situation, as there were also a lot of strange faces staring back at me – people who had heard about the incident and come to see me. I was so out of it and couldn't make sense of why all these people were allowed in my room. It was all really confronting for me – I mean, I had just tried to take my life, had woken up in hospital in excruciating pain and could barely move, yet I was expected to greet dozens of people every minute of the day and try to explain to them why I had decided to jump off the bridge.

The pain medication I was on initially wasn't nearly enough to dull the discomfort I was experiencing. My legs were pretty much disjointed from the hip sockets, and when I wanted to move, I had to pick up one of my legs with my hands and drag it to where I wanted it to be – it was the worst pain I've ever felt. I spent a lot of time in and out of consciousness due to the high pain levels and medication. I couldn't eat anything for days and had next to no energy.

There was absolutely nowhere to hide, which was making me feel worse. I desperately needed some privacy; I was crying out for it but being ignored. I wasn't even allowed to have my phone or turn the television on, because those around me were worried that I would hear and see what the media and the general public were saying about me. The reality was the world was actually showing me love and support. I've since seen all the messages and well-wishes that were posted to social media and sent to my private phone, and it was probably what I needed to read and see at the time. Instead of feeling all that warmth and compassion, however, I felt completely trapped, isolated and claustrophobic. At times, there were 200 people in the waiting room and spilling into the hallways. The floor I was on was jammed with people waiting to see me. It was a nightmare not only for me, but also for the nurses, doctors and hospital staff trying to tend to me and other patients.

By far the most shattering time came when my little brother, Ajak, arrived to see me. As soon as we locked eyes, he broke down crying, ran over to my bedside and hugged me and wouldn't let me go. It really broke my heart, and I can feel it breaking again talking about that moment now. At just 12 years old, Ajak was still trying to make sense of the world, and I think my actions really confused him. In his head he was probably thinking, *My brother just tried to kill himself*, and it would have been particularly hard for him to come to terms with, because he's always put me on a pedestal. Being so much younger than me, he watched on as I became somewhat of a celebrity and idol for many kids in our community, including him. We used to do a lot of things together when I started playing footy, when he was about five or so. Even when I moved out of home, I used to pick him up on my days off and we'd spend time together, go for long drives and just hang out. I was a bit of a hero to him and I think he realised when he saw me in hospital that everything in life is not necessarily what it seems. The big brother he'd thought was faultless and invincible was anything but, and was lying there before him, a broken and lost soul.

I struggled to get the sleep I so desperately needed to recover from my injuries. The drugs helped knock me out to a point, but every time I drifted off, a doctor or nurse would come in and wake me up to check my vital signs and pain levels. Other times, when I coughed or shifted in bed, I'd be woken by a sharp, intense pain unlike anything I'd ever experienced. It was excruciating. Each time I opened my eyes, a new person would be sitting or lying next to me. I had a lot of extended family coming in, like uncles and aunties, but on many occasions, I had no idea who the people in my room were. Some people were praying for me while others seemed mad at me and would bluntly ask, 'Why did you do this to us?' and 'Why did you bring this hurt and shame on your family?' It was almost like they were blaming me for their pain and disappointment. One time, I woke to find a woman lying on the bed with me. I had no idea who she was and had never seen her before.

It was such an invasion of my privacy, but I didn't have the strength to even utter the words, 'Can you please fuck off and leave me alone?'

There was a lot of tension building up between my family and Emily, too. I remember when I first woke up, I asked, 'Where is Emily? Where is she?' and one of the nurses got all awkward and immediately called my dad to come and speak to me. It became apparent that Dad was in full control of things, including who could and couldn't come in to see me – and to my horror, Emily wasn't on the approved list. He told me he didn't want Emily anywhere near me. This all stemmed from Dad struggling to make sense of what had occurred, and the fact that I hadn't told him about my struggles with mental health. He couldn't comprehend that I had gone to others rather than him, and that he hadn't been aware or able to help.

My parents were also frustrated because they hadn't been told what had happened to me for close to two hours after the bridge incident. They were really angry and hurt, and they looked to take their frustrations out on people who'd been aware of my mental-health battles – like Joey, Rory and the club's head doctor, Peter Baquie. Emily, though, copped the brunt of Dad's anger. He had put his foot down and wanted to control it all. Emily was treated really poorly, and I felt for her because she no doubt would have been experiencing a whole heap of different emotions herself. While all that was swirling around, I was stuck in the middle, aware of it all but unable to step in and resolve anything. It was all really exhausting and stressful.

Mum and Dad kept asking me why I had done what I had, and I could tell they were looking for someone to point the finger at. They couldn't, or wouldn't, accept that I had brought all of it on myself and, ultimately, I was to blame for my actions. It was particularly hard for them, because I don't think they had a good comprehension of what depression or mental health actually is. For them, when an incident happens like a car accident, there's someone to blame and someone at fault. There's a clear reason as to why one thing led to another. The hard part about mental health is that it doesn't always make sense to those who aren't experiencing the pain or trauma; it's sometimes illogical and hard to understand. So, looking at it from Mum and Dad's point of view, I can see why they were confused and felt let down by those closest to me.

While everyone was demanding answers from me about why I'd jumped off the bridge, I just didn't have the energy to go back in my mind and relive it all in an effort to explain my actions. In the end, I had a massive argument with my dad about the way he was treating me and Emily, and how he was allowing all these strangers into my room. I yelled at him out of frustration one morning, 'Just get out! Get everyone out of here, please!' and 'You're making things far worse in here for me and I can't recover! I need some sleep and time alone!'

My dad has always had a significant standing in the Sudanese community in Melbourne, and I started to get the sense that he was embarrassed by what I had done, so he was trying to find a cause that wasn't me – his son – to deflect the blame from our family. In some way, I thought my actions reflected poorly on him and his ability to run a happy and successful family. Initially, I thought he would have been appreciative of the support shown by everyone who came to the hospital, but perhaps he was ashamed by the sheer volume of people who knew what had happened, and he felt he didn't have the right to turn them away.

Two of my uncles were particularly harsh towards me, and I felt they really attacked me for what I had supposedly done to damage the reputation of the family. At a time when I was most vulnerable, they chose to berate me, which was extremely hurtful and disappointing. All I needed was people to just wrap their arms around me and show me they loved me, but that was too hard for some to do. My perception of what was happening was different to the reality. I look back now at the actions of those people at the time and don't hold any grudges, because I understand cultural beliefs and systems were in play. I realise no one had any experience with this sort of stuff, and to have a family member try to commit suicide would have turned all their worlds upside down. Also, I learnt that the Sudanese community will always seek to come together in times of crisis to help those in pain get through. The whole ordeal taught me a great deal, and that it takes a pretty strong character to stand up, put things into perspective, put others first and make sure everyone is okay – in the end, my mum was that person. During my worst times, when I couldn't hold it together in hospital and was crying uncontrollably, when I couldn't see a pathway back to my normal life, she was there by my side to comfort me and tell me that everything was going to be okay.

The conversation about my recovery had quickly turned to what kind of surgery I'd need and what option and course of treatment was going to be best for me. With all the emotion and anger, the number of people around and all their varying opinions, it was impossible for us all to agree and lock anything in. Making matters worse, the injuries I had needed to be fixed right away, so I didn't have time to waste. Peter Baquie was trying to arrange for a specialist surgeon to treat me in a way that would allow me to per-haps one day play football again. While trying to arrange that, he was fighting with my parents as they had lost all trust in him.

I really felt for Pete, because he is a man of the highest integrity, and while he knew about the mental battles I was having before I jumped, he also had a duty of care not to disclose that information to anyone without my consent – including my parents. I had demanded he keep those things private, and I had also withheld a lot from him and hadn't shown any signs that I would self-harm or try to take my own life. He was stuck between a rock and a hard place, and I think he did all that he could have done, under the circumstances, to help me.

Pete and the specialist we selected, Andrew Oppy, needed to make decisions on the type of surgery I required, and where all the pins, screws and steel rods should be inserted into my hips and pelvis. I clearly didn't have the capacity to make decisions for myself, so I was relying on those around me to make the right calls on my behalf. In the end, I didn't feel like I was being treated as a priority by some of the people closest to me, and I decided I had to take some control. That meant telling my dad to settle down or leave the hospital. Unfortunately, he took the latter option, as he was in a particularly combative mood.

There was genuine concern that I wouldn't be able to walk properly again, let alone run or play football, and it added another layer of tension to an already complicated and regrettable situation. If the surgeon opted to place a screw through my back area or sacrum, it would affect my movement and running gait for the rest of my life. That screw would seriously tighten the whole area that controls my running action, and I would have been severely restricted in what activity and sport I could do. There were some pretty big decisions to be made, and they were really hard to make while my parents were emotional and not thinking straight.

REFLECTIONS

Joey Halloran, Augustino and William Daw, Luke McDonald, Andrew Oppy

Like he was for the early stages of my new life in Australia, Joey was right by my side when I opened my eyes in hospital. He recalls the moment he found out that I had survived the jump and the scene that followed in the hospital.

After I had asked the police officer if Majak was okay, I had in the back of my mind that whatever he said would be carefully worded and designed to try to shield me from the reality of the situation until more support arrived. To my absolute shock, he replied, 'He's alive.' I couldn't believe it and said, 'Well, he can't be okay,' and he said, 'Look, he was talking to the paramedics and was awake in the ambulance.' I was convinced he would have been dead and couldn't believe he had somehow survived.

Emily and I went into the resuscitation room at the hospital to see Maj, and he was pretty groggy from all the meds they had pumped into him, but he was a lot better than he should've been – a hell of a lot better than he should've been. We called the North doctor, Bianca Scotney, and she

arrived not too long after and did some really basic testing to see how much damage he'd done to his neck, legs,
arms and spine. She was able to rule out some pretty
serious injuries, which came as a real shock as well. With
him being alive, I feared he would be a paraplegic or quadriplegic, confined to a wheelchair for the rest of his life.

We stayed at the hospital for the rest of the morning and
heard lots of different stories about how he'd landed, where
he'd landed and why he'd been able to survive. We heard
that he landed in a part of the river that's far deeper than a
lot of other parts under the bridge, but no one really knows
for sure what saved him – I think it was a combination of
fortunate events.

Over the course of the next few days throughout Majak's
recovery, people got distracted by his physical injuries and
forgot it was still a major mental-health issue he was fighting.
I just can't imagine anywhere else in a hospital setting
where a mental-health patient who had just tried to commit suicide would have that many people there. It was out
of control. Maj blew up a couple of times at his family, at
Augustino, and his family blew up at him. He was really
keen to know what the world was saying about him, which
I was pretty keen to protect him from as much as I could,
but at the end of the day, I couldn't shield him completely.

I know the news and commentary out there wasn't all
negative, but I just felt like he shouldn't get distracted from
what he had to deal with. For some reason, getting his
phone back to see the messages and media reporting was
a big priority for him. I suppose when you have the profile

that he does, you might want to know what people are saying about you. The one thing he said he wanted was to check his messages – he had a whole heap of unread messages, and I watched him scan through them and that was the end of the issue.

With a lengthy recovery and rehabilitation, Maj had to stay in hospital for a long time, which was actually a blessing in disguise for him, as it meant he had time to come to terms with things and sort out some of his mental-health issues with professional help around him at all times. He was taking some pretty positive steps, which gave us great confidence in him, because we were all understandably worried about what life would look like once he was discharged. Before he went home, he was cleared by the mental-health team, and they'd made arrangements for Emily to live with him. If Emily wasn't living with him, there would have been a few more red flags, but when there were times when I wanted to know what he was up to or had concerns about his wellbeing, I could always get in touch with Emily, so that helped.

When I look back on the night of his jump, Emily and I were the only people who had that feeling or the thought that Majak was dead. Everyone else close to him was able to wake up and know that he had survived. It's that five-minute drive, after hearing Emily was on top of the bridge and Majak was nowhere to be seen, and likely at the bottom, that was probably the most traumatic part of the whole night.

I don't think Maj will ever really know the amount of people he's inspired to keep on living and not give up.

We went out for coffee recently to a café in Altona, and there was a guy sitting at the table next to us. He didn't look like a footy fan by any stretch of the imagination, but he knew who Maj was. He got our attention and said, 'I've dealt with depression in my life and you really inspired me. Keep up the good work and thank you for all that you are doing.' It was a different sort of recognition that Maj was used to getting throughout his footy career, where he was only recognised as a footballer. I think he's inspired a lot of people with the way he was able to turn his life around.

As I've mentioned, there were some tense times in the hospital, and while I didn't handle the influx of people well initially – for obvious reasons – Augustino really helped me better understand people's motives for coming to see me.

A lot of people came to see Majak, to show my family and Dad respect, but also to share our pain and support us all. Culturally, when you mourn, you mourn together. If something happens, we're a collective society, and that's one thing I've tried to explain to Maj and help him understand why so many people came into the room from as far away as New South Wales, Brisbane, Warrnambool – just to wish him well. I told him, 'They really don't care about your status. They're not coming for you. They're coming for the old man, for the old lady and for the family unit because we're a collective society. If something happens to one, it happens to all of us. So, don't think because you're Majak, or you're the first Sudanese to ever play AFL, that's why they all came.'

Most of the people who came have known my father for a very long time. When we came to Australia, Dad had a hand in helping to bring a lot of Sudanese and, in particular, South Sudanese people here. He used to write their cases, present their situation to the Australian government and make the process easier for them. So, when they came to visit Majak in hospital, they said, 'William Daw is the man who helped us come to Australia, and he's going through a difficult time with his son. His difficult times are our difficult times.' It was an amazing gesture. I mean, what man would actually get here from Brisbane, or what woman would actually come from Warrnambool, to mourn with your parents? They came with the greatest intention, and that's what I keep on telling Majak. I told him that it was time for him to revisit his culture and rediscover who he is and where he came from, how we do things culturally, and how to balance both cultures.

Like in most cultures and religions, suicide is actually frowned upon. I mean, whether it's a Western society, or with Asian or African societies, people would actually say it's a selfish act. People were blaming themselves, saying, 'What got him to the stage of taking his own life?' Some said, 'Maj has got everything that he wanted in life, so why would he do such a thing? Why would he want to end his life, knowing where he came from? He could have died in Egypt, or been killed in Sudan, but God gave him a life.' A lot of our people are believers and they said to Majak, 'God gave you life. Why would you want to throw it away?'

On a personal level, I started to question myself too, and wondered if there was more I could have done. I asked him, 'Was it the pressure of being an elite sportsman? Was it the fame and everything? Was it a relationship problem? Come and speak to me. I am your older brother.' The first thing he said when I saw him in hospital was, 'I should have told you.'

We needed to give him time to recover, but with all the anger and blaming, it was hard for him. I had to tell my dad, 'Leave the poor thing. When the right time arrives, he will come and sit us down and tell us why. People deal with their demons. Whichever demon you want to call it, leave it at that, but then as long as he's right in front of you now, that's the most important thing.' We thank God he's still around.

As well as worrying about me, my parents were hurt that they didn't know what had been going on in my life. It certainly tested my relationship with my father.

I wasn't aware that Majak was going through difficulties, because he wasn't living with us. He didn't tell us. The thing that hurt me – too much – was that he didn't tell us he was suffering. We would have supported him. That gave me a shock, the thought that I didn't do something to help my child.

With the court case, when he was accused of rape, I was in Papua New Guinea for work, but he told me what was going on. I told him I would come back immediately to support him. He told me, 'Dad, I didn't do it!' and I said, 'I know, son.'

This time we couldn't support him, because his mother didn't know what was going on, I didn't know what was going on – not until we got that call from Joey, telling us that Majak was in hospital. But following that, there was hope. The hope that he would recover. The doctors did their part very well. It wasn't about how he could go back to football, it was about how he could survive.

That first moment was a shocking situation for us, but it happened. These things happen. That is life: there is pain, and there is the hope that things will get better.

What young people don't understand about their parents . . . They think if they're going through bad times, they cannot tell them, or tell anyone. They think, *My parents cannot do anything for me.* But no, it's not like that. Whether you're guilty of something bad, or have done something wrong, or you are struggling, in the heart and mind of your parent, you are still their child. If you are successful, if you are a failure, or whatever, you're still their child. You cannot take that out of their mind and their heart. You are still loved, no matter what.

Young people do not understand that the love of their parents cannot be described. It cannot be written down in books. Because of this, sometimes young people cannot feel this love. But the child is everything to the parents! Whatever is annoying a child is annoying the parents. Whenever their child is happy, they too are happy. Whenever their child is in pain or is suffering, they are also in pain.

I remember one time, when I was young, I told my mother that I didn't want to get married once I'd finished school. I told her that I wanted to join the rebel fighters in south Sudan. She asked me why, and I explained that I wanted to join the liberation movement.

She simply said, 'No! You are not going.'

I argued, 'But you have many children. If I die in the war, it's fine, you have other children to look after and love.'

She just repeated, 'No! You are not going.'

I didn't know in that moment that, even though my mother had many children, every single one of them had a special place in her heart. It's something I do understand now; I have nine children, and they are all very special to me in their own way.

It was a good thing that I shared what I wanted to do with my mother. She talked to me and I talked to her about going to fight in the war. She cried and was upset, and I realised that what I was going to do was not good for my mother. So any young people facing any problems: please talk to your parents and your family. If you don't talk, people don't know, and that means they can't help you. Everyone has their own sin; no one is perfect. But you will be close to perfect if you talk to people and allow them to help you. There is a lot of support around you.

One day a mother came to me and said, 'Thank you. Your son, Majak, helped my son, who was going to commit suicide.' She said, 'Without your son, my son would be dead now.' By recovering, Majak is now able to help other people. That's a beautiful thing.

My second family, the North Melbourne Football Club, was hit hard by what happened too, particularly those closest to me, like my teammate and great friend Luke McDonald.

Majak's mental-health battle was invisible to all of us at the North Melbourne Football Club who were close to him at the time of the incident. I've been mates with Maj for a long period of time, and I was as surprised, shocked, in disbelief – whatever word you want to use – as anyone.

On the morning after Majak jumped from the Bolte Bridge, one of my friends sent me a text message really early saying, *I hope Maj is okay . . .* I woke up to that message and thought it was very strange and obviously had no idea what it was about. Only the night before, Taylor Garner and I had invited Maj out to a Mexican restaurant for dinner, but he had declined because he was sick. I remember the sound of his voice over the phone: he was full of a cold and really stuffy and lethargic. I replied to the friend who'd texted me, *What are you talking about? What's up with Maj?* and he answered, *Oh, I'm so sorry, I shouldn't have messaged you.* I obviously pressed him further and asked him to tell me what had happened, and he told me there were reports running in all the morning radio programs saying that Majak had had an accident of some kind and had fallen from the Bolte Bridge.

I was in disbelief and in utter shock. I couldn't comprehend it at first and tried to call Majak's phone straight away, but of course, there was no answer, and it went straight to his voicemail. This panicked me further, but

I also had in the back of my mind that Maj wouldn't likely be awake yet and had been feeling ill the night before.

I made my way to training, unable to get an answer from anyone about what might have happened to Maj. I refused to believe that he had fallen from a bridge and thought it was just the Melbourne football-media rumour mill mis-interpreting something or getting wires crossed somewhere. But still, I felt sick to my stomach at the thought something may have been behind all the chatter.

The year before Majak's incident, 2017, was one of the best times of my life, because I lived with him as well as Taylor Garner and Ben Jacobs. We were such a tight-knit group and although we eventually went our separate ways, when certain guys moved out to live with their girlfriends, we kept an extremely close bond, and I know we will all remain best friends forever, even after we finish football.

Majak was heaps of fun to be around, and he always lit up a room when he walked in. That's why I couldn't begin to believe what I was being told about his acci-dent, because it just wasn't him. The Majak I knew always soldiered on with things and was the most resilient person I'd even met. I was around when he had his trial in the County Court, when he was unshakable in his determination to get through that ordeal and push on with positivity. He'd also been racially abused several times and had always brushed it off like it was nothing. He'd never expressed his feelings or told us that he was hurting or that something had upset him. When the chips were down for him, he'd always pick himself up, dust himself off and keep keeping on.

A lot of the other players were already training at Arden Street when I arrived on the morning that I'd heard Majak had been involved in a serious incident. We were training in groups (defenders, midfielders and forwards), and I went and found my dad, who worked at the club, and asked if he'd heard anything. He too was in the dark, but as the minutes ticked by, more and more people were getting wind that something bad was going on. Tension was building and emotions were starting to overflow. Some of the other line groups finished training and made their way upstairs to the administrative level of our club's facility to see what was happening – that's where all the big club bosses and executives work.

When I eventually got up to the admin level, I immediately noticed there was a funny air about the place, and it was eerily quiet. The club office space was usually vibrant and full of energy and noise, but on this occasion, it was anything but. It was clear at that stage something was amiss. There were a lot of closed office doors and worried looks on people's faces. I started to think there was truth behind all the rumours.

We were all wandering around, not sure what to do, where to go or who to talk to. I found Taylor and Ben, and we all just broke down, crying. The coaches and football staff ushered a small group of us, the ones who were closest to Maj, into the theatrette for some privacy. We all sat there and didn't speak a word to each other. Even though we hadn't been told anything official and nothing was confirmed, the fact Majak wasn't at the club or returning our messages or calls was enough to let us know the reports were accurate. We knew if it wasn't true and he was okay, then someone from the club would have told us and nipped it in the bud.

I started thinking about the night before, when we had asked Maj to come out to dinner, and I started second-guessing my actions and began to wonder if I could have, or should have, done more. Should Taylor and I have known he wasn't doing well mentally or was in some sort of trouble? Should we have gone over to his house to check on him? Should we have called the doctor and asked him to check in on Maj? Hindsight is a wonderful thing, of course, but it was hard not to feel some level of guilt or carry some blame. I wished Maj had told us what he was going through. We wouldn't have judged him, we would have just thrown our arms around him and given him a big hug and supported him through everything and tried to make it better. We are among his best mates; we are just so close with him.

We'd been sitting in the theatrette at Arden Street for about half an hour when the rest of the players and staff began to file in; an all-of-club meeting had been called and an announcement was about to be made. I felt like vomiting, because I feared what was going to be said. There was a lot of tension in the room, with everyone bracing for the worst. Our coach at the time, Brad Scott, walked in and stood out the front and addressed everyone. He looked nervous, which was very unusual for him. 'You've all no doubt heard the reports about Majak by now,' Brad said, or words to that effect. 'While we don't know much, we do know that Maj is in a stable condition at the Royal Melbourne Hospital after an incident overnight.' He went on to explain that the club had no information about what had actually happened to him or why it had occurred.

All around the room, people started crying and consoling one another. Brad continued, 'We know a lot of you will be in shock and you'll want to see him. As soon as we have more information about his condition and when visitors will be allowed, we'll let you know, but until then, our focus is on ensuring your wellbeing and health.' We were told to stay at the club for a period of time until the psychologist had a chance to speak with us all individually. While everyone was affected, some of us were hit harder than others due to our time at the club with Majak, and our closeness to him on a more personal level.

All I wanted to do was see Majak, but there were strict protocols put in place in the early stages, as he was being stabilised and treated for his injuries. He needed a pretty urgent operation, too, and was heavily sedated. That night Taylor, Ben and I caught up to support each other and process what had happened. It was like we were in a haze and nothing that was happening was real. By that stage, we'd been given a little more information about the incident and couldn't believe he'd somehow avoided death with such a huge fall. We all commented that if anyone could survive a fall that big, it would be Majak, because over the years we'd become so accustomed to him overcoming massive challenges and obstacles that normal people wouldn't get through.

After a few days, we were finally allowed to go into the hospital to see Maj. When we walked in, the entire hospital waiting room was overflowing with Maj's family and friends. There would have been more than 50 people in there, such was the level of care and love for him. We saw some of his family and friends who we'd met throughout the years and offered our support before we were escorted to his room. I caught a glimpse of him through the small window in the door and felt my breathing shorten. I didn't know if I was ready to see him yet. I didn't know how I'd react; I'd never had to confront anything quite like this.

I edged my way into the room with Ben and Taylor by my side, and approached Maj's bed. He was sleeping and his sister, Teresa, was watching over him. She gestured to us and encouraged us to come closer to the bedside. We spoke to her, found out how he was going and told her we desperately wanted to speak to him and see that he was okay. Without any warning, she gently pulled the oxygen hoses out from his nostrils for a brief second, which caused him to suddenly come to life. Maj coughed and spluttered and then slowly opened his eyes. It was like watching a miracle unfold when his heavy eyes opened and he recognised our faces. We were allowed a couple minutes alone with him, and my God, they were the best couple of minutes. He started apologising to us for what he'd done, but we stopped him and just kept telling him how much we loved him and told him he didn't have to explain anything and that he had nothing to apologise for. It wasn't long before he started cracking his customary awful gags and that's when we knew he was going to be okay.

Maj's recovery was unbelievable, to say the least. He made so much progress over such a short time. During one visit he was on his walking frame, which he was only supposed to use to balance himself and stand upright, but he got all confident when the nurses weren't around and tried to take a few steps and walk. We tried to tell him not to push himself too hard too early, but he just looked at us with that cheeky grin of his and did it anyway. It was at that moment that I thought, *He's gonna play footy again.* He's such a freak athlete and he just takes everything in his stride. Once he has a goal and puts his mind to something, nothing stops him from achieving it. He's so headstrong and determined.

Some of the highlights of my career have been Maj's little recovery milestones. There was the day he came to the club for the first time since being discharged from hospital. He was on crutches and told everyone he was confident of playing again. There was the time when he set foot on the AlterG [anti-gravity] treadmill in the gym and had his first aided run. When he ran across the ground unaided at Arden Street. When he played his first practice game in the VFL and, finally, when he played his first AFL game in 2020 – all these events were so significant; and while they're his milestones, they're also much bigger than that and meant so much to all of us who witnessed them.

The fact he tried to commit suicide doesn't change anything; not the way I feel about him or how I see him as a trailblazer and beacon of hope for so many people. He's broken down so many barriers for so many people over the years and will continue to do so for decades to come. Despite what he's been through, he's remained open and so kind to everyone. He's grown so much as a person and is now an amazing father to his little boy, Hendrix. I'm just so proud of him and I'll always consider myself so lucky to have him as a mate, and it will be that way forever.

I was fortunate enough to have the expertise of Andrew Oppy, my orthopaedic surgeon, who worked hand in hand with pelvic surgeon John Clifford to get me back on my feet.

I work at the Royal Melbourne Hospital on Mondays, Thursdays and Fridays, and because I'm kind of in charge, I get a twice-daily email handover every morning and every night telling me about all the admissions we have. When we get big trauma cases like Majak's come in, they could come up with a 'John Doe' type identification or another title like 'Foxtrot' or 'Sierra'. So that's their ID for the first 24 to 48 hours until they are appropriately identified. In the handover that I received in relation to Majak, it never said 'Majak Daw' – it only said 'unknown' – and it said something like, 'suicide attempt/jump from Bolte Bridge' and then went on to detail the injuries he'd suffered. It wasn't until mid-morning that I saw the news and realised that Majak had had an incident on the bridge the previous night or early morning, and was able to put two and two together.

When athletes are diving at Olympic level off the 10-metre platforms, you will always see a spray or stream of water that's designed to break the surface of the water below them and lessen the impact on their wrists and arms as they reach the surface. I presumed Majak had fallen into the water, and not into the muddy area at the edge of the river. Hitting the water from a significant height, around 10 metres or more, is like smacking into concrete. But with Majak, we're talking about a drop of about 25 metres with no broken surface water to help lessen the blow.

We know from experience at the hospital in the trauma unit over the years that if you pin-drop into water from a great height, you normally go right to the bottom of the river and end up hitting the ground, which normally breaks your heel bones. You can also break your pelvis and your spine. So, looking at Majak's injuries, we can sort of assume he's probably landed on a slight angle. Instead of going into the water in a perfect pin-drop, I'd say he was more leaning forward a little bit.

When we talk about pelvic fractures, if you know what the pelvis looks like, it's like a ring or oval-shaped structure. There are basically three different types of pelvic fractures: one is where you fall onto the side of your hip, and you squash your pelvis together; another one, which often occurs when you're riding a horse or a motorbike and you hit the front part of the pelvis and it springs open; then there's another one where the pelvis is forced upwards. But Majak didn't have any of those, which was remarkable. He had a minor combination of all of those injuries. I think what happened is, as he hit the water, his legs have taken all the moment of force and have driven his femurs up into his hip joints, and that's caused these cracks in the joints of both sides of his hips, and then he had some slight widening of the joint where the sacrum joins the spine and the ilium at the back of the pelvis.

Not long after I'd realised who the patient likely was, I received a phone call from the North Melbourne Football Club's head doctor, Peter Baquie, and then made calls to my training surgeon at the Royal Melbourne. He detailed the incident and the subsequent injuries Majak suffered and I said, 'Are you sure those are the only injuries he has? Is this all he hurt? If that's all he's got, then that is ridiculous.'

John Clifford was the pelvic surgeon on call at the time, so we took on Majak's case together. Normally, thinking about that sort of ring of the pelvis, if you fix the front of it, you can leave the back as is, but quite often, we like to insert a screw across the back as well to stabilise it. But with Majak, we were very reluctant to do that, because we knew it would affect his football career, because that screw would really inhibit any movement he'd have in the back of his pelvis. So, we deliberately left that and let that heal naturally. From a surgical point of view, it looks like a really big and complicated case, but in fact, it was one of the most minor surgeries you can do on the pelvis. We did it all through tiny cuts and put the screws up the front of the pelvis to fix it.

I mean, talking about these injuries, it's just amazing that he clearly didn't suffer anything serious with his abdomen, chest or head areas. I look after these types of patients every day or every second day, and it might be high-speed car accidents, suicide attempts involving people jumping off bridges onto roads, or jumping out of buildings, and the injuries sustained are always multiple. Recently, I operated on three patients who had broken every single arm and leg, and Maj comes in after that fall and all he's got are these little cracks in his pelvis – it's incredible and I still can't get my head around it. The biggest thing I've always said is that it came down to his pre-injury status, meaning his bone strength and muscles. His strength is what saved him. He was probably going to be stronger than any normal person given his genetics and training regimen.

Maj was put to sleep by the anaesthetists and we had him on a special operating table made out of carbon fibre, which means there's no metal in it that stops the X-ray machine from seeing what we need to see. John Clifford was on one side of Majak and I was on the other, and we put a little pin into each side of his pelvis, which acted like little joysticks so we could get control of the damaged area and move his pelvis and hips into the right position. With Majak's fractures we just needed to use the joysticks to compress the ring a little bit.

After we performed that reduction, which was relatively easy, the fixation was pretty straightforward; it's seriously like playing an advanced computer game to a certain degree. We had the 3D imaging of his pelvis, the CT scan that was done beforehand up on the screen, and we'd planned out where we wanted the screws to go. To get a straight screw up these corridors, there's quite a narrow point where it's got to go, because the bone turns and bends a little bit and we're putting a straight screw up it. It's all planned pre-operatively on the 3D imaging, and then we use the X-ray machine to make sure we're hitting the spots as planned.

Once we were satisfied we had the right plan, we ran a wire up each anterior column that makes the first pass. Once we were happy, on the X-rays, that the wire had gone into the spot we wanted it to go, we then put the drill over the top of the wire, and put in a screw over the top. We did all of that in a special way, so the wire and drill actually find their own path along the bone corridor. Bones are really hard on the outside, but inside is actually hollow. So, the screws were going into the hollow part. With a drill, it actually has a little bit of flex in it, so once we were inside the bone, we just had to go very slowly, because it could have easily drilled through the wall of the bone. If it got too close to a wall, we'd hope for it to sort of bounce off and find its way inside the bone.

Each screw was 140 millimetres long and 7.3 millimetres in diameter. They are specially made, and instead of having a standard screw you'd use at home, with a thread that runs the whole length of the screw, these screws only have a thread that runs halfway along. So, once the screw goes past the fracture site, it starts to grip. The end part of the screw, with the head where the screwdriver goes, then hits the edge of the bone that's hard, and can actually squash it. Maj had very tiny 1–2-millimetre gaps at the fracture sites, and we were able to compress and squash those, because that also helps the bone to heal.

John and I had a lot of discussions about this procedure. For instance, are we going to do more harm than good?

With Majak's right side more damaged than his left side, we could have argued the right thing to do was to go through his back and reduce the 1–2-millimetre gap and try to make it perfect, but to do that and put a huge plate and screws in would have been an enormous task. We also had to work out if that was going to make him better in the long term, or potentially not. With the option of inserting a screw at the back of the pelvic ring, we assessed the back of the pelvis and felt it was stable enough. If we'd put a screw in the back, that may have restricted his movement significantly, and we would have had to remove it at a later date, which would have meant more surgery, more recovery periods and more delays. Maj had very clean breaks as well, and they were very, very minimally displaced, which was again very lucky.

When I was talking to Majak before the surgery, I wanted to make sure that I painted a positive picture for him, which was really hard. I needed to explain to him that while it was a bad injury – a very serious injury – it's also one that I was very confident he would make a full recovery from. To me, it wasn't a huge injury, considering what we deal with on a day-to-day basis at the Royal Melbourne. It's just trying to manage the mental health side of things and encouraging a positive attitude, because you don't ever want to tell a patient who has just tried to commit suicide that they're now worse off. Unfortunately, that's the reality, and what we see quite often with our failed suicide attempts; patients come in and they're already in a bad place, we understand that, but now they have two broken legs, broken arms and a fractured spine or whatever else, and they're even worse off than they were before they attempted to take their life – how is that going to play out for them mentally?

Majak was lucky and I was able to tell him confidently, 'I'm going to have you back playing footy,' because that's the one thing he kept asking me: 'Am I going to be able to play footy again?' It's really hard as a clinician to say, 'Yes,' because even though that's our goal, it was a big injury, and I didn't want to give him a false hope, but I also needed to provide him with the right motivation. So, it was just a matter of managing that balance and saying, 'Look, we're going to do everything we possibly can to get you back on the football field,' and to try to set some timeframes that were reasonable and obviously achievable for him.

15

Thiär ku dhiɛc

Once I had my surgery, teammates and staff from the footy club were allowed in to see me, and that was also extremely difficult and confronting for me. I had been putting on a brave face and pretending nothing was wrong around them for years – acting all alpha male and macho – and now I was basically strapped to a hospital bed and laid bare for all of them to see. Again, there was nowhere to hide and nothing I could say to deflect from the fact that I had tried to kill myself. I had to own it, and so I did. Regardless of who came in, I told them the truth. I told them that some dark thoughts had got the better of me and I hadn't known how to handle it.

Being stuck in a hospital bed gave me time to think about where I was in my life, and it was clear to me that the position I was in was rock bottom. I couldn't get up or stand on my own two feet for a time. I couldn't walk around or even go to the toilet by myself. I know there would have been some people thinking the whole ordeal was me just seeking attention, but it wasn't that at all.

What I did wasn't attention seeking or even a cry for help. That might be the case for some people who try to take their own life and don't follow through with it, but in my case, I actually jumped off that bridge with no intention of coming back. I heard lots of different things about what I did: people told me that it was a miracle I was still alive; that I was lucky not to have smashed into the water head-first; that I had just missed slamming into a concrete pylon at the base of the bridge; that I should have become submerged in the thick mud at the bottom of the river and drowned – all these things were supposed to have happened, but none of them did.

For whatever reason, I was given a second chance at life. I had wanted my life to be over, and when I woke up and realised that I hadn't been successful, I knew I had more to give. That's a massive thing, and I knew I needed to do a lot of work to make sure I didn't go back to that dark place. I decided to reconnect with my faith, so I started practising Christianity and devoted myself to it a little bit more. I couldn't help but think that God had intervened in some way and saved me, because the chances of surviving a fall like that were minimal, yet, somehow, I did.

Sometimes when I'm out and about, I look at tall buildings, trees or bridges and I think, *I fell further than the top of that tree and lived*, and I can't wrap my head around it. If there is a God out there, thanks to him for keeping me around and not ending my life then and there. Everything that could have gone wrong went right for me, and I think I have him to thank for it.

I lay there for days on end, trying to make sense of everything that had happened, and it's pretty embarrassing being trapped there with people coming in who knew what I had tried to do. I eventually found comfort in just accepting responsibility for my actions and not trying to control who was going to come in and see me. I stopped worrying about what people might have been thinking about me or what they were going to say to me. In the end, I realised I had much bigger things to worry about. I had been unsuccessful in ending my life, but all the things that had pushed me to the brink before I jumped were still there – nothing had gone away, and I still had to deal with it all.

A lot of people were understandably worried that I would try to kill myself again – it was a genuine concern for them – and if I'm being honest, at that stage being so drowsy on ketamine and painkillers, I probably wasn't able to reassure them that I wanted to go on. Michael Inglis, my psychologist, came in and explained to me that many people wouldn't want to leave me alone or allow me to be by myself for extended periods, for fear of me doing something stupid again, and that they'd want to be around to protect me from myself.

Despite my urging him to go home, Augustino barely left my side, sleeping for nights on end in the waiting room at the hospital. His support was unwavering. Rory was the same – he barely left the hospital and put his life on hold to make sure I was being looked after. Joey, too, was amazing, as were all my siblings. I remember having a conversation with Joey about it and told him, 'Mate, you can't be with me 24/7. If I want to try to take my life again, I'll find a way. No one will be able to stop me, even you.' I said that not to scare him, but to reassure him there was nothing more he could have done for me prior to me jumping off the bridge, and there was nothing more he could do for me moving forwards either. I explained to him that I'd inevitably have to be alone at certain stages, and there was no preventing that. I was going to need space in my life, and I needed people to trust that I'd be okay – although I acknowledged that gaining their trust would be difficult. It's not realistic to think that people could be there guarding me, protecting me or making sure I was all right every minute of every day. I told him that no one could get me out of the situation I was in but me. I thanked him and the others for their support, but I was stressed out because I could see my situation was hindering them in their own lives, because they were putting things on hold that needed tending to. Some of them were missing work, not seeing their own families and forgoing an income just to be with me. It was at this time that I really felt empowered to take my life back and get some control over my destiny again, and to give my friends their lives back by extension.

All the pain I had been in prior to jumping from the bridge was now ten times worse, but I had to take every day as it came and couldn't allow myself to get too over-awed by it all. It was intense in hospital, and I lost track of time just because of the medication I was on. When I was awake, all I could think of was the pain I was in, and when I wasn't in pain, I was asleep.

The one person I haven't really mentioned yet, in terms of seeing her, is Emily. After all the infighting and blame games calmed down, she made her way in to see me. She gave me a hug and was crying, and I was crying. Some people have tried to blame her for what had happened, and I think that's really unfair. I know she was really hurt, both by me and some of the people around me. Because I either wasn't there or wasn't aware of what was happening, I couldn't stick up for her and protect her.

Emily and I also had the issue of telling people that she was pregnant again, because no one knew at that stage. I eventually told Joey and Rory, and then I told my mum and dad. Everyone was already all over the place with their emotions, and throwing that at them too was pretty huge. No one really knew how to take it or what to say. I think many of them feared that it wasn't the right thing for Emily and I to go through with, given what had happened, but we explained that it was going to happen, no matter what.

For the rehabilitation phase of my recovery, I was moved from the Royal Melbourne Hospital to the Epworth Hospital in Richmond. It was at that time that some people from a government agency, I think the Department of Human Services, came in to speak with me and Emily, because they'd been notified of my incident and the fact that Emily was now pregnant. The representatives spoke to us individually and asked if we wanted to go ahead with the pregnancy or terminate it. We were asked to give a rating from one to ten, one being the least keen and ten being the most keen to proceed with the pregnancy, and we both answered 'ten' without even speaking to each other about it. That was a really big driver for me to get my life back on track and to have something to aim for. The way I was looking at things was that I had less than nine months to get my shit together and prepare for the arrival of our child. Being a father was something that had once terrified me, but it now became my motivation to get better. I wanted to be in good shape for the birth, both mentally and physically – it was a huge driving force in the back of my mind.

I often think about the person who stood on the edge of that bridge and made the decision to jump off it. I think he was someone at the peak of his powers in many ways, but someone who had become lost in material things and allowed things to spiral out of control. I wouldn't say he was arrogant, but perhaps he got ahead of himself and forgot about the things that mattered most. He didn't realise that he was living in the fast lane and thought he was somewhat indestructible. He got caught up in it all. He got into the habit of ignoring his feelings and bought into various alpha-male behaviours. Drinking became a big problem for him, and he didn't know how to stop it. Some days he wrote himself off and didn't know why. He was going to every single party or event he was invited to, and he just didn't take good care of himself, in general. He started disconnecting from his family, going from visiting his parents once a week to once a month, or even less at times. He also started disconnecting from some of his really close friends, Joey and Rory. That person just thought he could do everything by himself. He lost his way and refused to acknowledge that he was battling depression.

The guy I'm describing above is the bloke who jumped off the bridge that night, and while I'd love to say that he's dead now, the truth is – as with all mental-health struggles – he can always come back. If I don't look after myself, there's no doubt he'll return to try to take back control. I'm doing my best to make sure he doesn't come back, being more disciplined to avoid falling into the same old traps. Sometimes I do make mistakes, and I know it's okay to do that, but I have to learn from them and move forwards rather than dwell on them and go backwards. Whenever I feel I'm on the brink of having dark thoughts or slipping backwards, I catch myself and say, 'It doesn't matter what's happening, you're in full control.' Then I either physically grab Hendrix if he's with me, or I FaceTime him if he's not with me, and everything automatically feels right again. He is my perspective, my grounding influence and my reason for being.

I've found it best to just keep my life really simple these days and try to be grateful for what I have and for all the support around me. I have an amazing family and I've got some equally amazing friends who really care about me. I don't try to take on too much disappointment. It's just all part of life, and I've realised it's okay if things don't go well or pan out exactly how I had planned. I always have another chance to make things right. I had to learn to love myself, and I do now. I love who I am, and I want to instil that in Hendrix.

I made a terrible and regrettable choice back in December 2018, but there's no shying away from it. Now, I always remind myself that no matter how hard things get, I'm not that person anymore. I've had a lot of time to come to terms with what happened to me and the decisions I made, though it hasn't been easy by any stretch of the imagination. Looking back now, I think the court case ordeal I went through tore me apart from the inside out – in ways I couldn't comprehend at the time. I was found not guilty, but as a result of the pain and torment I endured for years in the lead-up months and during the trial, and because of the brave face I had to show every day in public, I became really good at hiding my feelings and sweeping my issues under the carpet. I became great at ignoring the red flags, pushing them aside and just moving on to the next thing that grabbed my attention.

Having somehow survived my suicide attempt and being so lucky to have been given a second chance at life, I needed to accept the fact that I had major issues with my mental health, and that I couldn't go it alone anymore. I needed to work with the psychiatrists and psychologists, being nothing but honest with them, and ask for help from my family and friends whenever I needed it. I learned there was no point just 'seeing a psychologist' and ticking a box, I had to open right up and let them in, otherwise they couldn't help me at all. I can't hide anything from them or play down the issues in my life that I am struggling with. But it was also more than that – I had to be honest with myself, too, and accept my failures and weaknesses.

REFLECTIONS

Andrew Oppy, Alex Moore

My recovery was unique according to my surgeon, Andrew Oppy, who kept close tabs on me as I eyed a return to football.

All of the AFL players and elite athletes I have dealt with throughout my career always have a faster rate of recovery than a normal patient, because they have frequent access to treatment and physiotherapy through their clubs or institutions. But in terms of Majak and what we were dealing with, I don't think there have been any AFL players with those types of injuries before.

To come back from the type of surgery he had in the time he did would be easily three times faster than the recovery period of a normal patient in that same situation. Now, that's got to do with Majak in terms of his body, strength, his motivation, and clearly it has a huge amount to do with the support services available to him at the North Melbourne Football Club too – mental and physical. For example, the average person doesn't have an AlterG weight-bearing treadmill to run on every day, not to mention physiotherapy and massage.

The best way to describe how lucky Majak was to survive his fall and end up recovering fully after hip surgery is to explain that people like me simply don't see people after a fall of that magnitude. They die at the scene and never make it to us. The causes for that could be numerous, and what Majak somehow avoided were severe head injuries, which result in immediate unconsciousness and death; spinal injuries, particularly neck or back that can cause people to become quadriplegic or paraplegic; and abdominal and chest injuries.

If a person somehow survives all those things and makes it to us, we'd definitely be expecting multiple spine and pelvis injuries, and then, most likely, lower limb injuries, depending again on how they landed and what on. I think the water is the thing that sort of saves the limbs a little bit. Clearly if there's no water, it's the limbs like the ankles, knees and femurs that are just all gone. The pelvis, when it has a bad injury, can damage the bladder, but it's often the ribs that might damage the lungs. Then you've got the liver and the spleen, which are always at risk as well. They're the big things that could be at risk with those sorts of traumas and incidents.

I could never have recovered the way I did without the staff at the North Melbourne Football Club. The club really gave me every chance to have a normal physical life after my incident and put so much time, effort and resources into my rehabilitation.

I don't, for one second, take that for granted, knowing I was afforded so much more than the average person would have been. One of my great allies in rehab was former Cleveland Cavaliers strength coach Alex Moore, who literally walked me through my rehab program every step of the way.

Three weeks after Majak had jumped off the bridge, we were allowed to go in and see him in the hospital. I went in with Jona Segal, the club's head of high performance, and it was an extremely confronting sight for both of us. At that stage, Majak required a lot of support to even stand, and he wasn't walking. He had a walking frame and could stand, but only just, and only for short periods. He had to put all his weight on his left leg, because his right side had sustained the most amount of damage in the fall.

Surprisingly, he looked much bigger than I thought he would have. I thought he'd lose a lot of muscle mass, because he'd had three weeks of not only surgery and trauma, but three weeks of bed rest and hospital food. I was actually shocked at how much muscle mass he was able to retain. So, on the outside, he still looked pretty good, but what lay beneath the surface was a broken body and mind.

When I first heard what had happened to Maj, I was pretty shocked. I mean, I hadn't known Majak for too long, as I'd only just arrived at the club after seven years working in Cleveland with the Cavaliers in the NBA, but like everyone, I was shocked that it had happened. I never saw that side of Majak. I only saw the bloke who lit up a room when he walked in, who was always laughing and telling his terrible dad jokes, and someone I thought was generally in a good place and loving life, having come off a career-best season.

When I first saw him, my initial thoughts were that he was lucky to be alive and that he'd never play football again, ever. To be honest, I didn't think he'd even be able to get back to jogging or running, from what I understood and what I was told about the severity of his various injuries to his hips and pelvis. I thought we would get him, within about two years, to a point where he'd be able to walk without a limp. I didn't have a view in my head about him being able to run, particularly when we saw that he couldn't even stand without being supported, and was in severe pain when he did any weight-bearing activity. I mean, here was a guy in his late 20s in a hydrotherapy pool in hospital with a bunch of 65-plus-year-old men and women, barely able to move. I couldn't see a pathway forwards for him at that particular moment. It was really sad and confronting. But in saying that, we had to give Majak hope, because he was looking to us for positivity and to tell him, 'You'll be all right, mate, we'll get you back on the park in no time.'

When we started to contemplate Majak's rehabilitation, we had to work in with the physiotherapists and medical team at the Epworth Hospital, and allow them to do their post-surgery work and get him to a point where he was strong enough to even leave the hospital and be transferred into our care. As someone who had worked an entire career in sports and sports rehabilitation, strength and conditioning, there was no template for what we were about to deal with. We were guided a lot by the surgeon, Andrew Oppy, in terms of what Majak could and couldn't do, but at the same time Andrew admitted to us that he had not rehabbed someone with that type of injury back to high-level athletics or elite sport either.

It just became a simple progression program that we put in place, and along with Matt Turnbull, the then football club's head physiotherapist, it was a case of giving Majak a simple dose of exercise and then seeing how he responded to that. If he didn't respond well, meaning that he was in too much pain doing the exercise or pulled up too sore the next day or two, we would either back off completely and change the dose for the next time, or go slow until he recovered fully. If he was responding well, we would apply the same dose, and if he did respond well to that, then we would progress onwards with a little bit more load and slowly build him up from there.

It all started with Majak learning how to walk again, which was done first with the physios in the hospital and then with us at the club. A key to that was getting him to a stage where he could confidently put weight through his right side and be able to do simple movements on two legs. For example, we'd get him to do a basic double-leg squat exercise but only asked him to lower himself one-eighth of the way down, until he was proficient enough, and had enough mobility and strength to do movements that were akin to the appropriate movement patterns to walk. Then we'd progress him to single-leg strength activities and exercises.

Maj was still on crutches for the first three to four weeks when he got back to the club. He went from two crutches down to one crutch over a six-week period and then progressed to being able to walk unaided. Two weeks after he was on crutches, we were doing some basic movement work in the gym, and he got this cheeky look on his face and said to me, 'I reckon I can pull off a little jump.' I immediately said, 'There's no way you can jump!' and expected that to be the end of it, but it wasn't. He grinned and then did a little jump and cleared the ground by about 25–30 centimetres. I just looked at him in complete shock and said, 'We can't tell the physios that you did that, because you shouldn't be doing that yet!' I was absolutely shocked that he had pulled it off. It was one of those things that he probably shouldn't have done, but then again nobody really knew what he could or couldn't do, so it was pretty impressive.

At that moment, I had in the back of my head, *Maybe there's a chance he could run again*. We started to do some lateral work, where he would move from side to side. I had him just stepping back and forth, and I just saw him instinctively, over a three-week period, start to want to bounce sideways, to start to actually move more dynamically with some spring in his steps. That's when I definitely knew we would get him back to running. Maybe I didn't think at that point he'd play football again, but definitely things were looking up for him to be able to resume some sort of dynamic exercise or activity.

We would have Maj scanned thoroughly every four to five weeks, because the scans can take a little while to change in terms of fractures taking a while to heal. We had to respect the bone-healing process and we were very structured in how we went about his recovery program. But because there was no template to follow, we also had to be flexible, and between Matt Turnbull and myself, we had a simple formula and said, 'Okay, when he can walk properly and we are confident that his gait is fine, we will move him to a one-eighth squat with a double leg. When he can do a one-eighth squat, double leg, we will move to a one-quarter squat, double leg. When we're happy that he can do that, we'll progress to standing on one leg and see how he balances on that leg.' We had a checkbox system and, between Matt and I, tried to project when Maj would reach and achieve each goal, but each time we did, he exceeded our expectations by a long, long way.

Nobody could really relate to Majak's pain, because I didn't know of any athletes who had injuries to that extent. So, we were relying on him to give us feedback, and he was definitely in pain. The thing that we spoke about with him is that with this rehab, there was always going to be a small element of pain, just because of the nature of injuries he had, and there was always going to be some compromised mechanics in terms of his movements, because he had two huge bolts inserted through his pelvis, one on each side. For us, we just had to work around that and see how he responded. We accepted a three out of ten pain rating from him, because we knew that we weren't going to get a zero out of ten. As long as he was getting better and staying under two to three out of ten, we'd progress him.

The first time I saw Majak's X-rays was when I actually went to a doctor's appointment with him. It's an incredible X-ray, because it looks like he's a bionic man. Majak's ability to recover so quickly was pretty extreme. I haven't worked or rehabbed anyone who has healed that quickly from something that serious and delicate. Everything he did, I felt that a regular athlete wouldn't have been able to do that fast. Once I thought there was a chance he could run, I thought that, year one, hopefully we would have him jogging proficiently by the end of that year. If we had a second year at it, I thought we could get him up to being able to do football drills and in the third year, I thought that was where he'd get to play football again. He did all of that in a four-to-five-month period, which was just staggering by any measure.

Hopefully I never have to rehab that type of injury again, but even if I did have to, there's no way I could apply Majak's rehab template to anybody else. It was the same when he tore his pectoral muscle earlier in the year. I mean, he was ready to play within two and a half weeks of doing that. The crazy thing is, I'm stronger than the average person and he was beating my chest strength scores on our testing system within two weeks of having sustained the injury. So, he's pretty amazing.

While I was in charge of the physical side of Majak's rehab along with Matty, the mental side was something we had to be very sensitive of. Obviously, he'd jumped off a bridge and that was totally out of the blue according to those at the club. I was cognisant of making sure I was across how he was doing, so every day it was a matter of trying to get that connection with him and trying to find out what his motivation levels were like and how he was faring away from the club. I would ask him, 'How are you feeling? How are you doing?' and if he was having days where he was struggling a little bit or was down on energy, we'd get out of the gym and walk a couple of laps of the Arden Street oval and then call it a day. It was important that he had a schedule and a plan, but he needed to know there was some flexibility there too. There were probably six days, over that four-month rehab period, where we just completely scrapped the gym component of his rehab program and instead walked five laps of the oval and then sent him home. It was all about making sure that we weren't adding physical stress to mental and emotional stress.

I think the hardest part for Maj in the early stages of his recovery was that there was no light at the end of the tunnel for him in terms of getting back to playing football. If you do an anterior cruciate ligament (ACL) in your knee, it's 12 months, give or take a month or two either side, and then you can come back and play. With his injury, there was no template for him, so as a medical team and a strength conditioning team, we couldn't say, 'You will be back at this time.' From the very early days when he was in hospital, he told me he would play in April. While I knew that wasn't a possibility, at no point did I want to quash his optimism, because that's such a massive thing for someone in rehab – hope. A positive attitude makes a big difference with someone's recovery, and even when he didn't make his own April deadline, he was like, 'Okay, I'm going to play by May.' I was as optimistic as he was and became a believer six weeks into the process, because everything we had planned for, he was just far exceeding, so I just tried to make it as positive as I could. I think the worst thing you can do to an athlete is tell him or her, 'No, you can't.' Majak was so headstrong and determined to get back to a set point that I frequently said to him, 'Okay, if we can safely get you there by that time, we'll get you there.'

He's amazing. It's just incredible what he's done. Just to get back and play one game of football is amazing. He's unbelievable. I have a distinct memory of him in hospital and I was thinking, *This kid is not going to be able to walk properly*, so for him to actually play at senior AFL level is really amazing. He really defied the odds to survive, and he defied the odds to get back into the AFL. He's lucky that he has good genetics, but he also had to work incredibly hard for that comeback. He had to grind through some really painful gym sessions, and he had to live in an uncomfortable space for four to five months plus, where he didn't necessarily know that he was going to get the rewards at the end.

16

Thiär ku detem

Rory had just ordered from the menu of the restaurant we were in, Laksa King in Flemington, when his phone rang. He took it out of his pocket and glanced over at me before he said, 'Hi, Emily.'

Emily? I thought. My Emily? Why is she calling Rory?

'Oh shit!' Rory continued with urgency. He looked at me again and the expression on his face said it all. I grabbed my phone out of my pocket and saw that I had left it on silent and had missed a few calls and messages from her.

'Yep, okay. I'll get Maj to call you right away, don't worry,' Rory said, while making sure I heard him from across the table. Emily was already a week past her due date and I'd assured her I would have my phone handy at all times.

Before Hendrix's arrival in August 2019, I was back playing football in the VFL and felt great about where I was at in life. Although I'd had some hiccups along the way, with a few injuries, I had proven to myself and everyone that I was more than capable, both mentally and physically, to play at the elite level again. Before the end of the 2019 season, Scott Thompson announced his retirement, and without wanting to sound insensitive, I saw that as an opportunity for me to take back a key role in our defence the following year. Scooter was an absolute pillar of North Melbourne's defence for the best part of his 11-year career. He was always someone I looked up to and learnt a lot from as a defender. I had played alongside him and Robbie Tarrant for much of my breakout year in 2018 and had built a great relationship with him. So, while it was sad to see him hang up the boots, it also presented a good opportunity for me.

Although I didn't play in the senior AFL team that year, I was still part of the end-of-season celebrations. Our year officially ended on Saturday, 24 August, after the boys defeated Melbourne by five points in Hobart. Upon their arrival home that same night, the drinks started flowing and the week-long gatherings to mark the season that was began. By the time Thursday rolled around, and I had agreed to join my schoolmates at the Laksa King, I was already pretty stuffed, but I knew Emily's phone call to Rory meant that our baby was on the way.

I called Emily immediately and she told me she was going into labour, so I rushed home, which, thankfully, was only around the corner from the restaurant. Although I had been around many childbirths back in Sudan when I was little, men weren't ever allowed to be in the same room as the woman giving birth – even the father of the child – so I really wasn't sure what I was walking into. I had heard all the screaming and crying from my mum when she was giving birth to my younger siblings, but I had never seen what happened in that room. When my sister was born, I went into the room about an hour later, and there was still a mess everywhere and I nearly threw up. So, this time around, I was quite nervous and wasn't sure if I'd be any use to Emily given my weak stomach. I'd heard some good and bad stories along the way from other people whose partners or wives had given birth, and one thing that stuck in my mind was to try to be as attentive and comforting as possible. I did all sorts of stuff just to make Emily more comfortable. We had a large Swiss ball that she sat on to alleviate the stress on her body and back, I got her some drinking water and a heat pack, and I talked her through some breathing exercises. We went over our birth plan and called the midwife to freshen up on what we needed to do.

When it was clear the baby was on the way, we loaded up the car and went to the Royal Women's Hospital. As it turned out, if we'd had a choice, we couldn't have picked a worse night. We got there about eight o'clock and the place was packed. We were told they had 32 women there – some had already given birth and others were about to. Apparently, it was close to a hospital record. It meant we had to wait in the emergency area – and for a long time. Emily's labour began to intensify and she was screaming in pain. There wasn't much I could do, other than try to make her more comfortable and call on the nurses to help. When her water broke, I was freaking out inside, but I couldn't really do anything about it. I remember thinking,

Is this how it's supposed to be? I had imagined a much different scenario, but instead it looked like we'd be welcoming our baby into the world in a shitty little emergency room. We couldn't even get a bed; Emily was on a small trolley.

Emily's contractions increased, and one of the nurses told us it was time to find a bed upstairs in one of the birthing wards. Just when I thought the night had been dramatic enough, the obstetrician told us there was something wrong. Hendrix was close to coming out, but he was extremely lethargic and showing signs of fatigue. His heart-rate pattern had dipped, so the midwife placed a monitor on his head, called a fetal scalp electrode, which isolated his vital signs from Emily's and allowed them to monitor him more clearly. There were concerns that he wasn't getting enough oxygen, and it caused a few scary moments. Such was the feeling of concern in the room from the obstetrician and the midwife, we thought we might lose him. Another obstetrician was called in to help, and the urgency of their actions had me freaking out inside. I just had to focus on Emily and make sure she was coping.

At midnight, Hendrix's cries filled the room and he was delivered into Emily's arms. I watched everything and it was very traumatic, so to see him crying and moving his arms and legs was a massive relief. When I held him for the first time, I was overwhelmed with so many different emotions. I had come so far in my personal journey to be standing in that room with him. *Now I'm a father*, I thought, and I was already so in love. I was trying to compare him to me to see if we had the same features or anything.

I studied his little squished-up face and couldn't get over just how small he was. I was feeling a sense of relief and was really proud that I was now a dad and had the responsibly of looking after this little human. All the concerns I had harboured about being a father melted away as soon as I held him in my arms. I just stopped thinking about myself and was only concerned for him and his future. The fear of not being a good dad, and not being able to provide for him, was what had driven me to get my life back on track, and now that he was suddenly in my life, all I needed to worry about was making sure he was happy, loved, safe and that I would be a constant presence in his life.

Emily had done an amazing job, and she was understandably exhausted. She was being taught a lot of things that she'd never had to think about before, like how to breastfeed him and make sure he could latch onto her breast. There's no time to get used to things; the responsibility is yours straight away.

I rang my family and I told them the news. My dad was delighted and said, 'When I saw it was you calling, I knew straight away that Emily would have given birth.' He told me I was born around the same time at night as Hendrix, and that he couldn't wait to meet his new grandson.

When it was time to leave the hospital and head home, I was in charge of getting everything ready. I had a lot of stuff packed, like the pram, nappies and other items, but I had left the baby seat till last. It was the one thing that brought me unstuck – I had no idea how to clip it in. Looking back, it was quite funny, but at the time I was under the pump!

I was in the car for about half an hour, unable to figure out how to click the baby seat in properly. I'm just like, *I've had all this time to get it right, and I can't get it done!*

It was the most bizarre drive home. I was overly cautious and took it really slow on the road, because we had this precious cargo in the back. I couldn't stop looking at him in the rear-view mirror. When we pulled up at our house, my family was there waiting for us, and Dad pulled open the back door and scooped Hendrix up and took him inside. It was pretty special. I thought, *This is what it's all about. This is what I've been fighting for.* Hendrix's arrival put everything into perspective for me, and I think he did that for everyone close to us too. For those first few weeks at home, I saw just how many good people were in my life, and how many good friends genuinely cared about me, through their love of Hendrix and the support they offered.

I see my role as Hendrix's dad as someone who will help him be whatever he wants to be. I just want him to learn whatever he wants, and I'm always going to be there to support him. I'll teach him about good values and how important it is to work hard. I guess it sounds cliché, but if he does that, then a lot of things will just open up for him. I want him to have the same opportunities as I had and never want him to feel that he can't dream big and achieve great things.

17

Thiär ku dhorou

It sounded like paper tearing not once, but twice. Then came the first wave of intense pain. It was excruciating. I dropped the 60-kilogram dumbbells to the floor and cried out, 'Arrrggghhhhhhh!' The sound of the weights hitting the floor with force, coupled with my yelling, stopped everyone in the gym in their tracks. Shaun Atley was the first to rush over and help me.

'What happened?' he asked urgently.

'I think I've popped my shoulder or torn my pec!' I replied, still grimacing and clutching at my right shoulder to try to take some weight off the muscles and tendons. Our strength coach, Alex Moore, rushed to my side, and I told him that I thought I'd popped my shoulder.

'Tell me how you did it,' he directed me. I explained to Alex that I'd been doing a dumbbell chest press exercise, and I'd gone too deep with the movement on the way down, put too much strain on my right side and heard a few tearing or ripping sounds. He told me to go straight to the doctor's office. I made my way to the medical area, and I think I was in a bit of shock.

After my incident in December 2018, I had worked so hard to get my body and mind right for a return to footy. Just when I'd thought I was on the brink of a comeback in 2019, I had injured my hamstring in my third game of VFL and had been ruled out for the remainder of the season.

During the 2020 pre-season campaign, I was determined to train as hard as I possibly could to make a comeback in the AFL and complete what many people were calling a 'fairytale' recovery. I had left my hamstring issues from the previous season behind me and was feeling strong and confident in my body, so I was able to do a solid summer of training. I returned after Christmas still with a lot of work ahead of me to prove to our then head coach, Rhyce Shaw, and the other coaches that I was ready to play, but I felt I was in good shape for a possible return.

My form in the practice matches was fairly patchy early on. In the first game against the Bulldogs, I only had five possessions, but it was more about me getting back up to speed with the pace of the game than anything else. I dropped a few easy marks that I would normally take, but I still felt much better for the experience. It was like blowing out the cobwebs. The following game was against the Swans, and I fared a little better. Although I didn't fill up the statistics columns, I still felt that I was able to have a big impact on the game and helped us get the win. It was a big confidence booster for me, and I knew I needed a better showing to really push for a spot in the Round 1 side that was to take on St Kilda in a matter of weeks.

Like so many times in my life, curve balls were thrown my way. As my comeback edged ever closer, life started to become incredibly bleak for everyone with the COVID-19 pandemic sweeping the globe. Melbourne wasn't spared, and as we neared the commencement of the 2020 season, doubts were cast over the viability of sport around the country continuing. Following advice from medical professionals, the AFL decided to go ahead with the season's opening round but had to ban fans from attending.

Amid the gloomy backdrop, we forged ahead as a team and club, and prepared to kick off our season against the Saints. Rhyce told us all to block out the noise and conjecture regarding talk that the season would be postponed, and to go about our business as professionals. It was a case of it being 'all systems go' until we were told otherwise.

I was a mix of anxious and excited in the lead-up to the Sunday game, knowing that any day, I could be told that my dream and ambition to play in the AFL again had become a reality. When you're on the cusp of playing or breaking into the senior side, you become a little wary of the coach and his actions. At all times, you're anticipating he will pull you aside to say, 'You're in.' For me, that moment came before the weekly team meeting, where we break down the opposition, analysing what they're going to do against us and how we're going to combat their tactics and style of play. As we were heading into the theatrette at Arden Street, Rhyce pulled me into his office and asked for a 'quick chat'. My heart started pumping faster.

The look on his face gave me no indication as to which way the conversation was going to go, so I prepared myself for bad news.

'How are you feeling, mate?' Rhyce asked.

'I'm good. Ready to go,' I replied.

'It's been a long time coming, bud,' he continued. 'You've made some incredible gains since Christmas and we're gonna go with you this week. Well done, you deserve it.' As Rhyce delivered his message, he reached out and grabbed my shoulder and said, 'You've earned this, mate. Congratulations. What you've accomplished in getting this far, after what you've been through, is incredible.'

I was overwhelmed and pretty emotional, but kept my feelings contained, staying calm on the outside, and simply thanked him for having the faith in me and for giving me the chance to play again. We shook hands and had a little hug and then walked into the theatrette, where Rhyce confirmed the final team to the rest of the boys. He made specific mention of my inclusion in the 22, which was followed by an eruption of clapping and cheers from my teammates, coaches and the club staff.

After the opposition meeting, we trained, and then I called some of my family and loved ones to tell them the good news. Unfortunately, it was quickly followed by bad news, because that night, I didn't sleep well and felt under the weather. I knew I was coming down with something. With COVID-19 spreading, we'd been told to report any symptoms, no matter how insignificant they seemed, to the club doctor before coming into the club.

The next morning I called our doctor, Peter Baquie, and explained that I had mild symptoms of a cold, but I felt good enough to push through and participate in the main training session. To my disappointment, Pete ordered me to stay home, saying that under no circumstances was I permitted to come to the club, as there was a chance I could have COVID-19 and would spread it through the playing group and wider club. Rhyce told the media in an interview that day, 'It's just based on precaution. If he [Daw] came in with the same illness four months ago, he'd be training. He's got the sniffles, he doesn't seem too bad . . . Our docs have been fantastic in making sure we take all the right precautions. I've got no idea [if he will be tested for COVID-19]. I stay well away from that and let the professionals do their job.'

As it turned out, I didn't have any specific COVID-19 symptoms and therefore didn't qualify for a test, but the ramifications were still significant. Anyone with cold or flu-like symptoms, regardless of the type or severity, had to quarantine for a week away from the club and players, according to the AFL's COVID-19 rules. This meant I was unable to train for the whole week leading up to the Round 1 game, effectively ruling me out of contention to play. I couldn't believe that after all this time in rehab – almost a year and a half – a little head cold was going to stop me from returning. But it did. Showing little signs of improvement health-wise, I was told to continue staying home, and with each day that passed, I missed more crucial training sessions.

I watched the season opener against St Kilda on TV at home and felt extremely let down – I should have been out there. The boys pulled off a brave come-from-behind win over the Saints, despite being three men down on the bench due to injury. Just as the game finished, news started to circulate that the season was going to be postponed. It all happened so fast. One minute the boys were out there playing footy, and I was mentally preparing for Round 2, and then it was all called off. We received a message that evening from our head of football, Brady Rawlings, confirming the AFL had advised clubs that the season was to be put on hold, and that all players would be banned from going into their clubs from Monday until further notice. Text messages and phone calls from player to player followed, as we all tried to figure out what it meant for us. *Was there going to be a season at all? How long would we be in lockdown for? Would we be paid?* So many questions and so few answers.

The club opened the doors to our training facility for a short time on Monday and told all the players to come down, grab their personal belongings and empty out their lockers. Some of the boys also grabbed some gym equipment to use at home, not knowing how long we'd be locked out for. I grabbed as much as I could, including weights, barbells, dumbbells, medicine balls, training bands and an exercise bike – I was able to have a nice little gym set-up in the garage, but it wasn't anywhere near what I was used to. Days later, we all started to receive individual training programs to ensure we maintained our fitness and strength. My program involved a lot of running, some weights and the option to partner up with a team-mate who lived close by and complete some kicking and skills drills. That person was Sam Durdin. Upon receiving the program, I knew things were about to get even more complicated.

I separated from Emily in March, and we were living apart. I was looking after Hendy about three times a week, and my sister, Angelina, would come over to help out so I could train in the mornings. I'd do my running and come back to make sure Hendy was fed and had his nappy changed, and then I'd do my weights and attend some online team meetings – of which there were many!

Early on, I admit I was a bit stubborn and didn't seek much help from anyone, including my mum and dad. I thought I could do it all by myself. But in reality, when I had Hendy on my own, it was hard to really do anything productive. I couldn't just put him down and go and make myself a sandwich or cup of tea, or do some housework, or train – I couldn't really get away. Although he wasn't crawling yet, he could drag himself around on his tummy, and my house wasn't childproof. If I took my eyes off him, I'd find him pulling on chairs, opening the oven door or coming close to bumping his head on the edges of the coffee table, dining table or bed. I also wasn't getting the rest I needed, and as an AFL player, rest is critical for recovery from games and heavy training loads. Hendy would often wake up at midnight and not settle again until 3 a.m., and I would have to stay up with him. Being exhausted would then reduce my ability to train and attend the various team meetings we had online.

It was all a massive learning experience, because my life had gone from Emily and I doing everything together – sharing the duties of looking after Hendy and keeping the house neat and tidy – to us both having to do it alone on our days with him. I know that it was the same for Emily, but she was a lot smarter than me and had moved in with her mum. I'm not taking anything away from how difficult it was for her too, and I give her credit for accepting some help.

It came to a point that I had to reach out to my family for help too. At that stage, Hendy didn't have much of a relationship with my parents, purely because they lived so far away and it was hard to coordinate visits. If I took him over for a visit, and I walked out of the room to go to the kitchen, Hendy would cry until I returned. I had been wanting to improve their bond – so this was the perfect opportunity.

My choices were either to pick Hendy up from Emily's and take him to Mum and Dad's, which was more than an hour's drive each way, or suck it up and look after him by myself. In the end, I settled on doing this extra driving, and completing training and attending meetings in between. I spoke to our club's psychologist, Stephen Rendall, to ask what I could do to help build a better relationship between Hendy and my parents, and he said facial recognition was a key factor. Steve explained to me that Hendy was most likely thinking that I was going to leave him and not come back.

He was feeling like, *My dad does everything for me and if he leaves, what am I going to do?* Steve suggested I needed to build up a level of trust over time and make Hendrix realise that I would always return, and that everything would be okay. It was a case of some short-term pain for long-term gain, in that I needed to leave him alone with my parents, let him cry his heart out, and then come back to get him and take him home. Gradually over time, he would realise that I'd always come back. It was also up to Mum and Dad to distract him and entertain him when I left, so that he didn't miss me so much. Being a new parent, no one tells you this sort of stuff. You have to figure it all out and learn as you go. It's not easy.

Mum and Dad, and all my brothers and sisters for that matter, were so supportive and helpful. Everyone was willing to give me a chop-out with Hendy and help me not only look after him, but also give me the time and ability to focus on my career. Now, Hendy loves my dad – I think he can see the similarities between me and him – and he absolutely adores my mum. It makes me so happy to see that they have such a tight bond with him, and I know that I can leave him with them and he'll be happy, safe and loved. It also helps that he was the first grandson in the family – before Hendy there were four granddaughters.

Seeing their relationship flourish has also allowed me to see a different side to my parents, as grandparents. I would describe my dad as very proper; he's always dressed in slacks, a tucked-in shirt and polished shoes.

You rarely see him in tracksuit pants, but when Hendy comes around, he'll get down on the floor and play with him, roll around laughing and make silly noises. I've never seen him do that before. It's such a satisfying feeling to see that unfold. I get so much joy out of seeing them all together, and they get just as much joy out of spending time with him too.

With a new arrangement in place for Hendy, I was able to attack my training and preparation with a renewed energy and drive. Being alone for training was an unusual environment, and our team drew inspiration from track athletes who've always had to train alone. Our football program relied on self-motivation, a level of trust that each player would do the right thing and, most importantly, hard work. There was a lot of running and not a lot of kicking or skills work that could be done. I'll admit there were some tough sessions in the program, and some days where I didn't feel great or in the mood to go as hard as I would have if I'd been training with my teammates. It's much harder to train alone; you tend not to go as hard, because you have no one to compare yourself to. For example, if you are running with someone, it's like a race, and you can see how hard you are working depending on whether you're in the lead or behind.

After several weeks, Victoria started to get a better handle on the COVID-19 situation, and we were finally allowed to come back to the club, but with some heavy restrictions in place about what we were allowed to do and who we were allowed to train with. In the early stages, we could train in groups of seven with one coach only, which made it really hard to work on things like our game plan. We had to have our temperatures taken upon entry to the facility and were required to fill out a daily health survey. We were tested for COVID-19 twice weekly and all staff had to be tested one to two times per week as determined by the AFL.

All players and staff were required to complete a mental-health screening with our psychologist and complete a risk assessment – this included details about each person's living arrangements to determine if they were at risk of contracting the virus from someone else at home. A letter from the AFL said:

> If 'high risks' in your living arrangements are identified, and if all other alternatives have been fully investigated and are deemed impossible, this may include the player or staff being asked to live somewhere else for a temporary period. This option will be avoided if at all possible. If a change to living arrangements is required, players will not be responsible for any costs, and the club and the AFL will need to consult the AFLPA before making any decisions or changes.

Even access to our club building was severely restricted. Entry and exit was via one set of doors only and player arrival times were provided for each day as part of the daily schedule. Each area and room in the building had capacity limits, which were clearly marked at each entry point.

Players and staff weren't allowed to complete any form of exercise prior to attending the facility, and we had to shower, dress ready for training and attend the club directly from home. Day-to-day living also had to be altered for anyone returning to work at the club. We were told we had to avoid contact with any individual who was not in the club or our household, and like the rest of the state, we could only leave home for essential reasons, set by the state government.

We were specifically prohibited from doing activities including surfing, golf, fishing or boating; allowing social visitors into our home (including our garage or yard), or going to a friend's house for a meal; sitting down in a café for a meal or coffee; going for a picnic in the park; taking kids to a playground; going to work at another job outside football; going to university in person; and doing volunteering or community work.

On the first day of our return to training, I misread the groupings and thought I had to be at the club at 8.30 a.m. sharp. I lined up outside the door with some other players and waited to be called in for our temperature test. Ben Brown, Mason Wood and Jack Mahony were ahead of me, which I thought was strange, because they were all forwards and I was a defender. I got to the front of the line and walked up to our second club doctor, Bianca Scotney, and had my temperature taken. Then someone yelled out, 'Maj! What are you doing here? You're not due for another four hours!' I was so confused and asked to see a training schedule. I scanned the training groupings, found my name and saw that I was in fact early – I was supposed to have arrived at 12.30 p.m.! Normally I would have just hung around the club until our training group started, but under the new protocols, I wasn't allowed and was sent back home. It wasn't a great start, but it was a lot better than being late.

After a few weeks under the new rules, we all got used to training in small groups and still had some solid sessions. The AFL allowed one day a week of contact training, which meant we could conduct some match simulation sessions. The first match sim was hard work. No one was quite match-fit just yet, and I struggled badly. I was defending against guys like Nick Larkey and Tristan Xerri – two young forwards with plenty of talent – and also had big ruckman Tom Campbell rotating through me. While 'Larks' and 'X' were highly skilled and strong, I usually had their measure, but on this day, the tables turned and they towelled me up big time. I had a shocker and just couldn't get into the game. I was on the weaker team, and the ball was being bombed into my area frequently, with precision. Larks and X were on the end of several kicks and booted a heap of goals between them. It didn't look good for me at all.

I left the track feeling flat and dejected. I thought to myself, *Am I that far off it?* and started doubting whether I had worked hard enough on my home training program. I was pretty pissed off with myself during lunch and then had to do my weights program in the afternoon. When I walked into the gym, I knew lifting heavy was a good way to take out some of my disappointment and frustration.

One of the exercises I was scheduled to do was a dumb-bell chest press. For those who don't know, for this exercise you lie on a bench on your back and push a dumbbell in each hand from your chest up into the air until your arms completely straighten, then you slowly lower the dumbbells down to your chest. These two movements are called a 'rep-etition', or 'rep', and we do eight to ten reps to make up a 'set', then three to four sets of any one exercise. I loaded up the dumbbells with 60 kilograms on each side, which is fairly heavy for me, sat on the bench and heaved them onto my knees, lay back and started. It was in the middle of my third set that I heard the tearing of my right pectoral mus-cle and felt the pain.

I now know the pec injury occurred because I hadn't lifted weights that heavy for a long time, due to the COVID-19 lockdown period. I had been too arrogant or confident, trying to lift too much too early. It was a weight I had lifted in the past; and, in fact, I had even done a few reps at 70 kilograms, but I clearly had a lack of condition-ing leading into this particular gym session. My maximum bench press was 162 kilograms, and I'm glad I didn't try to take my anger out on that exercise, because it could have been a much worse injury. Strength coach Alex Moore felt guilty, because he was in the gym supervising, but it wasn't his fault. I'm responsible, not him, for loading up the weights and pushing myself way too hard. I knew what I was doing and had simply bitten off more than I could chew.

I walked to the doctor's office and told Peter Baquie what had happened. I tried to take my top off but could barely lift my arm to get it over my head. Pete helped me manoeuvre it off, and then he examined my chest and saw how my right pec had caved in where the tear had occurred. It looked slightly deformed. Pete was extremely worried, as he knew all too well that this injury could spell the end of my career. Being someone who had been there for me after my fall, he knew how important getting back and playing in the AFL was to me. In fact, I would say it wasn't just my goal, it was a goal shared by everyone who had helped me get back to full fitness. My pec started to swell up pretty bad, and the pain was increasing as time wore on. We applied some ice to the area to reduce the inflammation and pain while Pete called a radiologist to arrange some urgent scans.

Our head physiotherapist, Matt Turnbull, came over and did some tests with me to assess the damage. He told me it wasn't looking good. I could hear Pete and Matt talking, and the word 'surgery' was being mentioned a lot. I started to realise that my career was likely over. I felt overwhelmed, with mounting pressure weighing down on me. I had recently split up with Emily, I had Hendrix to raise, and I had no idea what I'd do for a job without footy. I was thinking the worst and it got to me. I started crying. Rhyce Shaw must have heard the news about my gym mishap, and he came down to the doctor's office and comforted me. He put his hand on my left shoulder and told me not to get caught up thinking about a 'worst case' scenario just yet. He said, 'Let's get the scan done and get all the answers before we jump to any conclusions. Only then can we make a decision on the best course of treatment for you.' Rhyce's words resonated with me, and I forced myself to lift up my chin and start thinking more positively. He was 100 per cent right; there was no use worrying until we knew how bad the damage in there actually was.

My scans showed some torn tendons had retracted underneath the pectoral muscle, meaning they'd need to be dragged out and reattached through a surgical procedure. Thankfully, some of the other tendons were still intact. Dozens of conversations with the doctors and physios followed, then we sought the opinion of some specialists. In the end we were given two options: have surgery to repair the damage or allow the injury to heal naturally. Surgery would have meant the season – and likely career – was over for me, due to an 8–12 week rehabilitation period. After my hip and pelvis injuries from the fall, I couldn't afford to become deconditioned and not have any load bearing through my bones, as it would simply take too long for me to get back into shape. The non-surgery option, on the other hand, would mean only three to four weeks of rehab and the chance to get back for some games before the year was over.

I had to consider the functionality of my arm, too, because a big part of my game is marking and spoiling the ball – if I was unable to fully extend my right arm, it would severely impact my effectiveness on the field by taking away one of my main strengths. One specialist was keen to operate, and I initially agreed with him. I didn't want to have any lingering issues post-football and felt it was best to fix it right away – even if it meant I'd have to hang up my boots. Normally in this situation, the club would direct a player on what to do, but my situation was different. I was 29, out of contract at the end of the season, and hadn't played for two years – so the decision was mine as to which path to take, knowing that one would likely be the end of football for me. It felt really uncomfortable having to make that choice, but the club wanted me to be in complete control of my future.

I spoke to Rhyce and our head of football, Brady Rawlings, and told them I was leaning towards surgery. I could tell by the looks on their faces that they didn't agree with me at all. Doubts crept in, so I asked more questions and started to sway back the other way. After a lot of deliberating, I decided not to have surgery. Ever since the rehab from my injured hips and pelvis, I've vowed to always attack everything with conviction and determination. I knew that if I could put up with the pain in my shoulder and pec, I could push hard in rehab and get back quicker than the specialist's timeframe. A few days after the injury, I went to the gym and did a push-up to show everyone that I was committed to playing again. Alex Moore took me aside and said, 'We can do this, but it's gonna be hard. It won't be comfortable but I'll get you through.' He was right; rehab was painful but bearable. We had to reactivate the muscles and get the pec functioning again. I just had to trust Alex and do whatever he told me to do, even if it didn't feel quite right.

Following the theme of the year so far, we got word from the AFLPA that the AFL was making plans to relocate

some teams to other states, because the COVID-19 situation had flared up again, particularly in Victoria. There was
a chance that all ten Victorian teams would have to flee
the state so that the competition could resume. The league
feared if we were stuck in Victoria, no games with teams
from other states would be played due to government border restrictions and lockdown laws. Everyone was briefed
on the possibility of us moving interstate for a period that
was likely to be about 32 days, and we were told that we
didn't have to go if it wasn't viable. The AFL, the AFLPA
and the club were very clear that they understood every
player had different situations and responsibilities to consider, and it was not a 'one size fits all' approach.

I had a big decision to make, and everything revolved
around Hendy: do I leave him and miss out on watching
him grow up? Do I run the risk of missing his first birthday,
which was only months away? Or do I have an obligation
to go interstate, resurrect my football career and do everything I can to get another contract, so I can ensure he has
what he needs in the future? I was torn. Before I could
even think about leaving, I chatted to Emily to see if she
could manage things on her own. Emily was fantastic and
told me she'd support me either way, which took a huge
amount of pressure off me. With her blessing, I decided the
best thing to do was to go on the trip and give it a go. If it
didn't work out for me or Emily within the first few weeks,
I would just pull the pin and come home. I figured I'd do
my best to force my way into the team, but leave the hub
if it became obvious that I was being overlooked for a spot

in favour of younger players. It was the best outcome and enabled me to give my dream of pulling on the boots again another shot.

I thought back to my childhood in Sudan, Egypt and even in Melbourne, and thought about the choices my dad had constantly had to make. A family man at heart, he always wanted to be with us, but on so many occasions, he had to leave Mum one-out to look after us, so he could work and bring in money. That meant him leaving us in Egypt for many months, and when we came to Melbourne, he'd often have to fly back to Sudan for weeks or months on end. When Dad wasn't around, other family members, like my older brothers, stepped up to help Mum out. I knew I could call on my family to help me out this time too.

With no contract to lean on for the following year, or any idea about what line of work I'd be able to undertake without football, I decided it was best to stick to what I knew and did best – football. I told myself that it was in Hendy's best interests to have his dad doing what he loved for as long as he could. In the long run, me playing footy for as long as possible would serve our family best.

On Monday, 6 July 2020, I said goodbye to Hendy and headed to the club in North Melbourne with my bags packed for the next month. We bused to the airport and flew out to the Gold Coast, where 'hub' life began.

In the early weeks of being in our Queensland hub, I felt like I was in the 'football wilderness' or limbo, where players who can't seem to break into the senior side find themselves – a place where you don't know if you are close to getting a game or not. Add to that the fact I was away from my family and loved ones, and the frustration of it all started to get to me. I was still battling to come to terms with my decision to chase being an AFL footballer over being physically present in Hendy's daily life. He was ten and a half months old when I left for Queensland, and I knew he'd likely be celebrating his first birthday without me. Although we were initially told that our stay in the northern state would only be 32 days long, within a week of being there, the AFL advised that we'd have to stay for 60-plus days, due to the worsening COVID-19 situation in Victoria.

It was a massive blow, and the unexpected news sent shockwaves through our club and all the other Victorian clubs that had abandoned their home state to keep the competition going. I don't mean to sound like a sook, but we'd agreed to go Queensland for a month, and then the goalposts were shifted and we had no say in it at all. Everyone had a different situation to consider, whether that be kids, family or even pets that they had left behind on the understanding they'd be back in four weeks, so to have the length of time effectively doubled was significant.

For me, it meant my hopes of being back in time for Hendy's birthday were all but dashed. I again had to weigh up my options: if I wasn't close to getting a game, I felt the right thing to do would be to leave the hub and ensure I was back for his birthday. However, if I was close to getting back into the senior side or if my selection was imminent, then I would stick it out. The only person who had the answers I was looking for was the coach.

I asked Rhyce for a catch-up, and he invited me to have a chat one night after dinner at our hotel. We met up the back of the dining area, and I told him what was on my mind. 'I need some honest feedback about how I'm going and whether I'm close to getting a game,' I stated.

Always honest and upfront, Rhyce pulled no punches and hit me squarely between the eyes. 'We can't trust you out there yet,' he declared. 'We just don't think you're fit enough to give us what we need down back. We think it's best if you train with the forwards from now on, as that's your best chance of earning a spot in the side. We can use you in front of goals and in the ruck.'

Although it was hard to hear that I'd be going back to play as a forward and ruck, at least I had something I could work on with my forward craft, fitness and running capacity. I immediately sought out our head of strength and conditioning, Jona Segal, and asked him to help me somehow improve my aerobic conditioning. Rhyce telling me to train as a forward wasn't ideal, as I'd hoped to be recognised as a key defender for the rest of my career. Players who get swung from one end of the ground to the other, also known as 'swingmen', never seem to get the same recognition as those who stay in one position throughout their careers.

As I've mentioned earlier, I really felt like I was best suited to the role of a key defender and had already proved that I could be one of the best backmen in the competition. Unfortunately, I had no grounds to argue and simply had to do whatever the team needed, which was to turn myself back into a forward. With Robbie Tarrant and Josh Walker playing some great football for us in defence, there wasn't a spot for me. At the other end, our leading goal-kicker for the past four seasons, Ben Brown, was struggling for form and had only managed a handful of goals, while our next key forward, Nick Larkey, was out with an injured foot. The coaches needed to shake things up and were looking at swinging Josh Walker forward or using me instead.

I kept training as hard as I could, but it was a difficult time. As the weeks went by, I wasn't even named as an emergency player on the team list. Despite Ben Brown's continuing struggles, the coaches persisted with him, hoping he'd turn the tide and bag a few goals. I played in a few practice matches and performed pretty well but was still being overlooked. To keep going like that and not be rewarded – or feel like you're on the cusp of being rewarded – makes it hard to keep the fire burning inside. Add to that a year and a half of rehab, and I was mentally exhausted.

Already at my wits' end and considering leaving the hub, I received some alarming news from Emily. Seven of my family members, who had all had recent contact with Hendy, had tested positive for COVID-19. My mum, sisters Angelina, Sarah and Mary, little brother Ajak, brother-in-law Emmanuel and niece Awur had all contracted the virus. Emily called me on her way to take Hendrix to a clinic to be tested. I was beside myself. I was told Emmanuel, who is married to my sister Teresa, and who works in a factory for a packaging company, had unknowingly brought the virus into Mum and Dad's home, because my parents were also helping him and Teresa out with some babysitting. Somehow my dad and Teresa avoided the virus.

I felt helpless as there was absolutely nothing I could do from the Gold Coast to help out. I considered asking the club to get me on the next flight home, but Emily told me to wait until we got Hendy's test result back before making any rushed decisions. At that stage, my biggest concern was Hendy's health, and I couldn't care less about my football career.

The next day, Emily called and told me Hendy's result was negative, but he'd had to have another test in 14 days to ensure he was clear of the virus. I was so relieved but still felt bad for my other family members who had tested positive. I spoke to Teresa, who was actually pregnant at the time, and was reassured that they were all asymptomatic and not sick at all. It was just another bump in the road for me to get over.

Rounds 6 and 7 came and went, and I still hadn't had a sniff. Ben Brown was still battling to hit the scoreboard and had only eight goals to his name after Round 8. As a team, we weren't going well, and the calls for team changes were coming from all corners of the media and our fan base. We were on a six-game losing streak and had only won two games for the year, those being back in Rounds 1 and 2.

Despite training hard, performing well and seeking out the coach for some clarity, I was really no closer to knowing whether I was on the right track. Again, I considered going home early. The last thing I wanted to do was waste spending precious time with Hendy on something that was never going to happen. I've always been someone who could take honest feedback and could have copped it if Rhyce had just told me that they wanted to play others ahead of me. In the back of my mind, I knew I had to play seven games to trigger a contract extension, and we only had nine games remaining in the season if we weren't going to make the finals. It meant the window was closing on my football future, and fast.

REFLECTIONS

Shaun Atley

My teammate Shaun Atley thought I would have to spend a fair bit of time away from football after he witnessed me tear my pectoral muscle.

I remember him getting through the first set of three pretty easily during the session. He was doing the heaviest weights available, which wasn't unusual for Maj. It was during his second set that a group of us who were in the gym at the time heard him scream. It wasn't a yell, like you often hear when someone lifts heavy and is using all their power and strength to get weights up, it was more of a scream. We looked at each other and thought, *Something bad has just happened*, and rushed over to see if he was okay.

When I asked what he'd done, he calmly said, 'I've just done my pec,' and walked off towards the medical area where the docs and physios work. His pec looked very deformed, like it had caved in. Usually, as we all know, Maj has perfectly rounded pec muscles, but this one was now sagging down a fair bit. You knew just by looking at it that he'd done some serious damage and it wasn't good at all. I thought it could have been career over for him, as did a few other people at the club.

18

Thiär ku bët

My usually structured football schedule had been anything but in 2020, and the random nature of things was putting extra pressure on Emily back home in Melbourne. The club's demands on players are already onerous, and as bad as it sounds, families and loved ones have to take somewhat of a back seat when the football pre-season and season are in full swing. We can spend up to eight hours a day training most days of the week, as well as attending club appearances, conducting football clinics, going to community camps, fulfilling sponsor requirements, and attending hundreds of team and individual meetings. When we travel for games, we can be away for up to four days, and our scheduled one day off a week is never the same day each week.

With COVID-19 throwing a spanner in the works, requiring the club to move to Queensland, Emily sought to clear up our separation arrangement through a mediator. We'd tried to sort things out on our own, but she was keen on using a third party to resolve any differences we still had. An online mediation session was booked in, but I later learnt it clashed with our main team meeting ahead of our Round 9 game against Adelaide. I spoke to Rhyce, and he told me to sort out my private business and he'd brief me later on the team meeting. I'd had my half-yearly review with the coaches the day before, and no one had foreshadowed me getting a game anytime soon, so I wasn't too worried that I'd be jeopardising my chances of being selected. If anything, I felt even further away from a comeback. I walked away from that mid-season review extremely flat and knew I would likely have several more weeks on the outer, trying to fight my way back into the team.

To my surprise, the mediation session was very straight-forward, and Emily and I were on the same page with much of what was discussed. She just wanted some reas-surances around custody of Hendy and security in terms of child support, which I was able to provide without any problems. With that all squared away, I raced off to rejoin the team for main skills at an oval in Maroochydore. At the start of each main training session, we all form a circle and have a quick chat about what we want to get out of the day. We called that ritual 'Mob', which is the collective noun for a group of Kangaroos.

Rhyce stepped forward from the circle to address the group and declared that Ben Jacobs would be taking part in his first skills session for some time, after battling with concussion-like symptoms from head knocks and other issues way back in 2018. That news was met with applause and cheers from all the players and staff. I saw that our media team was filming and thought they were there to capture that moment, but I was wrong.

Our captain, Jack Ziebell, took centre stage and said he had some more news to share with everyone. 'Today, I'm fortunate enough to present this to everyone. One of our own has been through a pretty substantial period in his life, no doubt. But we've all been a part of the journey,' he announced. 'It's been 706 days since he last played AFL football. We've seen his journey; we've seen how much work he's done to get back to this point. It's been an incredible journey, and this feat that he's going to achieve this weekend is going to be one of the great stories in AFL footy.' He paused and looked right at me and continued, 'Join with me in congratulating the big fella!' Another eruption of applause and cheers broke out, and I was swarmed by my teammates.

The day I had been dreaming of for so long had finally come. The boys were jumping all over me, hugging me, rubbing my head, patting me on the back and celebrating the occasion wildly. They too had experienced my every hiccup, and every time I had been knocked down, they had all helped me get back up again. I couldn't have done it without them, and to celebrate with them in that way was special. I was so overwhelmed with emotion and pure joy.

After all the excitement, the realisation hit me that I still needed to get through the session unscathed. The last thing I needed was to injure myself at training and have my return to the AFL put on hold yet again. But I couldn't go easy on the track either and knew that I had to train hard and put myself through some more physical punishment. I knew in myself that I had done all the work to get my body right and to the point of being able to compete for two hours in one of the toughest and most demanding sports in the world. If I held back at training, I would have lingering doubts in the back of my mind. I needed to test myself out and prove once again what my body was capable of. My confidence in my body and what I was able to do was rewarded during training, and I got through with no issues whatsoever. In fact, I trained better than I had in a long while.

After the session, I sat down with our media team to record an interview, and I opened up a fair bit on what it meant to me to be selected after spending so long on the sidelines. I told our media boss and the co-writer of this book, Heath O'Loughlin, who interviewed me, that it had been a testing few years for my character and resilience. My achievement showed how I could bounce back from setbacks. I also paid tribute to all those who had helped me along the way. 'It's the ultimate reward for my hard work personally, and with my mental-health battle,' I told him. 'I realised when all the boys got around me that I couldn't have done it myself. There's so many people involved. The footy club, my family, the doctors, my psychs, S&C [strength and conditioning] staff, and having the backing of Shawry [Rhyce Shaw] is huge. Shawry didn't really give me any idea the last few days, but it was the best way to be able to have that really organic moment with my teammates.

It was pretty special having someone like Ziebs telling me in front of the group that I was going to play. He's been there with me the whole time. There were times when I wondered when my moment was going to come. The work I've done with the psychiatrists was to not try to take on too much. I just had to take each day as it comes. Who would have thought that I'd be making my return up here and not in front of my family? But when I set my goals of making my return to AFL footy, it didn't matter where and when it was going to happen. I can't wait to get out there and repay the club for what they've done for me. Giving me a contract last year, not knowing whether I was going to play or not, was huge.' I also realised that I would be playing for the first time since becoming a father and said, 'It's amazing. I love my little man, I'm so proud of him. He's growing each day. He's starting to say "Dadda" and that sort of stuff. Luckily the game is in the afternoon and he can see me on telly. I love being a dad to Hendrix.'

By the time I got back to my room and looked at my phone, I saw dozens of missed calls and hundreds of congratulatory text messages. I didn't even have the opportunity to call my parents before the news was circulated in the media and they found out that I was playing – but that's fine, it's the way things are these days with social media and the like. I eventually got to talk to them, and they were so thrilled for me.

Despite all the carry-on and messages of support I received, I didn't really get a chance to reflect on the significance of the occasion and what it meant to other people.

I made a concerted effort not to buy into the hype too much, realising I had a game to play and a job to do. I didn't want to just go out there on game day and be mediocre – I wanted to show the footy world that I had a lot of time left at this level. The other side of it was the emotional toll it would have taken. If I got too absorbed in the excitement and celebration, it would have worn me out to the point where I wouldn't have had the energy or mental capacity to play.

I had learnt from previous experiences that I had to play things down and not get too wrapped up in small wins, for my mental wellbeing and peace of mind. When I had hit small milestones in my recovery from my hip and pelvis injuries, I had always kept my eye on the bigger picture and focused on the hard work still to come. I had also learnt that if I tried to respond to every phone call or text message from those who reached out to me to wish me well, I would be too exhausted to do anything else.

So, with another comeback box ticked and hundreds of people sending me messages of congratulations for being selected in the North side, I had to put my virtual blinkers on and narrow my focus. I had to trust that all those people awaiting a response from me would know I had received their messages and was thankful for them. It's not that I want to disappoint people, I've just learnt that it's okay if people feel disappointed, and that you just can't please everyone all the time.

In this case, I needed to come to terms with the fact that I was playing, rest up and do all my preparation for the game, including getting through the final training session of the week. I had to be selective with who I put my energy into – those people being Hendrix, my family members and my teammates. When I had the opportunity to duck off and spend some time alone, I'd leave the phone in my room and escape from it all.

After the final training session of the week, we had a two-hour bus ride from our accommodation in Maroochydore down to the Gold Coast. It was the perfect time for me, on the day before the game, as I was afforded some more alone time and just sat back and enjoyed the ride. Although I was relaxed and feeling good about the game, I didn't sleep a wink that night. The excitement was just too much for me to handle. It had been a massive build-up, and I'd been so close to playing so many times and it just hadn't happened. I couldn't believe it was going to finally happen tomorrow.

In truth, playing is the easiest thing about footy – you just go out and play. The hardest part of becoming a footballer again had been teaching my body and mind how to play again and doing all the training and education. It was a massive tick for my mental health, because me getting back onto the football ground was me getting back to the best version of myself, and getting back to what I had done best before everything unravelled back in 2018.

A lot of people had doubted whether I'd make it back to football, even my mum and dad. They weren't actually concerned with me getting back to playing football – their only expectations for me were living my life to the fullest, being happy, being a great father to Hendrix and even doing something as simple as being able to walk again. I was the only one who expected I would come back and play footy. And the reason for that? Because it was proving to myself and other people that my life didn't have to stop or go backwards because of what had happened, that you can rebuild your body and mind and pick up where you left off. Yeah, rehab had been incredibly hard, but playing again, for me, would be like a massive 'fuck you!' to my mental-health battles. We all know how low I was and what had become of my life, so I wanted to rediscover the best version of Majak Daw and prove that mental health is a battle people can conquer.

Not many people talk about suicide, so let's be clear again: I tried to kill myself. It isn't easy for me to write, say or talk about that. But I have many clear memories of the time I was lying in that hospital bed in pain – broken both mentally and physically – and of all the people who came to visit me and how much what I'd done had affected them. I'll cherish the power of their concerns, care and love for the rest of my life – it will never go away. The genuine hurt in people's hearts gave me the motivation to get back and be the best version of myself.

I know so many other families have been through similar situations, but their loved ones weren't as lucky as I was to have survived. I've learnt to accept what happened, and I have an opportunity to show that my suicide attempt doesn't have to define me forever, hold me back or keep its grip on me. If others want to take bits and pieces out of what I've achieved or done along the way and draw some level of inspiration from that, then I think it's great and encourage it.

And if I hadn't made it back to playing football again? Yeah, I think I would have been bitterly disappointed, but I would have known deep down that I'd left nothing on the table. There were so many hurdles along the way and I had leapt over most of them. But if that last one had been unattainable for me to get over, then I think I would have been at peace with that, knowing I'd given my all. I would have played practice matches, VFL games and AFL pre-season games, just not actual games for premiership points – so it would have been a pretty good effort regardless.

When we arrived at Metricon Stadium on the Gold Coast, I walked past the property room and saw the property steward, Carly Fox, laying out my jumper with the No. 1 on the back. The manufacturer's tag was still attached, and it looked so fresh and vibrant because it hadn't been worn yet. I went over and grabbed it, feeling a rush of energy course through my veins. I know it sounds cliché, but you have to earn the right to pull on the North Melbourne jumper, and I, of all people, felt I had done that over the past 18 months or so. I think some players take wearing the jumper for granted, but it would be impossible for me to do that given what I had been through to get to this stage.

The vibe in the rooms was electric, and I tried to absorb every moment as the clock ticked down to the first bounce of the ball. Like riding a bike, I slipped back into my pre-game routine from 2018 with ease. I got my ankles strapped, had some physio treatment and sat in the team meeting.

Rhyce's pre-game speech, about an hour and a half out from the game, didn't mention my comeback at all, which was great. I didn't want to get too overwhelmed or fired up that far out from the game. Rhyce focused on a cycling documentary we'd all watched together, which told the story of a young rider, Esteban Chaves, who overcame many challenges to win a race for his team through sheer grit, determination and selflessness. Rhyce was trying to instil in us that out there on the field that afternoon, mistakes would be made, but if each individual played his role and went when it was his turn to go, then we would be successful and win the contest.

We were playing the winless Adelaide Crows – the worst performing team in the AFL that year. However, we weren't going that well either, having only won two games out of the eight we'd played so far. Most punters thought we'd win, but the Crows had played some good football and only narrowly lost to Essendon the week before. We knew we'd have to be at our best to beat them.

Before every game, we have a tradition at North Melbourne – all the players go into the locker room and stand in a circle, shirtless, and we all pull on our jumpers together. On this occasion our acting captain, Robbie Tarrant, came forward to rev us all up and make a pre-game speech. He congratulated Shaun Higgins for playing 100 games for the club and then looked over at me. 'Maj. We all love ya, mate,' he said. 'It's an amazing effort, we're really proud of ya. Let's get out there and let's give him a chance. We've gotta get the ball going forward.' There was some clapping and words of encouragement for me from the other boys as we all pulled on our jumpers together. It was such a great feeling to pull mine on again – some 706 days since the last time I had worn it in an AFL game.

Although only a small crowd was allowed in to watch the game, because of COVID-19 restrictions, I was still full of nerves and excitement as we ran out onto the ground. Despite it being my first game back for some time, the Crows did me no favours, playing two-time All-Australian defender Daniel Talia on me. I managed to get my hands on the ball twice in the first quarter for two kicks, and another three times in the second quarter. The pace of the game was challenging, and I really had to suck in some deep breaths to get from contest to contest. No matter how hard you train in the lead-up to any match, nothing can quite prepare you for the speed, explosiveness and physical output required.

In the fourth quarter, we were leading by about 40 points, and I had my first opportunity to kick a goal. I had worked myself into the game and was having an impact around the ground and in the ruck, but I really wanted to hit the scoreboard to make it a fairytale return. My chance came with about 15 minutes left, when Shaun Atley broke free from congestion just outside our defensive 50. He sprinted forward with the ball and took a bounce. I had led up towards him then doubled back towards goal. Shaun read my mind and kicked the ball over the back of my opponent, Talia, and safely into my hands for a mark about 30 metres out from goal on a slight angle. Shaun Higgins yelled out to me, 'Maj! You've kicked goals like this more than a hundred times!

You know what to do, mate . . . just back your routine in and kick through the ball.'

I tried to block out all the noise and the significance of the moment and walked back towards the 50-metre line to begin my run-up. I felt quite relaxed and confident. I took a deep breath and started my approach. After a few steps, I increased my pace, and when I felt the time was right, I dropped the ball onto my right boot and swung my leg through. The ball came off my foot perfectly. I didn't even have to finish watching the ball sail through the middle of the goalposts – I just knew it was going through. I clenched both fists and yelled, 'Yeahhhhhhhh!' as my teammates came running towards me from every part of the ground to celebrate. There were hugs, kisses, pats on the head – you name it, I copped it from the boys. It was a very special moment, probably the best moment of my career.

We won the game comfortably and I was humbled by the messages of support I received from the Crows as we shook hands. I did an on-ground interview with Ben Dixon from Fox Footy and spoke about what had unfolded. 'It's been two years since I played and there's no better feel-ing than winning, but I think over the past few years, the battles I've gone through, it's worth it, winning with your teammates, my family at home watching,' I told him. 'I haven't been able to do it by myself, there's been so many people involved, the footy club has been amazing, the wider public, even when I was in hospital, the hospital staff there they looked after me. I was pretty strong early on and had the support of the club, the club doctors, the psychs who

have worked with me, the strength and conditioning staff –
I told them, "This is what I want to do, I want to come
back and play," so they backed me in and they helped me
get here. It was tough at stages, a few injuries here and
there, hammy, pec, but nothing beats playing AFL footy
and that's why I wanted to do it so much.'

North Melbourne coach Rhyce Shaw, speaking about
my comeback goal, said, 'We were just waiting for it
because it was such a special moment. We knew it was
coming at some point and he wouldn't miss because he is
such a deadeye shot at goal.'

Speaking on Fox Footy before the game, AFL legend
Dermott Brereton put it like this:

Majak tried [to commit suicide] and so often we hear,
'Why did he attempt that?' We have a problem at the
moment with COVID, ten times as many people have
taken their lives this year already. It is a massive problem, ten times the amount. We hear so often, 'He had so
much to live for, why would he do it?' They're all questions we ask. This is a bloke who almost did it, tried to
do it, went bloody close to taking his own life. What
made me emotional, he's got a chance to reclaim that
life. Today, whether he plays well, good, bad, poorly.
He has reclaimed his life today. For everybody that has
family that have done it, this is a snapshot into their life
of what their loved ones who took their lives could've
done. They could've succeeded again in life with the
right support around them. That's why I congratulate

North Melbourne and Rhyce [Shaw] for the support
around this young man. That man, he could've been a
memory. He could've had his plaque in a funeral par-
lour somewhere. But his flesh is living and breathing,
he is living proof people can reclaim their lives. What
makes me upset . . . I'm so proud of him. I barely know
him, I've met him two or three times. A lot of people in
my circumstance – thousands, hundreds of thousands
of people who have a close link to someone who has
taken their own life, who love their footy, and in some
small way would live through this today. It's heroic
what he's done. Well done, Majak.

19

Thiär ku dhoŋuan

There was so much excitement and hype surrounding my first game back, and even the few that followed that. But as I've learnt during my time in football, people move on pretty quickly, and my little honeymoon period was soon over, as the pressures of keeping my spot in the team returned. I never expected to be gifted any games, but I was very keen to get an opportunity to play as a defender at some stage and prove that I still had what it takes to be an effective backman. I didn't feel comfortable playing forward, having not trained in that position for a few years, and thought it was a bit unfair to expect me to excel in that position right away.

After three consecutive games against the Adelaide Crows, Geelong Cats and Melbourne Demons, my spot in the side was in jeopardy. We'd lost the last two games pretty badly, and while I'd managed to kick a goal in each of them, it wasn't enough to satisfy the coaches that I was going to help us win the next game. After being out for two years, to be on the cusp of being dropped after only three games was disappointing, to say the least. I hadn't really gotten the chance to prove anything or find any continuity, and I wasn't the only player struggling for form. Where we were at as a team didn't help, with only three wins for the season. I know no one gets a green light to play every week, but I still felt I was being treated harshly.

We had a five-day break between our game against the Demons and our next game against the Brisbane Lions. It became clear to me very quickly that I was on the outer. Rhyce eventually told me that I'd be an emergency for the Lions game, as there wasn't a spot for me in the 22. It was a pretty strange week, and it was pretty hard to take, I guess. He told me the reason I'd been left out was because of my forward-half defending. The coaches felt I wasn't doing enough when our team didn't have the ball, and I wasn't putting enough pressure on our opposition. I made a concerted effort not to be too disappointed or show my frustrations to anyone, but I was a bit flat for a few days.

I had kicked three goals in three games and felt like I was getting better with each game, but the coaches wanted to see more from me. The most frustrating thing for me continued to be where I was playing. All pre-season I had trained as a defender, and I know that's where I play my best footy. While I understood there was no spot for me down back, it was still frustrating. I found playing down back a lot easier than playing as a forward, because it worked to my strengths. While I could play forward, back and in defence, the fact that I could be thrown into these various positions made it hard for me to settle in one spot – like so many other players have the opportunity to.

With Ben Brown out of the team and our season completely off the rails after only three wins, the club shifted its focus to the youth, and getting games into the youngsters to set them up for the future. First, they needed another key forward to help young Nick Larkey and wanted to have a decent look at young developing ruckman Tristan Xerri – so he got the nod over me. Down back, they wanted to pump some games into another youngster, Ben McKay, and have him play alongside Robbie Tarrant and Josh Walker – so he got the nod over me too. Second in line with 'youth' on his side as a defender was Sam Durdin – so he was in line ahead of me. Suddenly, I was back in football's no man's land; something I couldn't have seen coming three weeks earlier when I'd played my comeback game.

I asked for another meeting with Rhyce to get more clarity on why I was being dropped, and he explained again that my defensive efforts simply weren't good enough, and that the coaches and club wanted to see if some of the younger players had what it takes to play in the AFL. I begged him to back me in and give me another chance, but he said his mind had already been made up. I had the sense the club was moving past me and that those in control had no intention of offering me a new contract. The roller-coaster continued. My contract situation was starting to play on my mind now, with time quickly running out. As I have mentioned before, the automatic trigger clause in my deal required me to play at least seven games and

I had only managed three, with just five games to go in the season. Again, all I could do was stay positive and show the coaches that I was a good team player and was willing to train hard and do whatever it took to get back into the side.

On the day of the game against the Lions, a few guys needed to pass fitness tests. Early in the morning, Luke McDonald, Robbie Tarrant and Josh Walker were all put through their paces by the medical and strength and conditioning teams to see if they were in good enough shape to play. As an emergency, I was told to be ready in case any of them failed to get up for the game. About an hour out, Luke McDonald was looking iffy, and I started to entertain the possibility that I might come in to replace him in defence. But it wasn't to be. Luke is one of those players who will never miss a game, if he has a say in it. It would take a very serious injury for him to miss a game.

The boys fought valiantly against the Lions, one of the ladder-leading teams in Round 12, and lost by only one point. Even though it was a loss, given the number of young, inexperienced players we had in the team, it felt more like a win. I knew a performance like that would mean I had zero chance to regain my spot in the team, unless there were injuries, but I was happy for everyone and for the club regardless.

I had to wait another two weeks before I earned a recall in Round 14 to play against the Gold Coast Suns. Little did I know at the time, it would be my last game for the North Melbourne Football Club. The Suns had started their season well but faded away and were now, like us, wallowing near the bottom of the ladder, with only four wins and a draw. We were still on three wins and had lost our last four games in a row. With Gold Coast being a young side, we were expected to beat them, but from the outset of the game, things weren't going to plan.

I started up forward alongside Nick Larkey and felt completely off the boil. Sometimes you feel great out there and everything is clicking, but on this occasion it was the opposite; it was one of the most frustrating games I had ever played in. I had so many opportunities to impact the game, but I fumbled the ball or dropped easy marks. I just felt so completely off. As a team we weren't playing together, and it felt like we had no game plan, systems or strategies to counter the Suns.

We were down by 9 points at quarter-time and I felt exhausted. I was trying so hard to find the footy and make something happen. One of the assistant coaches, Jade Rawlings, absolutely sprayed me. He pulled me aside from the forwards' huddle and said something along the lines of, 'You're playing for everything here, Maj! You need to pull your finger out and do something. You're not playing up to the standard right now. Your career is on the line and we need to see more from you! Get in the game!'

If you speak to any players, past or present, they'll tell you that when you're playing, sometimes it just feels like you're not trying hard and everything's going well, but there are other times where you're absolutely trying everything and nothing is going right for you – this was one of those games for me, and the spray I copped didn't help. It made me pretty flat, because in my mind, I was like, *Are you serious? I'm trying everything I can right now. We're getting absolutely smashed in the middle. Nothing is working and you're blaming me?* There were a lot of other players who weren't performing up to standard, so I felt unfairly singled out, but that's football.

In the second quarter, things got even worse for us. I was still struggling, and so was the team in general, as the Suns' lead blew out to 25 points. We headed into the half-time break low on confidence, with the game being played on their terms. In the third quarter, I started on the bench and was called on to give our main ruckman, Todd Goldstein, a break about five minutes in. I was on the ground for only about five minutes before I was told by our runner, Jona Segal, to come back to the bench as Todd was rested and ready to come back on. Normally I would have stayed on the ground after such a brief stint in the ruck, and would have rotated to the forward line, so it was strange to be told to come off again that soon. I was getting cold on the bench as the clock ticked down. I looked over to our rotation coordinator, Josh Humphries, who was sitting near me on the interchange bench and asked him who I was going on for next.

He replied, 'Let me check with the coaches, sit tight.' He made a call up to the coach's box through the two-way radio and had a brief discussion with one of the coaches, but didn't confirm anything with me.

'What'd they say?' I prompted him. 'Who am I going on for?'

'Just sit tight, mate,' he said again.

It was strange, and I knew something wasn't right. Our game is so demanding and taxing, and rotations are extremely valuable, so it didn't make any sense to have me sitting for this long while other players were desperate for a rest. I waited a few more minutes and got Josh's attention again. 'Am I going back on? What's going on?'

Josh looked at me with an expression that said, *Don't shoot the messenger*, and replied, 'I don't know, mate. They haven't said. I've asked the coach, and he told me to hold you on the bench for now.'

My heart sank and I felt hopeless. The message Josh's words sent me was painful to hear.

The siren sounded to mark the end of the third quarter, and I slowly made my way onto the ground to join the boys in the huddle. I felt completely out of it, and my interest level in the game had plummeted to an all-time low. There was no suggestion that I'd be returning to the field of play for the fourth quarter, and deep down, I feared my papers had been stamped. Since we were down 34 points and showing no signs of coming back to win, I felt the coaches could have thrown the magnets around and tried something different. I could have played down back, and someone like Josh Walker or Robbie Tarrant could have gone forward to try to jag us a few goals and spark a come-from-behind win. It was a time to throw something different at our opposition, or at least show that we were prepared to shake things up – clearly what we'd been doing for the previous three quarters wasn't working.

To my further disappointment and embarrassment, I started on the bench again for the final term. I waited and waited, and there was no rotation for me. I asked Josh one last time if I was going to be going back on, and this time he had an answer. 'You're done for the day, mate. Sorry, that's the coach's decision.' *Whack*. It was like a punch to the guts. I was essentially being told that I was of no value to the team anymore, and me being on the ground would do more harm than good. It was a huge insult, and while I didn't want to sulk or feel sorry for myself, at the same time, I didn't know whether to cry or be angry or just take my boots off and walk down to the rooms. I was hurting, absolutely broken. The game had turned from bad to worse: we managed to kick just 3 points from half-time until the final siren. We were thrashed by 63 points, and because of the way I was treated, I felt like all the responsibility was on me. While the whole team had been humiliated, I felt I had been humiliated on another level altogether.

The Gold Coast game really summed up the entire experience in the Queensland hub for me. It was deflating and unrewarding, and I felt like I never had a real opportunity to resurrect my career. I was constantly asking myself, *What am I doing up here?* since I was rarely playing. Instead, I would have to drive an hour or more to play in practice matches for different teams. There were games where I'd rock up, and I would be thrown another club's jumper and told to fill in for them, because there was a lack of numbers. I'd play against my actual teammates, and wouldn't get the chance to play our game plan or show the coaches I deserved a spot. I never felt like I was given any honesty and was instead being dragged along to make up the numbers.

A few of the boys who were also out of contract felt as dejected as me, and one night we asked if we could have a few afternoon drinks and watch the horse races. The coaches and leadership group allowed it, but only for a set time. As is often the case with footballers and alcohol, things got out of hand and we broke our curfew by several hours. What had started as a small gathering grew significantly, and even some players with contracts joined in. Having more people involved meant more noise, and eventually, we were busted and the party was broken up abruptly. The next day we copped it from the coaches and leaders for playing up and disobeying team rules.

I didn't get another opportunity to play another game for North Melbourne, and our season ended in Round 18 with just three wins, in Rounds 1, 2 and 9, for a total of 12 premiership points. We were a shadow of the club we'd once been. I had obviously missed the trigger clause in my contract, meaning my destiny was in the hands of the list management team, which included the head coach, Rhyce Shaw, and head of footy, Brady Rawlings.

With our hub stay coming to an end, player exit interviews were scheduled for the day after our last match, a Friday. Being in jumper No. 1, I was first cab off the rank at 7.15 a.m. I walked into that meeting knowing it was all but over for me at the Kangaroos. I'm not sure how much impact the partying a few weeks prior had on the decision, but I was told I wouldn't be getting another contract. I was respectful and said, 'Look, yeah, no worries. Thanks for everything you guys have done for me this year and the way the club has supported me throughout my mental-health battle.' That was it. Our player welfare manager, Neil Connell, was waiting for me around the corner, and we went for a walk. I remember thinking, *So, this is how it ends*. I'd always imagined playing at least 100 games for North Melbourne, leaving a long-lasting legacy and getting my name on the locker. But I'd fallen short. It was pretty hard to take in.

I was grateful to be given the opportunity to speak to the players that afternoon and thank the people who had been there for me. 'It's obviously pretty disappointing that I'm not going to be around going forward,' I told them. 'I've been at the footy club a long time, 11 years, I got drafted together with "J Mac" [Jamie Macmillan] and "Cunners" (Ben Cunnington). It's [my career] had its highs and lows along the way. I played one final, and I think I played 54 games in 11 years, so it's quite a humble career, but I'd just like to thank this footy club for giving me an opportunity to be the first [Sudanese-born] African to play in the AFL. It's something I will always hold close to my heart. I've made some really good mates at this place. I'll miss the locker room banter and some of my dad jokes. It just didn't work out the way I wanted it to this year; there's been challenges I've gone through. Boys, good luck going forwards and just make sure you look after each other around this time – there's gonna be guys who are not gonna get offered contracts going forwards. Cherish your friendships.

Thanks, Shawry for all your support, and Brady. The last few years obviously haven't been easy for me and I can't thank this footy club enough for what they've done for me.'

By the end of that day, another ten players were cut from the North Melbourne list, so I couldn't feel sorry for myself for too long. It's a brutal business, footy. One minute you're part of the furniture and so invested in everything that's happening at the club, and the next minute you're out. I had gone into footy knowing that my career could be over as quickly as it had begun, but it didn't lessen the blow. I was so fortunate to have been on the list for 11 years and lucky to have played 54 games with the Kangaroos. At the end of the day, the industry is all about winning; it's an environment that demands success, and if that's not happening, changes get made and people lose their jobs. As harsh as it is, that's what you've got to get your head around and accept.

20

Thiërrou

I couldn't hold it in any longer. I stepped aside to try to let it out discretely, but there was no avoiding drawing attention to myself – plus there was the noise I was making. It was my first training session since leaving North Melbourne, and I was vomiting my guts up.

It was my fault; since that nightmare in Queensland, I had done no fitness work. For so long, I'd been Majak Daw the AFL footballer, but then I was Majak Daw the former AFL footballer, and it scared the crap out of me, to be honest. I had seen close to 100 players get delisted from the club in my time and have to find a new career, and even though you know it's coming, it hits you like a sledgehammer when it's your turn. While, deep down, I had probably known I was a slim chance of getting another deal, it had still shocked me to hear Rhyce and Brady tell me I was done.

One of the first things you do after a conversation like that is call your manager and see what they think about the chances of getting a deal elsewhere. Shane Casley told me a few clubs had told him they felt I was worth having on their list, but with resources being taken away from teams because the AFL needed to save funds after the extra costs due to COVID-19, and the reduction of list sizes and the football department soft cap, these clubs couldn't commit to a list spot for me. Adam Ramanauskas (Rama) was working the phones too, but no one was calling back with good news.

My life used to be so structured, and everything I did was scheduled or controlled by someone at the footy club. When I went from having that to nothing at all, it was hard to adapt. I struggled. I was used to having a certain time to go to sleep and a certain time to wake up. I was used to training all the time and keeping my body in shape. Without a reason to do all that stuff, I just stopped. Most days I'd just sleep in until 10 o'clock, because there was no pressure to do anything. I had days where I was pretty bored, especially when Hendrix was with Emily; my parents and my friends were all at work. I hung out with my former North teammate, Joel Crocker, a fair bit – he'd also been delisted and wasn't doing much either. I caught up with some friends I hadn't seen for ages and did some day trips down the coast, but I really didn't know what to do with my time.

Luckily, soon after I'd gotten the bad news from North, Heath O'Loughlin told me I would likely be able to work as an ambassador at The Huddle. He urged me to pick up the phone to the CEO, Cameron McLeod, and let him know I was keen on helping him out with their various programs and activities. The Huddle is a not-for-profit organisation that was the brainchild of former North CEO Eugene Arocca and businessman and philanthropist Peter Scanlon. The North Melbourne Football Club built The Huddle in 2010, when it redesigned its Arden Street headquarters. The aim was to have a designated part of the facility set aside for the community and dedicated to helping migrants and refugees integrate into society, engaging through the power of sport.

The work the staff in The Huddle did was always something I could easily relate to, having only found my feet at MacKillop College after I'd picked up a football. The same philosophy was adopted by The Huddle – that sport can bring people of all walks of life together and help break down barriers. In most years, The Huddle would see about 5000 students and hundreds more parents and other people seeking help with their education or career. My role would be to work with these families and students, and promote The Huddle and what it does so that more people could benefit from its offerings.

The idea of working at The Huddle really excited me, but I wanted to fully extinguish my chances of playing footy again before I agreed to work there. I entered myself into the 2020 Rookie Draft, hoping a club would throw me a lifeline, but I didn't get picked up. The same thing happened in the Pre-Season Draft. My AFL dream was all but over. It didn't take long for the phone to ring, with local clubs enquiring about my availability. Donald McDonald sounded me out about playing for his side, Old Scotch, in the Victorian Amateur Football Association (VAFA), but my brother Anthony was playing with Brent Harvey at North Heidelberg in the Northern Football League (NFL), and I couldn't resist that. I was pretty keen to get Hendrix down to a local footy club and bring him to training and games so he could experience grassroots footy, and North Heidelberg seemed like a family-oriented place, where training was pretty casual and only twice a week.

I spoke to Boomer a fair bit about expectations and how to approach my first training sessions, and he said, 'Look mate, to be honest, you can come down and do a few drills. It's just really casual. Don't be trying to go really hard in the first month or so. Ease yourself into it.' It was nice that he said that to make me feel more comfortable, but being an ex-AFL player, I did feel some pressure to stand out during my first run with the team.

I made my way to North Heidelberg's home ground as the sun was going down and was introduced to my new teammates. There were a lot of Under 17s and 18s, and they were just so excited. They asked me a lot of questions about footy and what it was like playing in the AFL for North. Their enthusiasm and the way they sort of looked up to me made me feel like I had to train well and almost be a leader, which is not something I'd really had to do before. In my playing career, there were always more senior and experienced players taking the lead and I just had to follow what they were doing.

At that first session, we split up into three groups and rotated through various drills, including some sprints.

I knew I was unfit, but I didn't think I was *that* unfit. I did my best to get through, but the sprints brought me undone. There were a lot of sprints and it was pretty hard – I hadn't trained at that intensity for a good four months. I wasn't used to training at night, either, and had become accustomed to an afternoon nap in my 'retirement'. My head started spinning and my stomach felt heavy and uneasy, and I walked away from the group and hurled.

It was bad enough spewing in front of the young players, but then it became apparent that Boomer had shared the news with my former teammates at North, because I started getting text messages from them. *Boomer said you threw up at training. Hahahaha!*

After a few more training sessions, I started to get back into the rhythm and my fitness levels increased rapidly. I had trained for about a month and just started getting familiar with the guys when everything came to a complete halt. I woke one morning at about 8 a.m. to my phone ringing. I rolled over to see who was calling and saw that it was Rama, my manager. I didn't think it could be anything urgent so I rolled back over and dozed off for a few more hours. When I was ready to get up, I checked my phone and saw that Rama had also sent through a text. *Would you be keen to go and train with Melbourne for the next month?* I had to do a double-take to make sure I wasn't seeing things.

I wrote back, *Haha. Are you serious?*

Yeah mate, I'm serious. Have a think about it and get back to me in a couple of days.

I couldn't believe I might have another opportunity to play AFL after missing out via the Pre-Season and Rookie Drafts. I knew Melbourne was having a bad run with injuries to their key position players and needed back up, but I had no idea I'd be considered. But there was some hesitation on my part about not being fit enough – the thought of making a fool of myself and being humiliated. I think that was a natural reaction, because I hadn't trained at that level for a long time.

Later that day I took a phone call from Melbourne's list manager, Tim Lamb, who arranged a Zoom call with their senior coach, Simon Goodwin, and head of footy, Alan Richardson, as well as a few other coaches. That call was quite confronting. They wanted to know if a comeback was something I really was interested in and if I'd be committed to another crack at the AFL. They asked things like, 'If you were to come down, how do you think you'd go? Would you be committed to training hard?' I told them that I felt I had much more in the tank and plenty to offer, that the fire was still burning and my desire to keep playing was still there. Rama told me to be honest with them about how unfit I was so when I was asked about that, I just said, 'Look, I've trained a bit, but not that much. I'm very unfit.' They were surprisingly okay with that and told me it would be a slow build to get me back to where I needed to be in terms of my fitness. 'We're not going to put your body in danger or make you do anything you're not prepared to do yet.'

About half an hour after the Zoom meeting ended, Simon Goodwin rang me and said, 'Mate, look, we're going to give you the opportunity to come down and train with us.' I really couldn't believe it, but I was still so hesitant. Did I really want to go through with this? I didn't have long to ponder what was happening, as the phone immediately rang again. It was one of Melbourne's fitness coaches, letting me know what I'd need to do before I joining the group, including getting a COVID test. Then I realised I had to start calling other people who were relying on me, like Boomer at North Heidelberg, and the staff at The Huddle, where I'd just started working a week earlier. I was actually really excited about doing something different, but then this opportunity with Melbourne came along when I least expected it and it was just too good to turn down.

I was supposed to start at Melbourne on a Monday, but my COVID test was delayed by two days, during which I trained with legendary AFL figure Mark 'Choco' Williams at a local oval near his place. On the Wednesday, I went down and trained with Melbourne, where I was introduced to the guys but not allowed to do anything with the main group yet – I just wasn't ready. I would be doing a lot of running on the sidelines for a couple of weeks before integrating into full training.

I was so sore. I think the first couple of sessions I ran about 7 kilometres. At one stage it was so hard I contemplated running off the track, getting my stuff from the change rooms, hopping into my car and leaving. I knew how hard pre-season training was, but I was playing catch-up and could see just how far behind everyone else I was.

They'd all done full pre-seasons while I'd been sitting on my arse.

It was really challenging in those first few weeks, but I stuck at it. Footy training is demanding physically and mentally, particularly towards the end of sessions when you feel like you've got nothing left. I remember sitting in meetings after a big session, knowing I still had weights to do, and thinking, *I've got so much work to do, and I don't know if I'll ever get there.* I had some open dialogue with the head of strength and conditioning, Darren Burgess, and the physios, and let them know how I was feeling all the way through. I just had to trust them and know that the work they were giving me was going to hold me in good stead. I guess muscle memory is a good thing, because my body picked it all up again pretty quickly. I gradually integrated into some sessions with the main training group, which was really fun.

If training wasn't hard enough for me, then getting there made life even more difficult. When I agreed to train with them, I didn't know Melbourne were based at Casey Fields, which is in Cranbourne East, in Melbourne's south-east. For me, living back in Werribee, it was a pretty ordinary place to get to; usually it was a bit less, but some days it took me two full hours just to get there. It was a massive commitment, given I hadn't been guaranteed anything would come of it.

With the AFL season around the corner, Melbourne's VFL side began playing practice matches, which enabled me to show the club I still had what it takes to play at the

AFL level. Before the first game, in Footscray, my car broke down and I was 40 minutes late to the ground. I freaked out and was like, *Fuck. Of all the times this could happen, why today?* I managed to get some help to get going and, thankfully, I didn't miss any of the game. But it was a bad look. I was stressed out, although part of me thought, *Well, you know what? There's nothing you can do about it. Surely they will understand it was out of your control.*

I went out and played. I was a bit rusty. I was moving all right, but just running under the ball a lot and didn't have great touch. I played limited minutes but felt good. I was starting to pick up the game and the momentum of it when the fitness staff said, 'That's enough, Maj, you're done for the day.' I was a bit worried about being pulled from the game early. When this happened to me in Queensland with North Melbourne, it didn't end well for me, so I feared they thought I just wasn't up to it.

It was around half-time, and I was summoned to a meeting with all the coaches in one of the coaches' boxes upstairs. Simon Goodwin asked me why I was late to the game. When I explained that my car had broken down, he said, 'Look, mate, is this going to be a regular thing?' Obviously, when I was younger and had just started my career at North, I used to be late to meetings and training a fair bit, so I felt he was making sure I wasn't going to repeat any old behaviours. I reassured him that it was not going to become a regular thing. I added, 'I still have the desire to keep playing footy, and I really want Hendrix to see me play. He's my purpose and my inspiration.'

It was strange to open up to people I'd just met, but I couldn't afford to hold back in that moment. They needed to know if they were bringing the right person into their organisation. I left the meeting none the wiser, and still didn't know if I'd done enough to earn a spot on the list.

We had a recovery session the next day at St Kilda Beach and the coach called me to the front of the group. 'Boys, we're offering Majak a spot on our list!'

I had thought this moment would feel like back in 2009, when I was picked up in the Rookie Draft, but it was different. Although I was super excited, I knew the clock was ticking. If I wanted to play AFL footy again, I still had a mountain to climb.

REFLECTIONS

Brad Scott, Shane Casley, Sonja Hood

I set out to achieve a lot in my football career and feel that I accomplished a lot. Former North head coach Brad Scott was there from the beginning of my AFL journey.

Through no fault of his own, Majak's career hit many speed bumps or hurdles. Regardless, I would say his career was an unmitigated success – in terms of the things that could be controlled. I used to say that I wished I had coached former Carlton and North champion Jarrad Waite from 18 years of age. But the thing is, Waitey comes from a famous football family, and he'd had a footy in his hands since he was basically born.

In the same way, I wish I could have coached Majak when he was growing up and put a footy in his hands early on. The mind boggles at what could have been, if we hadn't had to backfill basically 14 years of childhood with a footy in his hand. The Majak Daw we saw in 2018 is the Majak Daw we could have had as a 19-year-old, and then extrapolate from that what the next ten years of his career would have looked like – it's a scary thought to consider just how good he would have been. That's my opinion of what it could have been, and it's so unfair to say that he had unfulfilled potential because that's just circumstance. You go through his background, what he's been able to achieve, and in 2009, 1 per cent of people would have thought that Maj was going to make it. The fact that he played a single AFL game was a success. The fact that he took a massive hanger in the first 15 seconds of his first game and kicked a goal is a Cinderella story. If he'd only done that, it would have been a huge success, based on where he was coming from.

Our main focus at North was always, *How do we protect Majak from the scrutiny, expectations and pressure that have been placed on him?* Everyone wanted a piece of him, and it's still going to be the case to this day, long after his football career is all said and done. The AFL is going to want him, The Huddle will want him, the North Melbourne Football Club will want him, and countless other community organisations tied to multiculturalism will want him. He's such a nice guy that he won't say, 'No,' to any of them, and that stems back to the lying episode as well. He wants to please; he's a genuinely nice person. The thing about being a professional athlete is you need to be quite ruthless in your ability to prioritise what's important. And that's really hard when you've got competing priorities.

Players are expected to be role models in their community, and that was particularly magnified for Maj. He's got very close family ties, and he was being pulled in so many different directions. I think North did as good a job as it possibly could in shielding him from it all, but no one, out-side of North Melbourne or Maj's family, had any idea about the pressures that were being put on him. Even without the playing accolades, he had the profile and the recognisability of our highest profile players. He had more pressure on him than just about any other player on our list.

Many people believe I will leave a lasting legacy, and one of those people is my manager, Shane Casley.

I think for what he's been through, footy is a thing that is mentally and physically draining for all players. I've had some elite AFL players – and champion AFL players – who have retired with a year to go on their contracts because they said they were 'mentally cooked'. I always wanted Maj to leave the game satisfied and look back on his time in a positive light. My son finished playing footy, and he was sick of it; he hated footy. I don't want Maj to have that feeling. I don't want him to look back and say, 'I hated my footy career.'

I'm just so proud of the bloke he's become – he's such a genuine, good guy and everyone who meets him or talks to him gets that feeling from him. I just hope that he can set himself up, be happy and get back on track financially. At the end of the day, you're a footballer for only a very, very short part of your life, and he'll be recognised long after footy for the other things he does, not just for what he did playing footy. I'm proud of his career and what he was able to achieve. With all that scrutiny, all that pressure, all the things he's been through, he still played some really, really good footy. He wasn't just a bits and pieces player, either; he was a very good AFL player.

From a football legacy point of view, the number of people who look up to Majak as a role model, and the role he played in those Sudanese gang wars, is remarkable. Maj was a high-profile AFL player, and whether he liked it or not, people asked for his opinion. People wanted to put him up there as a role model and make him an ambassador for the game. I'm sure he's helped a lot of kids, because when he gets in front of people, he's impressive. He speaks well, he speaks with a lot of passion, he's very likable, and when you listen to him, you believe him. We won't ever know just how many people he's inspired, but we know of a lot, and not only in the Sudanese community, but people like Dermott Brereton, who was in tears during Majak's comeback game – and he's a hardened AFL guy who has seen pretty much everything. Maj has touched a lot of people, and I think he's improved a lot of people's lives.

I worked with a lot of people on and off the field throughout my AFL career, and one of them was Sonja Hood. When I first met her, Sonja was the general manager of the North Melbourne Football Club's community arm, The Huddle, and we have maintained a strong relationship since. Sonja witnessed all of my ups and downs, and is perhaps as best placed as anyone to sum up my AFL journey and life to this point.

When I think of Majak, one word comes to mind immediately: resilience. He's like one of those inflatable toys that you knock over and they bounce back up again, and no matter how many times you knock it down, it pops back up like nothing happened. He has hit some unbelievable barriers and roadblocks in his life, ones that normal people wouldn't get through, and he pushes through them, looks back at them and says, 'I'm not doing that again,' and off he goes. It is extraordinary. I think about the things that he's gone through in the time that I've known him, and any one of those things would have finished an ordinary human.

And it's not like he's only had to endure one major event or trauma; he's had several. Some of us go through life not having any, so he's had more than his fair share. Who gets through a public rape trial like that? Who gets through being stood down by his teammates and told to go and find a job because he's not welcome at the club anymore? Who survives lying to an AFL coach or having your picture on the front page of the paper every day because you've had the temerity to go out with someone else's ex-girlfriend? And that's before we even get into any of the stuff he suffered with racism – he suddenly had to be the poster boy for that hot topic, whether he wanted to be or not. In amongst all of that, he's trying to learn a game that he'd only just picked up a few years before going pro. There has always been this expectation on him that never applied to anyone else in that position, but he's shouldered that load and pushed on.

I remember doing a sports women's lunch panel in Ballarat when Majak was still a rookie, and before he played a game of footy, and the very first question I got was about Majak Daw. I said to the hundreds of people in the room, who weren't all North Melbourne supporters, 'Before I answer that, can I get a show of hands from those of you who have actually heard of Majak Daw?' Every single person's hand went up. I followed up with, 'Now, hands up who can name another rookie on a club list that you don't barrack for?' Not a single hand went up – not one. Majak was under a phenomenal amount of pressure that nobody else had.

I think the media were pretty foul to him for an awfully long time. I think those images of him walking out of the water at the beach after a recovery session were unfortunate. That reporting was set up as, 'Black men are here to take your white women.' Majak was seeing Emily, who was this young, white, petite woman, and the ex-girlfriend of a white teammate, and the picture of Majak was of him mostly naked walking out of the water looking huge. The whole messaging was about predation. It was awful. Majak wasn't looking for that kind of publicity, and he and Emily weren't doing anything that invited that kind of media scrutiny. He hadn't played a game yet, and it was all because he had a white girlfriend; if he'd had a black girlfriend, nobody would have cared. The whole thing was awful. And watching the response of teammates who were jealous about the fact that Majak was someone who was widely recognised and they weren't – I think some of the more senior players on the list at that time dealt with it really badly, actually.

Majak has been held to a different standard than everybody else, because there's been this view that he's had a free ride or an easy run, and therefore he had to prove himself twice as much and work twice as hard as everybody else. So, going back to that word resilient – that's what he's always been. Majak would say, 'If what I need to do is to become better at marking, then I'll come down to the club and do twice as many marking sessions as everybody else and become better at marking. And if I need to become stronger at tackling, then I'll do twice as many tackling sessions as everybody else and become stronger at tackling.' You could never knock his work ethic but that's not what people tended to talk about.

Early on, I don't think the playing group really understood how tough it was for him, and they were more worried that Majak was getting ahead of himself, because of media hype that he hadn't generated or even asked for – it was unfair. When Majak was racially abused during a game in Tasmania in 2014, the media pack that was supposed to be following Hawthorn on their community camp drove from Launceston to Hobart to ask Majak how he felt about the fact that someone in the crowd had said something racist, which he hadn't actually heard. We had Drew Petrie and Scott Thompson on either side of Majak so we could push through the media pack. It was awful; it was physical and awful.

At North Melbourne, there was no one else on our list who was getting that kind of attention, or that kind of pressure to suddenly have an opinion on something. Then off the back of that we had the AFL come along and say they wanted to roll Majak out at every opportunity, to use him as the face of racism in Australia. But he didn't want to be the face of racism. He just wanted to get better at football and try to get a game like everyone else. He was never allowed to just focus on footy, even though that's all he wanted to do.

At football clinics and club appearances, the attention on him was intense too. It was ridiculous. It wasn't just that people wanted to be photographed with Majak; they wanted to touch him as well. If he was in any way agoraphobic, it would have been overwhelming. But it never overwhelmed Majak. He was always so gentle, very respectful; almost too respectful and almost too gentle. When I went to see him in hospital after he broke his pelvis, one of the first questions he asked was about me and my kids – and he remembers the names of all his friends' children. His main concern was, was I okay?

He was the 'mirror test' for a long time. When kids looked across the fence and saw Majak out there playing in the AFL, they saw someone from the same background as them, or from a different background than the rest of us. I look at every one of the African players who've come after him, and they're there because he made that possible. And that's a huge burden to carry. It's hard to think of anyone else who has been as genuinely pioneering as Majak. He was a leader and a role model when he was an 18-year-old, when he had no ability to be a role model or a leader. He could barely manage his money and couldn't even get to training on time – not because he was hopeless, but because he was 18.

I think back to his court case, and I can't imagine what it must have been like for him to go through that and be in a situation where you are being reported on and talked about on the front page of the paper, every day. And then when it's done, it's never really done because that became a thing that defined him. Afterwards, he took no time off and went straight back into training and tried to have a normal life. That's Majak right there: 'I've looked at it, I've gotten through it, it's finished, so let's move on.' When he jumped off the bridge, the first thing he said to everyone when they went in to see him was, 'I'm going to play footy again.' My reaction to that was, 'Right, of course you are. You're Majak Daw.'

I sincerely hope he actually spends some time working out what he wants for himself, rather than what everybody else wants for him. I feel like he spent such a long time responding to what everybody else wanted of him and from him: his family, his friends, his girlfriends, his football club, his manager, the media, the AFL, the African community – the list goes on. Everybody has a view on who he should be and what he should do. I'd really like to hope that he's got a view and is allowed some time to have formed that view and act on it.

Maj was such a joy to be in footy with. He's one of the people that you walk out of your experience at a football club and say, 'That's someone I would never have got to spend time with otherwise and I have valued every interaction.'

A letter to Majak

We visited you in hospital when you were broken and barely able to speak.

We witnessed your first steps following the fall.

We saw how utterly exhausted you were after your first walk down the hospital corridor – you went 5 metres and couldn't go any further.

We watched you grow in strength, mentally and physically – day by day, week by week.

Suddenly, the doubts about you being able to walk again began to fade.

Working tirelessly on yourself and your strength and fitness, you kept performing little miracles.

Your first aided jog on the treadmill was mind-blowing. Your first unassisted run was awe inspiring. Your first game in the VFL was incredible.

More barriers were thrown up along the way, and you were humble yet determined and undefeated. You kept knocking them down with resilience and a willpower rarely seen.

We all watched on as you did what no one thought was possible – you played AFL-level football again.

But you didn't just do it for yourself, and you couldn't have done it by yourself. You did it for all those struggling to make it to tomorrow and for those helping others make it through each day.

Your incredible feat is a reminder that no matter how tough things get, life is worth living and being kind to each other can make a difference.

Majak, I love you, am blessed to know you, and am so proud of you. I'll never underestimate what you achieved and what you continue to achieve every day.

Your friend,
Heath O'Loughlin

Acknowledgements

Not a day goes by that I don't feel sorry for what I put my family, friends and loved ones through, and not a day goes by that I don't stop to think about how lucky I am to have so many truly amazing people in my life. That they still care for me and love me means the world to me.

The level of support I've had during some truly tough periods has been overwhelming, starting with my parents, who put their own lives on the line to give me and my siblings a better chance at life. The selflessness and unconditional love they've always given us has been the greatest gift. Everything they've been to me growing up, I try to embody as a father for Hendrix. I know if I can follow the example my parents set for me, Hendrix will always be okay. Mum and Dad: thank you for everything you've given me and taught me. Thank you for not judging me when I've been at my worst, and for always showing me the way forward. You are my guiding lights and I will forever follow you.

To my brothers and sisters: Peter, Augustino, Anthony, Teresa, Mary, Sarah, Angelina and Ajak, I love you all dearly and look forward to raising our families together. Mum and Dad moved us to Australia so we could all be together, and I am so proud to be your brother. Thank you for always believing in me.

Emily, looking back on all the fond memories we forged together, it was amazing. Thank you for your kind heart and how much you cared for me when I was at my worst. But the best thing to ever happen to us was making such a beautiful little boy. That will forever keep us together.

To my little man, Hendrix: you are my absolute world. There is nothing I love more on this earth than you. You are my inspiration, my motivation and my heartbeat. You will always have my unconditional love, support, encouragement and guidance. I can't wait to see what you do with this amazing life you have in front of you.

I've made a lot of friends along the way, but I will be forever indebted to my closest mates, Joey and Rory, who saw me as a vulnerable young boy in a foreign country and took me under their wings. Without your kindness, generosity and ability to see me for who I am, I would never have made it this far. You embraced me as a mate from the beginning and provided me with security and confidence during some challenging times growing up.

Dani and Hop: thank you for all you have done for me over the years. The guidance you offered me from a young age to this current day has been invaluable. You've given me love and care, and shown me what it means to be a family man.

I can't single out anyone from North Melbourne, so to all the players and staff: I felt so loved and welcomed by you all. When I stepped foot inside the club – a place I knew little about – I was very hesitant to be myself, but you all accepted me and helped me grow, not only as a player but as a man. Thank you for having faith in me and for putting up with all my dad jokes!

To all my coaches: thank you for having belief in me as a player. To Brad Scott: thanks for instilling some valuable life lessons in me. You are by far the best teacher I've ever had. Josh Drummond: thank you for your patience with me when I was learning and adapting to a new role. Alex Ishchenko: I appreciate your support throughout some of the toughest times in my life. You always believed in me more than anyone. Darren Crocker: you were always hard on me in the early days, but I know it's because you saw the potential in me. I know how much you cared about me, and I'm thankful for all the time and effort you put into my development. Gavin Brown: you are such a gracious man and your teaching methods helped me so much throughout my football development. Rhyce Shaw: I know you went through some tough times too, but when I was at my lowest point, you were there for me. Thank you for taking the time to visit me in hospital on multiple occasions and for genuinely caring about me.

To the specialists, doctors, nurses and staff at the Royal Melbourne Hospital and Epworth: thank you for your meticulous care and support. You took immense care of my wellbeing, making it possible for me to walk again and do what I love most.

To the North medical and training staff of Jona, Alex, Matty, Christian, David, Alister, Matt, Josh and Tania:

thank you for constantly going above and beyond in your roles.

To Peter Bacquie: there will never be a better doctor than you, and I am forever indebted to you. What you have done for me and my family will never be forgotten.

Michael Inglis: the work you have done with me to get me back to enjoying life again is enormous. From the day we started to unpack everything to the time I came back to play, your encouragement and guidance has been incredible – thank you.

To the TLA team of Shane, Adam, Susan and Sally: I appreciate the constant support and friendship we have built over the years. Thank you, Susan, for helping and guiding me through a really difficult time.

Sonja Hood: you took me in and treated me like your own child. The care, support and constant advice has been invaluable, and hopefully I can pass it all on to Hendrix.

I was terrified about sitting down and opening up about certain chapters of my life for this book. I spoke to Brent Harvey, who had written a book with Heath O'Loughlin in 2016, and he encouraged me to talk to him about writing mine. It wasn't until I spoke with Heath that I knew I had nothing to fear in putting my feelings and emotions down on paper. I felt so comfortable speaking to Heath about things I'd never discussed with anyone before – all under the premise of helping others with their mental health. Locked away together in the Queensland AFL hub, we spent so many hours chatting about my life, my failures and my successes. It was cathartic for me, to say the least.

ACKNOWLEDGEMENTS

Heath, thank you for helping me through this and making it easy for me to open up – you did a great job.

To Alison Urquhart, Johannes Jakob and the wonderful team at Penguin Random House, thank you for helping me tell my story the right way.

I hope those who are struggling will read this and realise there's always a way out of the darkness and into the light. Speak to your loved ones and open up to them about your feelings. Never be too proud to ask for help, and know you're never alone.

Discover a
new favourite

Visit **penguin.com.au/readmore**